JAPAN STUDIES
Studies in Japanese History and Civilization

Prince Ito

Prince Hirobumi Ito

PRINCE ITO

BY

KENGI HAMADA

SANSEIDO CO., LTD.

1, Jimbocho, Kanda, Tokyo

1936

Reprint edition published in 1979 by

UNIVERSITY PUBLICATIONS OF AMERICA, INC.
Washington, D.C.

ISBN: 0-89093-267-0

Library of Congress Catalog Card Number: 79-65475

Manufactured in the United States of America

PREFATORY NOTE

The author desires to express his deep indebtedness to Count Kentaro Kaneko, Privy Councillor, for having graciously examined the manuscript, particularly those chapters dealing with the constitution of Japan and with those activities of the Meiji era of which he was not merely an interested observer but an important participant. To Mr. Midori Komatsu, veteran authority on the subject of this biography, he is no less grateful for having gone over the whole manuscript and made valuable suggestions and corrections.

He also wishes to thank Mr. Ken Yanagisawa, Director of the Cultural Affairs Bureau of the Japanese Foreign Office, and Mr. Tadao Kuwabara, Chief of the Enterprises Section of the Tokyo *Nichi Nichi*, both of whom have given generously of their time and service in helping to place this modest work before its readers within the present covers.

CONTENTS

BOOK I
THE FIGHTER

CHAPTER I
GENIUS AND THE DEVIL

I

A little pale-faced boy of seven stood listening bravely as his playmates, garrulous and mischievous, formed a ring about him and called him many abusive names. "You are a green calabash," they teased, "a green, green calabash!" They repeated this over and over in sing-song fashion, their faces gleaming, their tiny throats crooning lustily. Suddenly they came to the chorus, viciously. "Go and drink some wine," they rasped, "and get more red, red, red in the face!"

The boy did not cry; he was not the crying kind. Instead, there was a broad grin on his face: a broad, inexplicable grin. For with all the pallidness on his cheeks, this youngster had a solid head crammed with precocious wits, and he swiftly improvised a scheme—a bold, diabolical scheme!—to get even with his tormentors. "Let us all get together," he invited, with a friendly enough gesture, "and play war." The boys, nothing loath, accepted. A born leader, he divided them into two groups, taking particular pains to assemble those who had been loudest in their abuses under one group, which he characterized as the "enemy," and assumed command of the other.

Anon, the free-for-all began! The little commander was all for strategy. Feigning flight, he enticed the "enemy" into a tangled heap of dry miscanthus. Thus for a while the game of "war" became a game of "hide and seek." Suddenly he disappeared. When he returned there was a piece of burning wood in his hand. With this he set the trap afire. There was a series of crackling sounds, the disquieting smell of burning leaves. Within the little labyrinthine trap there was a great commotion.

Most of his little adversaries found no difficulty in disentangling themselves, but the flames spread with such rapidity that all of them were thoroughly frightened before they found their way out.

Thereafter his little friends regarded him not merely with respect, but with a certain measure of awe.

This astounding incident, with curious variations, is said to have occurred in the little village of Tsukari in the province of Choshu while Japan was still sleeping her sleep of centuries. The child, when provoked, was known to reveal strange proclivities. Often the village people were shocked beyond words by the manner in which he accomplished little feats of wickedness befitting a lad twice his age. But beneath this reckless instinct there reposed a mind capable of extraordinary concentration even for one so incredibly young—a mind which, if diverted into virtuous channels, could be made useful and productive of the most amazing results. The village pedagogue opined that the youngster was a distinct prodigy compounded of a rough admixture of genius and the devil. He prophesied that the future of one so obviously gifted was certain to embrace immeasurable possibilities; that he would some day blossom forth into a great national figure, but that, failing in this, he would develop into one of the most detestable scoundrels of history.

A singular lad, the circumstances of his coming into the world had been even more singular still. For over three years before his birth his parents had made daily pilgrimages to the Tenmangu shrine, for the Great One would not bless them with a child and they must seek with prayers to regain His favor. And as though their fervent supplications had been answered, the child in whom was centered the happiness of two lonely and virtuous souls was conceived shortly thereafter. But those of the neighboring village who reveled in the sensational and possessed a voluptuous bent for purveying the scandalous, refused in this particular instance to believe in the efficacy of prayers. A rumor of their own concoction soon found a wide circulation in which this child was represented as the offspring of a wandering Buddhist pilgrim. Those, however, who boasted of a more imaginative turn of mind gossiped that the father, having been attracted by a mysterious cry to the nesting place of the larks close to the Tenmangu shrine, had discovered a man-child wrapped in swaddling clothes—a smiling, gurgling bundle of palpitant humanity that was as sparklingly fascinating as a monumental jewel—and believing him to be a gift of the gods, had taken him home and adopted him. Years afterwards when Hirobumi Ito became the brightest star in Japan's firmament, these strange tales were taken down from the ancient shelves, dusted, dressed in a new and more appropriate garb, and foisted upon the imagination of a pious and gullible world.

Like Lincoln's, his birth, on September 2, 1841, occurred in a humble abode in a place far removed from the center of progress and enlightenment. Tsukari, the place of his birth, bore every traditional stamp of an uncouth medieval village. It nestled on a rugged plain between the brooding slopes of sinuous mountains. Separated from the provincial capital by some sixty miles of primeval forests and sombre streams and isolated patches of human habitation, it presented an aspect of deep and stolid loneliness. Its population was composed mainly of destitute farmers who tilled the grudging earth and wove the priceless expectorations of the silk-worm. It was a far outpost of the redoubtable Choshu Clan, loyal supporters of the dispossessed Emperors.

Koto, the lad's mother, was the daugther of a plain citizen of the village named Akiyama. She was of a stern spiritual mould. Though capable of abiding affection, she was conscious at all times of that strong sense of duty toward husband and child which has become a religion with the women of her race. Much of the child's spiritual growth in later years owed its origin to the rigorous discipline of this staunch and loyal mother. His father, Juzo Hayashi, is listed in the ancient records as a farmer. But it is also a matter of record that he was descended, however devious the ties of blood, from the famous Kono of Shikoku and from many other samurai and a few swashbucklers who did considerable fighting and distinguished themselves in the service of their lords. Kono was in turn descended from Prince Iyo, third son of Emperor Korei (290 B.C.—214 B.C.). All these evidences of distinction, however, belonged so irretrievably to the remote past, between which other and less distinguished family strains had been absorbed, that they contributed nothing whatever to Ito's status at birth. Officially, he was rated and accepted as nothing more than a traditional farmer's—a *hyakusho's*—child.

2

His family was meanwhile in straitened circumstances. The father, a man of some influence in the village, held a temporary position of trust and responsibility in the government office at Tsukari. Through sheer carelessness on his part, coupled with his ignorance of mathematics and of accounting, a deficit had occurred in the funds left in his keeping. Though there was no criminal act involved, he found it more agreeable to his conscience to leave the village. He thus went forth to seek his fortune in Hagi, the Choshu metropolis, leaving his wife and child in the care of his wife's parents.

At first he did menial work entailing great physical hardship in the homes of well-established samurai and their squires. But his passion for hard work soon won for him a recognition which eventually earned the berth of "substitute" to Mizui, hereditary squire to the house of Kuramoto. This constituted his first upward step in the change from the status of a lowly commoner to that of a samurai.

The heir to the Mizui title was an invalid, and in order to safeguard against a possible extinction of the family name, a relative, Buhei Ito, was adopted as heir in fact. Soon afterwards, however, Buhei retired in favor of the legitimate heir. He then purchased the title in the possession of Nibei Jugawa, an impecunious samurai to whom economic salvation seemed more desirable than the abstract rewards of rank. This enabled him to establish the samurai house of Ito. Through the early contacts made while associated with Mizui, Buhei had been deeply impressed by the stranger from Tsukari, and being himself heirless, adopted him to succeed to his newly-created title. In this manner the knightly surname of Ito replaced that of the commoner, Hayashi. Thus the little prodigy of Tsukari became, as it were automatically, a potential samurai.

With this extraordinary turn in the family fortunes, the child Ito and his mother decided to join his father at Hagi, and the long trek over the lonely mountainous trails began. There were no vehicles in those days which conveyed human freight except palanquins of various shapes and sizes used by the lords and warriors and other privileged individuals who were in a position to requisition manpower. Others were obliged to accomplish their journeys on foot. Ito and his mother walked; at least his mother did most of the way, for the trek was a long and tedious one and the child must frequently rest his weary feet. At such times his mother carried him on her back in a primitive contraption designed by the farmers for carrying firewood. It was in this picturesque fashion that they entered Hagi.

3

The real, earnest and intensive work in the life of Ito had its humble beginnings soon after this family re-union took place. The child was nine years old. He was growing fast. His natural craving for knowledge must be gratified. But the family exchequer was in no wise blessed with such plenitude as to permit a sturdy, growing boy to wallow in the luxury of a life of leisure. He was, therefore, made to go to work in the homes of wealthy samurai. His work consisted in going on errands and serving as a handy-boy about the house. The work allotted to such youngsters in Japan, then as now, is no sinecure, as those who have survived the ordeal can testify. Through the hot, sweltering summer days, the days of seemingly endless rain, and the bitter days when the pitiless snow sweeps across the wintry towns, these boys, scarcely ten years old, trudge across the toilsome paths, drawing water from the abysmal well, hewing firewood for the stove and the bath-house, carrying bundles, doing the marketing, and running on errands that often take them to distant villages across hills and dales.

While thus serving at the home of Sohee Ibara, Ito refused to eat the cold rice left over from the previous family meal, such as is usually allotted to menial servants. This was rank mutiny. Nevertheless the meaning of justice had already filled the young toiler's heart, and he was determined to risk a dishonorable discharge for the sake of the principle involved. Fortunately, the maid of the household, to whom he bared his little soul, was a kindly woman. She had often admired the hard-working child and marvelled at the breezy insouciance with which he entered upon tasks requiring an adult's muscles and the patience of a Job. The child, moreover, possessed a remarkably genial disposition, and in her womanly breast there had entered a great affection for him. And so, out of pity and affection and at the risk of her own position, she managed to feed him clandestinely whenever possible with fresh warm rice and plenty of it.

His fertile brain was meanwhile beginning to absorb the rudiments of a crude but nevertheless profoundly esoteric system of education. There were in those days no formal institutions of learning such as exist today. The government, under the Tokugawa Shogun, was interested primarily in the enhancement of military prestige and in the glorification of a philosophy of life grounded upon a peculiarly Nipponese system of chivalry known as Bushido. While the Galahads of medieval Europe fought with lances and courted the smiles of their favorite ladies beneath the flourishing banners of knighthood, the samurai, their prototype in Japan, fought for their lords with double swords and expressed their emotions in classic poetry. Preparation for such a life was often an exclusively personal affair. It was frequently attained by first attaching oneself to a scholar and later serving a sort of apprenticeship to an elderly samurai. Ito's first effort along this line found expression in a conscientious devotion to his grand-uncle, Keiun, a superior priest in a Shingon temple. Most of the scholars of medieval Japan were found among the Buddhist and Shinto priests. In the absence of professional pedagogues, these worthies performed the tasks of a tutor, specializing in Japanese and Chinese classics. But even this form of instruction, meagre as it necessarily must have been, Ito was privileged to acquire only after the day's gruelling toils were over.

A few years later he found his way into a group of about seventy ambitious lads studying under the able guidance of Goroemon Kubo, where he soon distinguished himself as a budding scholar. It was a tradition at Kubo's always to divide the student body into two distinct groups of about equal mental capacity, and only those who ranked among the first five pupils in scholastic attainments within each group were given the close personal attention of the master. Competition was uncommonly keen, for these young scholars represented the cream of Choshu's hopeful adolescents, and all of them dreaded the stigma of mediocrity. It was characteristic of Ito not to concede the title of superiority to anyone. He succeeded in almost every instance, but there was a frail-looking lad named Yoshida who invariably topped him. There was something inexplicably, almost divinely, superior about the latter's mental powers which even Ito, able as he was, could not overcome. This brilliant, hollow-chested youth met an early death, too soon for one so filled with promise.

Ito's favorite subjects were history and political science. Many of his achievements in later years received their direct impetus from his early admiration of Rai Sanyo, premier historian of the Japanese middle ages. Ere long he developed into a finished logician in matters political, putting to shame many an able adult who attempted to explore the depths of his growing mind by engaging him in highly sophisticated tête-à-têtes.

CHAPTER II
MAN OF DESTINY

I

To the youthful Ito, who had now reached the thirteenth year of his life, the coming of Commodore Perry in 1853 and its significant implications, followed closely by the advent of Admiral Stirling, of Vice-Admiral Poutiatine, and of other Western emissaries, meant the beginning of a career filled with excitement, with ambitious adventures, with revolutionary activities.

Japan was in the throes of a cataclysmic confusion. Perry's historic mission had caused tremendous repercussions in every nook and corner of the land. The Emperor, Komei, and his Court, the immemorial victims of the Shogun's dictatorship, suddenly emerged from their shell of helpless desuetude and refused, with all the militant powers at their disposal, to sanction the act of the Shogun's Government which brought the two hundred and fourteen years of foreign exclusion to its humiliating end. From Kyoto the cry of "Son-o Jo-i!"— honor the Emperor and expel the barbarians—reverberated through the nation. While thus denouncements and recriminations flew thick and fast between Kyoto and Yedo, Townsend Harris, the first American consul to Japan, landed at Shimoda, and Japan found itself in a still greater quandary. Harris's arrival was certain to be followed by countless hordes of other unwanted alien residents, whose number would increase from year to year. Might not this be merely another ruse with which to defraud the nation in the manner of the early missionary exploiters? And would not their initial efforts be followed sooner or later by the advent of a mighty armada, of other and even more powerful armadas, bent upon conquest and spoliation?

During this agitated period the Shogun's Government, acting under Lord Ii's influence, behaved with remarkable sobriety. Factional animosities wherever possible were overlooked, and a general appeal was transmitted to the leading Clans of the country, regardless of their traditional allegiance, to prepare for any national contingency which might arise and to defend their respective coasts. The Choshu Clan was especially urged, solely on the strength of its merits as a fighting organization, to guard what was then considered the most strategic coastline of Japan—the Soshu district.

Soshu constituted that strip of territory extending from Kamakura to Miyata and watered by the romance-laden Sagami bay. It formed the bulwark of the Shogun's capital, protecting the latter against a possible invasion from the sea. Here Perry had made his first historic landing. Harris had chosen it for the scene of his debut. It was a part of Kanto, the center of national activities and the cynosure of the political geniuses of the day.

The glory inseparable from a defense of this coastline and the brilliant opportunities of service it afforded attracted some of the most conspicuous figures of Choshu who merited renown, not only as warriors, but more particularly as scholars of the first rank. Among them was Ryozo Kuruhara, a virile young samurai with honest convictions and an unimpeachable character. Kuruhara was placed in command of a little band of some thirty-five samurai who were dispatched for service in Miyata. To this young leader Ito attached himself as aide. He was at the time sixteen years of age and on the threshold of his life's career.

Kuruhara was a true patriot. He had a profound knowledge of Japanese history and of his particular milieu. He loved military discipline because of its simple austerity. A brilliant logician, he was always prepared to defend his views with his life. He was known, moreover, for the unmitigated aversion which he harbored against personal defeat in any form, for defeat connoted physical and intellectual imperfections. Whatever cause he espoused, he did so from honorable, unadulterated motives. Usually it was with great credit to himself. He quickly discovered young Ito's singular aptitude for the two-fold life of a samurai. Through the passionate assiduity of master and pupil, he succeeded in drilling his protégé with a discipline that was at once rigorous in its physical ordeals, noble in its literary and moral aspirations, sympathetic in its application. It was a truly Spartan discipline exercised in an extraordinarily scrupulous fashion but superimposed by a deeper sense of humanity.

Ito's intellectual pursuits, however, were confined necessarily to those precious moments when his duties did not require his undivided attention; and such moments were few and far between. It was Kuruhara's usual custom to rise at an early hour. He would then rouse his youthful charge from a slumber all too brief and teach him history and the classics under the faint light of a waning candle. The classics embraced almost every conceivable aspect of human conduct. They represented a distinct philosophy of life, a tradition, a code. No samurai could justly appreciate and defend the invaluable heritage of his forefathers without immersing his spiritual and intellectual being in its sublimated depths. To achieve such a life was thus a task involving something infinitely more exacting and profound than that of becoming a mere soldier.

Such a life, however, was not without its thrills, particularly as the increasing turbulence of the times engendered by the coming of the foreigners and the burst of revolutionary activities at the seat of the Imperial Court filled it to the brim with all manner of hazards. Differences of opinion between the Emperor's supporters and those owing allegiance to the Shogunate, even in places far removed from the center of disturbances, were sharp and distinct. Sword duels which frequently developed into dangerous riots were precipitated at the slightest provocation. The handful of Choshu troops under Kuruhara's command literally seethed with royalist convictions and aspirations. But the eyes of the law, as prescribed by the Shogunate, directed a most penetrating surveillance which it was suicidal to defy. This behooved all patriots of the royalist persuasion to use the utmost discretion in expressing their views, whether in the privacy of their own barracks, as in the case of Kuruhara's detachment, or in the two rival capitals, or even in the far-flung provinces where recruits were added daily to the augmenting list of potential revolutionists. But the more hazards it involved, the more attractive did the life of a samurai appear to Ito. He was just passing through that stage in life when the consciousness of danger serves merely to whet one's imagination and to spur one on to reckless adventures.

This period of apprenticeship for Ito was of short duration. But it was more than compensated by the glowing opportunities of contact it afforded with the leading patriots and with the great issues of the day. This aided him immeasurably during those formative years and prepared him for what was yet to come.

2

Political events, in whose bewildering complexities and their ultimate solution Ito was later to apply the full measure of his singularly fertile mind, meanwhile proceeded on their inevitable course. Townsend Harris, ensconced in a temple at Shimoda, entered upon his difficult mission of inaugurating an extensive political and commercial relationship with Japan. The Shogun's Government had as yet formulated no definite policy as to what precisely should be Japan's permanent answer to this form of encroachment by a Western nation. Furthermore, the psychological receptivity of the average Japanese, be he a loyal subject of the Shogun, a reactionary, or a royalist, had been so developed that he could not contemplate without serious misgivings a situation in which foreigners would be permitted freely to live in his country. Harris, however, let loose a magnificent barrage of diplomatic powder, and after a series of exhaustive deliberations with the Shogun's Councillors, he succeeded in completing the draft of a commercial treaty. Signature was postponed at the request of the Japanese until the approval of the Imperial Court had been obtained. The Shogun's Government, possessing only a scant knowledge of the revolutionary movement gaining strength in Kyoto, gave Harris to understand that this approval would be secured as a matter of course. Little did he realize that a stormy dissension which was destined to plunge the nation into a stupendous holocaust ending, inevitably, in the overthrow of the Shogunate, was to follow in its wake.

To Ito, the little samurai's aide at Miyata, Harris's negotiations meant only one thing. He was as yet too young and
inexperienced in the affairs of the world to pass judgment upon
so momentous an event. But he was growing fast, his mind
was alert, he was eager for knowledge, and under Kuruhara's
tutelage he was being rapidly initiated into the typical Choshu
point of view. Choshu had nothing but inordinate contempt
for the Shogunate. Every concession granted the foreigners
was thus seen through jaundiced eyes. Harris's latest feat in
particular was construed as revealing a cowardly and dishonorable strain in the Shogun's Government. Beset by such overwhelming influences, and with no opportunities for perceiving
the struggle through other perspectives, Ito had very little
occasion to believe otherwise. His first contact with national
politics was in consequence made under the disadvantage of
age-old prejudices. But the time was slowly approaching when
he would be free from the shackles of Clannish loyalty; when
he would be able, independently and of his own volition, to
observe the march of events from a more detached point of
view. Until then he must live and learn.

He remained at Miyata for a year, at the end of which he
was at liberty to return to Hagi. Kuruhara, fully convinced
that the lad deserved a higher form of instruction, recommended him to one more able than himself.

The figure of a heroic soul, brilliant and passionate, shines
forth from the dark and bloody pages of history. It is the
figure of a Choshu prophet whose adherence to his lofty convictions was beyond the comprehension of his persecutors and
whose invaluable life was snuffed out all too prematurely to
enable him to materialize his dreams. It is Sho-in Yoshida,
than whom there is none greater among the tragic martyrs of
Japan.

This was the man to whom Kuruhara, himself a disciple,
recommended Ito for further instruction in the classics.

Sho-in was first of all a royalist. Hence his anti-foreign
complex was in reality merely a vicarious expression of his
enmity against the Shogun's Government which, in reopening

the country to foreign intercourse, had ignored Imperial sentiment and opposition. He had, as a matter of fact, a secret and unbounded admiration for the Westerner's science. So much so, that in urging the expulsion of the foreigners from Japanese soil he advocated the use of their own superior weapons of warfare! Such a policy, however, could not be adopted by Japan without coming inevitably to grips with her conflicting national commitments—without adding gratuitously to the confusion of the times. And in those dark hours of futility he made a momentous decision. He resolved that he would himself go abroad, that he would himself take the initiative in making an exhaustive study of Western civilization. But there were insurmountable obstacles. To leave the country was a crime punishable by death. Nothing, however, daunted the fearless Sho-in, who was determined to turn criminal, if by so doing he could ultimately benefit his country.

He first proceeded to Nagasaki where he planned to board one of Poutiatine's ships of war for points out West. But when he reached there, the Russian fleet had already cleared the port. He returned, bitterly disappointed, to Yedo. Then his hopes were kindled anew, for he soon learned that the American fleet was anchored off Shimoda preparatory to making an extended visit to Hokkaido. Setting out at once for Shimoda, he succeeded in boarding one of the vessels on a dark and stormy night, only to be rejected by the Commander, who declared that he would not be a party to a criminal conspiracy against the government of Japan. Despite Sho-in's pleas for secrecy, the matter was immediately reported to the Shogunate officials. This, together with his belongings which were discovered on a drifting boat on which he had rowed to the battleship, served as sufficient proof of his guilt to warrant arrest and incarceration. His life was spared because his offense did not go beyond making a frustrated attempt to break the seclusion law. His position of influence in Choshu and the sinister power behind the Choshu movement to overthrow the Shogunate also accounted not a little for the apparent leniency on the part of the Yedo authorities. He was later released on parole with the understanding that he should thenceforth devote himself solely to educational work. He returned to Hagi and became master of the Shoka Sonjuku, where he surrounded himself with a group of the Clan's most gifted scholars.

Young Ito, returning west from Miyata and equipped with a mind rich with the brilliant impressions of the eastern tumult, entered the portals of the Shoka Sonjuku and began at once to receive the fiery influence of Sho-in's astounding mind. The distinguished master and the eager pupil were quick to discover in each other a community of interests, of ideals, of aspirations. Sho-in was tremendously impressed by this young recruit, and the thought raced through his mind, like water through a mill race, that here was a budding genius gifted with those very attributes of leadership which would enable him to succeed where he himself had failed in diverting the nation's course from the terrible fate to which it was obviously headed. Ito, Sho-in decided, was Japan's man of destiny. And having so decided, he proceeded to instil into this raw youth those imperishable convictions which burned in his breast.

CHAPTER III
TYRANNY

I

Soon afterwards Ito, though still a youth of eighteen, was dispatched by Sho-in with five other young samurai on a strange mission to Kyoto. Wild and incredible rumors, apparently based on authentic reports from the two rival capitals over the latest developments with respect to the foreign situation, had seeped in with astonishing persistency, conveying an ominous portent to all loyal supporters of the Emperor. Ito's mission was to investigate these rumors, to sift the facts from the myths.

The facts, he found, were in themselves unprecedented in their national and international significance. The fate of Townsend Harris's commercial treaty hung precariously in the balance as Lord Hayashi, the Shogunate's special envoy to the Imperial Court, and Councillor Hotta, the man who was responsible for the drafting of the treaty, hastened to Kyoto to present an exhaustive analysis of the pressing circumstances under which it had been concluded and requested, vainly, for Imperial endorsement. The Shogun, Iesada, was meanwhile sinking rapidly on his death-bed within the Yedo castle. A violent controversy over the appointment of his successor between Nariaki Mito, senior Lord of the Tokugawa dynasty, a reactionary and hater of foreigners, and Lord Naosuke Ii of Hikone, the acknowledged power behind the pro-foreign faction, threatened to disrupt the ranks of the Shogunate itself. Then word came that the fleets of Great Britain and of France, having succeeded in subjugating the will of China, had forced her to sign new and undesirable treaties; that they were about to proceed to Japan to wrest a similar victory. Townsend Harris, who had anticipated such a move and repeatedly warned the Yedo Councillors against it, threatened to go to Kyoto to make a direct appeal to the Emperor, little knowing that the place was a hot-bed of anti-foreignism. Out of this welter of dissension and despair Lord Ii, having received the death-bed endorsement of Shogun Iesada to become Tairo—a position approximating that of Regent in every essential particular— emerged as virtual dictator. Lord Ii, assuming sole responsibility, authorized the signing of Harris's commercial treaty in open defiance of the Emperor's known opposition. He met the demands of the envoys of Great Britain and of France with a similar pacific treaty. He foisted young Iemochi Kii to the position of Shogun. He meted out cruel and arbitrary punishments to all the leaders of the anti-foreign persuasion who had dared obstruct his policy. Victorious, unmolested, dreaded, Lord Ii was now supreme.

The rumors, Ito learned, had merely provided a highly fantastic twist to the inevitable aftermath. Lord Ii's name became one to conjure with. The story of his phenomenal rise to power and his subsequent use of extremely tyrannical methods spread like the proverbial wildfire throughout the country. The news, intensified, exaggerated, and distorted by the fatuous populace with every mile it traveled, brought terror to the hearts of the masses. Lord Ii, so the tale ran, had developed a mania for usurpation, and was now on his way to Kyoto to abduct the Emperor! A prodigious army of retainers flanking his triumphal march was prepared, the tale continued, to annihilate the active leaders at the seat of the Imperial Court who betrayed hostility, or were suspected of spreading enmity, against the Shogunate.

But the Imperial Court, Ito discovered, to his own relief, was hardly cowed by such rumors. Stern disciplinary measures were contemplated to bring the Yedo dictator immediately to a proper sense of respect for the Emperor. The hour had come when the Emperor must re-assert his sovereign rights with implacable firmness. Two Imperial emissaries were at once dispatched to Yedo to convey a resolution to the Shogun's council, demanding the presence of Lord Ii or the heads of the three Houses of Tokugawa at Kyoto to make a formal acknowledgment of the Emperor's supreme authority. Kyoto, meanwhile, waited impatiently for the response from Yedo which did not come.

2

During his brief sojourn in Kyoto Ito met Yanagawa and
Umeda, two of the most brilliant leaders of the militant royalists. The spirit of revolt permeated their entire beings. But
this revolt was of a sublimated order, for it was rooted in the
very essence of the Yamato traditions. They had sworn in
their own peculiarly solemn manner to restore the Emperor
to his rightful position as the supreme ruler of the nation, in
fact as well as in name. Ito's young mind was still in a formative state, and a mature appraisal of the complex feud in
which the foreigners played, unwittingly, a significant rôle,
was impossible. But this magnificent movement developing
in Kyoto and the personality of the leaders who engineered it,
impressed him tremendously. He returned to Hagi with a
heart filled with a holy sense of patriotism. He decided that
thenceforth he must so prepare his life as to be able dutifully,
wisely, unceasingly, to fight for the restoration of his Emperor.

Soon afterwards Kuruhara also returned to Hagi. But his
homecoming was effected under circumstances less conducive
to glory than those under which he had originally set out for
Miyata. For he had been suspended from his duties by Choshu's bureaucratic chiefs and made to suffer the stigma of official displeasure. His offense lay in the fact that he had incorporated into Choshu's military system certain improved
methods of discipline derived from recent contacts with the
foreigners, such as drilling and the use of drums and other
standard military accoutrements. Like Sho-in, he had been
among the first to realize the singular effectiveness and the
obvious superiority of Western military practices, and he could
think of no convincing reason why they should not be utilized
by Choshu's troops. Nor was the personnel of Choshu's general staff averse to these innovations. But he had essayed to
apply them to the troops under his command without first
seeking the official sanction of his chiefs, and for this he had
received the latters' stern rebuke and his own summary dismissal.

His retirement from active duty, however, was only tem-

porary.   No sooner had he returned to Hagi than Choshu's
military system was revolutionized, with ironical suddenness,
through a universal adoption of Western methods.   Kuruhara,
thus vindicated, was quickly reinstated to his command.   Furthermore, he was ordered to proceed at once to Nagasaki, there
to engage in a thorough study of these methods under Dutch
tutelage.   He chose twenty young samurai to accompany him
on this mission, chief among whom was Ito.

The city of Nagasaki occupied a unique place in the history
of Japan.   It was the great western gateway through which
the ebb and flow of the picturesque tides from foreign lands
passed in colorful review.   Here the sea-meandering foreigners
obtained their first intoxicating whiff of the mystic shores of
Cipangu.   It was the haven of the storm-tossed foreigners
seeking refuge from the terrible typhoons which swept the
China coasts, the coveted goal of ambitious traders, the first
and only city of the Empire that betrayed any semblance of
an international character.   Although the enforcement of anti-
foreign regulations had been rigidly carried out in other cities,
Nagasaki had always been somewhat exempt.   Always a sort
of benevolent slackening of the reins had been allowed to prevail there.   The Dutch traders, who pursued their legitimate
tasks in a commendably unobtrusive fashion, were the most
exemplary foreigners who sought their fortunes in this quaint
city.   They exerted a profound influence upon the social and
cultural aspects of the life of the Japanese.   Even their language was assiduously assimilated.   They served as capable
and faithful intermediaries in the development of Japanese
contact with the foreigners, as purchasing agents supplying the
matchless creations of Western genius, as instructors both civil
and military.

Here Ito and his comrades, under the vigilant superin-
tendence of the resourceful Kuruhara, himself a diligent student, succeeded in mastering, through the aid of Dutch experts,
a rudimentary knowledge of that vast accumulation of Western
experiences which simplified warfare with such devastating efficiency.   For a year these quaint converts of the West, housed
in the pretentious estate of the Lord of Choshu, grappled un-

relentingly with the knotty, unfamiliar tasks placed before them. All commands and instructions were issued in the Dutch language; hence a mastery of the language was an essential prerequisite. Their loose native gowns replaced by an ill-fitting foreign attire, their short stubby feet enveloped in ungainly shoes in lieu of the native wooden clogs, but topped with the customary "chom-mage" coiffure, these young men met the prying eyes of a hotly disapproving society and knew the inward terrors of ridicule. The spectacle of these oddly picturesque figures shouldering the massive guns and marching clumsily to the shrill tune of the fife and the ponderous beating of the rackety drums, presented a ludicrous appearance upon the stolid background of centuries-old national habits and customs. These scenes marked the frail and awkward beginnings of an inexorable metamorphosis which was soon to transform the mystic somnambulist of the East.

During the course of his training Ito made a careful study of the manufacture of firearms. He marvelled at the amazing precision with which these fighting paraphernalia served the ends of human destruction, how thoroughly they drilled death-dealing holes through the enemy forces at long range, if operated skillfully. So he made a hurried trip back to Hagi with a few samples and presented them to the Lord of Choshu for consideration as future weapons of warfare. Lord Mori, no less convinced of their tremendous efficacy, received them with approbation.

Soon after his return to Nagasaki Ito, the main essentials of his training completed, accompanied Kuruhara and his comrades back to their native fief. Upon arriving at Hagi, Ito met Takayoshi Kido, the young leader of Choshu, through Kuruhara's introduction. Kido, who was the latter's brother-in-law, was about to depart for Yedo on an important mission, and through Kuruhara's solicitation Ito became attached to him as aide. This meant that he was about to re-enter that vast political battleground of the east where the nation's destiny still hung in the balance. It meant that he was about to plunge headlong into the fierce conspiracies which were soon to involve the nation in a mighty conflagration.

3

Upon his arrival at Yedo Ito was beset by the first great sorrow of his life. For the rumors which had first sent him on that mission to Kyoto had actually materialized, not in the abduction of the Emperor, but in the prostration of the Imperial Court under Lord Ii's direction and the arrest, punishment, and beheading of its most eminent leaders, including Sho-in himself.

The crime for which Sho-in received the death penalty was a peculiarly paradoxical one. His own position was clearly evinced in the two brief poems which he composed during those precious moments preceding the falling of the fatal sword. One was a parting message dedicated to the members of his family. It expressed a tender sentiment which was without parallel in beauty and poignancy, revealing a boundless love, an immaculate conscience, and a profound commiseration for the frailties of human judgment. The other was a public declaration, a message for posterity in which he affirmed in his own masterful fashion that he was about to die for his country. By so doing he was violating neither the trust of his ruler nor that of his fellow-beings. He was dying in the performance of his duty to his Emperor whom he conceived to be the rightful ruler of his country. All this, however, was in contradistinction to the claims of his executioners, who characterized his activities in life as those of a pernicious culprit.

Ito and his new master, Kido, set foot in Yedo in time to receive Sho-in's remains from the Shogunate authorities. The two, together with Iida, a Choshu physician, attended to the preparations of his burial. Kido first disrobed himself, and with the "juban," or innermost garment, which he wore, he wrapped the lifeless form that once contained Sho-in's animated spirit. Then Iida, who followed next, covered it with his own "shitagi," or mid-garment, of black silk. Over all this Ito placed his own silken sash, the "obi," to complete the ceremonial robes of the deceased. Thus outfitted, Sho-in's remains were placed in a casket and lowered into his tomb close to the graves of other distinguished royalists whose spirits

had preceded his.   It was a sorrowful moment for the youthful
Ito.   It filled him with an added sense of the tyranny of the
Shogun's Government, with the ever-increasing spirit of revolt
against this tyranny which animated the faithful followers of
the Emperor.

4

The estate of the Choshu Clan in Yedo boasted of a unique
institution known as the Yubikan.   It was here that Choshu's
embryonic scholars and budding knights on duty in the Shogun's capital pursued the arts of literature and military conduct.   Here the great Kido had his being.   Here he established his Yedo headquarters whence he directed Choshu's immense
under-cover revolutionary activities.   Here, too, Ito spent the
next few months to perform his duties as Kido's assistant, and
found the opportunity to resume his studies which constant
travel in the interests of his Clan had so often interrupted.

Sometime later Kuruhara also made his appearance in Yedo,
this time to assume the rôle of head of the Yubikan.   Thus
the three valiant sons of Choshu, one a leader of men, another
a scholar of the first rank, and the third a youth of great promise—all faithful, upstanding disciples of the late Sho-in, all
destined to become nationally important figures, and all bound
by close personal ties—lived under the same roof and dreamed
together of great things yet to be achieved.

CHAPTER IV
CONSPIRACY

I

From this period onward Ito, no longer a mere adolescent, shouldered his responsibilities as a full-fledged warrior. Thenceforward he was a revolutionary royalist engaged in hectic intrigues and conspiracies, not merely against the Shogun's Government, but also against the foreigners whom the latter had permitted to trade and to reside in Japan. His first assignment was an exceedingly ambitious one, which nearly proved fatal.

Lord Ii, modernist and tyrant, was finally stabbed through the folds of his palanquin while en route to the Shogun's palace to commemorate the "Jomi Sekku" or girls' festival. But his successor, Nobumasa Ando, who sought to inaugurate a more pacific policy, adhered, unfortunately, to the principle of "Kobu Gattai"—a union of the civil and the military, and hence an entente cordiale between the Yedo and Kyoto Governments—which was to have been realized by the marriage of Shogun Iemochi to Princess Kazu, sister of Emperor Komei —a most unwelcome solution to all militant royalists. A plot to assassinate Ando was in consequence formulated under Kido's leadership, of which Ito, though he was not numbered among those delegated to do the killing, became a willing accessory. The murder, however, was frustrated, Ando having escaped with a slight injury, and five of the six swordsmen put to death. The sixth would-be executioner, Mannosuke Uchida, who had been unavoidably detained, attributed the death of his five comrades and the failure of the plot to his own involuntary negligence; and in order to make proper atonement in true samurai fashion he disemboweled himself at the Yubikan.

This brought the Shogunate authorities hot on the trail of Kido and Ito. They were at once suspected of complicity in the Ando assault and summoned to the Kitamachi headquarters for a stringent quizzing. Kido preferred to maintain a discreet silence lest he be forced into confessing something which might be used to incriminate him, and Ito, though he was manifestly unfitted both by age and experience to attempt such a feat, acted as defense counsel.

The investigation turned into a wordy combat in which the wits of this seemingly presumptuous young rogue were pitted against those of Lord Kurokawa of Bitchu, a seasoned official representing the Shogunate's department of justice. Ito built his arguments around a particularly strong alibi, a procedure which the West holds somewhat in contempt but whose efficacy in the legal vicissitudes of this country was still to be proven. So cleverly did he manipulate the facts surrounding his and Kido's movements during the Ando assault that the elderly official failed utterly to find an effectual loophole through which to penetrate the bluff. There was nothing the latter could prove against the prevaricating young warrior, nor on the arch conspirator, Kido. The two were thus absolved from complicity in the crime.

2

In releasing them, moreover, the Shogunate was actuated no less by circumspective scruples. For its advocacy of a conciliatory union with the Imperial Court—the "Kobu Gattai"—was being received by the Choshu Clan with mixed feelings which indicated that hope for its ultimate reception was not altogether lacking. But Ito, following in the footsteps of his superior, threw discretion to the winds. He himself proceeded to aid in the wrecking of even this slender hope.

Ever since he had become Sho-in's pupil and subsequently Kido's aide, he had joined the ranks of the extremists in thought and deed. Like all upstanding extremists, he was now irrevocably committed to the destruction of the Shogunate, at whatever cost. To him, as to his comrades, no compromise was acceptable. He would not cease to conspire against the Shogun's Government until every vestige of its power and influence had been reduced to smithereens; until the Emperor, triumphant and unassailable, had been securely restored to his immemorial rights.

The Shogunate's hope rested on the work of a liberal group within the Choshu Clan headed by Uta Nagai, diplomat and propagandist, who favored the entente. Nagai occupied a prominent place in the Choshu council, and his pleas for unification were based on the hope that a reconciliation between Kyoto and Yedo would lead to a consolidation of the nation's entire military strength, which was now disrupted by Clannish feuds, and which was so necessary in coping with all eventualities incident to the foreigner's penetration. Lord Mori was persuaded to support this movement, and with his permission Nagai attempted to enter into negotiations with the Emperor's Court for its adoption.

But Kido's extremist comrades, notably the group headed by Kusaka, anticipated his move by precipitating a strong counter movement at Kyoto. Here Ito, whence he departed as Kido's assistant, took a spirited part in the campaign. Violent, impulsive, destructive, he became a boldly conspicuous figure, preaching revolution, creating warlike disturbances in order to rally the lukewarm pacifist royalists beneath the extremists' sanguinary banner.

Nagai, arriving with high hopes, made an elaborate attempt to revolutionize public opinion in Kyoto before beginning negotiations. But everywhere, with the extremists dominating, he met with a scurrilous opposition. Pressed by his own embittered clansmen, he fled from the city. But he did not proceed very far. He lingered in the outskirts of Kyoto, hoping to intercept Lord Mori, who was heading westward, and to confer with him over the possibilities of reviving his ostracized doctrine. When his whereabouts was reported to the extremist headquarters, Ito, in common with all true extremists, became violently enraged over his incredible persistence; and with that hot-blooded impetuosity of youth which knows neither fear nor mercy, he joined a little band of warriors, five in number, who started out on a hunt for him. He thus became a would-be assassin determined to take the life of a distinguished fellow-clansman whose only offense was that he persisted in preaching a political doctrine at variance with his own. The only reason why he failed to fulfill his homicidal mission was that Nagai had finally become aware that his life was being sought after and had expedited his flight by deceiving his pursuers and by achieving an extraordinary burst of speed, which carried him beyond their avenging swords.

The irony of it all, as Ito had occasion subsequently to discover, was that no less a person than Kuruhara, his erstwhile master and teacher, had himself become one of Nagai's staunchest supporters, and that when the Imperial Court repudiated the "Kobu Gattai" by adhering to the extremists' anti-Shogunate, anti-foreign policy, this upstanding soldier-scholar had taken the only step compatible with the code of a samurai: he had disemboweled himself. It was not an easy matter for Ito, with his young and headstrong sense of patriotism, to reconcile the thought that he had sought the life of the man for whose principles his own benefactor—the man who had initiated him, after the most exacting personal sacrifices, into the arduous role of a samurai—had given his life in vindication.

3

Much as he felt its dramatic impact, this realization did not, however, deter him from carrying out his militant vows with the same relentless zeal, and with the same unswerving belief in their righteousness. Because of his daring, his deft swordsmanship, and his proven ability to talk himself out of difficult situations, he was now delegated to undertake the most dangerous mission of his life.

The Shogunate under the direction of Lord Kuze, successor to Ando, now drifted slowly into a state of innocuous docility. But the extremist royalists would not consider its forcible dissolution until it had first nullified the foreign treaties and driven the foreigners out of the country literally at the sword's point. Meanwhile they proceeded to commit a series of reprisals to cripple the power of the Shogun's Councillors. Lord Ii's son and heir, who succeeded to the lordship of Hikone, in particular, was deprived of the greater portion of his fief. Apparently as a protest against this outrage, a vast army of

Hikone warriors, it was rumored, were plotting a coup d' etat
against Kyoto.   Their scheme was to abduct the Emperor and
hold him as hostage pending a suitable redress of their grievances.   Elaborate repairs on the old Hikone castle were being
made, the rumor continued, in order to provide fitting quarters
for the royal prisoner.   Two Choshu warriors had been dispatched at different intervals to investigate the truth of this
story, but they had found nothing stirring, either in the vicinity of the castle or in other parts of the fief to warrant belief.
This spying business was a perilous affair, and both had returned to Kyoto without caring to probe any further into its truth
or falsity.   But the rumor persisted, and Ito's mission was to
proceed at once to Hikone and there conduct an exhaustive
investigation of all evidences which might either bear out, or
forever set at rest, the disquieting reports.   To return with
anything less than the absolute truth meant dishonor and death
by his own sword.

He thus became a spy, and he acquitted himself in faultless
fashion.   Traveling under an assumed name, he revealed a
fictitious front calculated to divert suspicion.   He took up his
quarters in the very home of a Hikone clansman in the immediate proximity of the castle.   He remained there for some
length of time.   He put up such a magnificent bluff that he
was able continually to conduct his search unmolested.   The
castle came under his observation for days and weeks.   After
all this sleuthing he found the castle to be innocent of any
suspicious movement which might indicate that a coup d' etat
was being planned, or that preparations were being made to
accommodate a royal prisoner.   In the end he was convinced
that the rumored story was a hoax.   When he returned to
Kyoto and presented his findings to the extremist headquarters,
the rumor, its credibility definitely discountenanced, ceased to
circulate.

4

Having successfully undertaken his mission as a spy, Ito
now turned destructionist.   His destructionist activities were
aimed at the foreigners, at the British in particular, whose

newly-constructed legation house at Gotenyama in Yedo he regarded, like others of his faction, as an alien monstrosity and must consequently be demolished. It stood, this British edifice, on hallowed ground, alone among the ancient pines and venerable temples. Not only was it, to him, a desecration of the primeval beauties of Gotenyama; it was built by foreigners who had come to reside in Japan by virtue of treaties concluded by the hateful Shogunate and to which the Emperor had refused endorsement, and thus had no ethical or legal right to exist!

A few of his comrades had previously departed for Yokohama to attack the foreign diplomats there, only to be severely reprimanded by young Motonori, the Choshu Heir Apparent. With them he now kept tryst in an old warehouse of the Sagami-Ro at Shinagawa near Yedo to devise a plot to raze the British "monstrosity." Details were arranged and assignments made. Together they went to the Yubikan to prepare "yakidama," an explosive used by the Japanese for incendiary purposes.

One dark night they invaded Gotenyama: twelve inscrutable, diabolic plotters, each carrying his share of the explosives. Severing the strong barriers which protected the legation quarters, three men immediately set fire to the building by hurling the "yakidama" into various nooks and corners. The others followed suit. Ito stationed himself outside to fight off would-be fire fighters. Only a lone guard appeared on the scene, but he was frightened off by Ito's gleaming sword flashing in the firelight. Within a few minutes the building was in flames.

BOOK II
THE REFORMER

CHAPTER V

BAPTISM

I

This incendiary outrage proved to be the last of Ito's acts of conspiracy—and for good reasons. He was about to enter upon an amazing series of adventures that opened new vistas of a civilization incomparably superior, which revealed the utter futility, if not the utter imbecility, of exploiting the foreigners as an issue over which to put an end to the Shogun's rule. A great and lasting metamorphosis presaging a new understanding of Japan's destiny was, in short, about to come over him.

The Choshu extremists, moulders of the Imperial policy, finally compelled the Shogun and his Councillors not only to proceed to Kyoto with the utmost humility and acknowledge the Emperor's supreme authority, but also to pledge and to avow the forcible expulsion of all foreigners on May 10, 1863. This expulsion act was to be emblematic of the forcible nullification of all the foreign treaties concluded by the Shogun's Government in defiance of Imperial opposition. But meanwhile these revolutionists had disclosed one mounting inconsistency. While professing an irreconcilable aversion to all foreigners, they had repeatedly betrayed an increasing interest in things foreign, particularly with respect to methods and weapons of warfare. The Kuruhara mission to Nagasaki to study Western military tactics under Dutch tutelage, of which Ito was a member, was the result of their first recognition of the desirability of adopting the Westerner's ways. From then on they had established secret connections with agencies devoted to foreign trade and carried on an extensive importation of firearms from abroad. This in itself was a violation of those very principles which constituted the basis of their attack upon the Shogun's dictatorship. Then in 1862 they purchased a mammoth steamship from Jardine, Matheson & Company of Yokohama.

To purchase the steamship, despite the suggestion of supreme hypocrisy, was a simple enough matter, but to operate it with safety and precision was quite another. Other than hired foreigners no one possessed any knowledge of the complicated machinery which propelled it. They were thus completely at the mercy of foreigners; and in view of the fact that their own men were the ringleaders of the anti-foreign faction in control of the nation's destiny at Kyoto, it was obviously suicidal for them to continue to rely upon foreign assistance. From this state of affairs sprang the belief, within as yet a relatively small group of radical thinkers, that their own men must go abroad to make an exhaustive study of the Westerner's complex science—of the science of operating steam-driven vessels in particular. Three deserving samurai, Inouye, Yamao, and Nomura, were thus secretly commissioned to undertake this study.

While arrangements were being made to secure the necessary steamship connections to Europe, Ito became aware, for the first time, of the contemplated journey abroad. Quick to grasp the tremendous possibilities of this mission and the unprecedented opportunities it afforded to see the world, he decided at once to have himself included among its personnel. Knowing, however, that the Choshu council would not consent to any further increase, he succeeded in joining the fortunate trio by having recourse to a number of ruses, chief of which was his pretext that the Shogunate authorities were hot on his trail for some manufactured offense and that he must consequently seek temporary shelter in foreign lands. Endo, another aspirant to worldly knowledge, was also in the end permitted to depart, thus increasing the number to five.

On the evening of May 12, 1863, the five boarded a little foreign freighter bound for Shanghai. Since it was imperative that they use every precaution in eluding the surveillance of the Shogunate officials, they hid themselves in a coal hatch until the vessel departed. Five days later they reached Shanghai.

Here they disembarked, and with roseate hopes sought out Jardine, Matheson & Company's Shanghai Office, where they

presented their credentials, preparatory to securing passage on
a Europe-bound vessel. But here they encountered their first
stumbling block. When inquiries were made by the officials
of the Company as to the real purpose of their trip, their inability to speak the English language gave rise to a serious
misunderstanding. The only English word with which they
were able to associate their mission was "navigation." This
word they uttered in reply, to the best of their doubtful ability, confident of its conveying adequately the sense of the
phrase, "to study the science of steamship navigation." But
the officials of the British firm construed it otherwise. Believing that these quaint visitors from Japan were bent upon studying the practical aspects of navigation—to become, in a word,
plain sailors—they forthwith assigned them to two little
freighters bound for London with a cargo of Chinese tea.
The little ambitious group thus parted company, Ito and Inouye starting out courageously on a tiny vessel of three hundred
tons, while the other three followed them on a larger ship a
week later.

For Ito and his companion the stark disillusionment came
soon after embarkation. The master of the vessel, instead of
treating them as passengers, followed scrupulously the instructions from the agents at Shanghai and put them immediately to work scrubbing the decks, and performing such
other menial duties as were required of an ordinary seaman.
For their daily rations they were given salt meat and stale
biscuits, such atrocious food as they had never before tasted.
Obviously they were being taught "navigation" from the
ground up and in that traditional fashion of the sea, where
the stern, often brutal, disciplinary measures of those in command have wrought havoc with the human soul. Being unable,
however, to communicate their protest against this treatment
in a lingo comprehensible to the ship's master, they were compelled to suffer in silence.

Here were two young samurai, occupying an exalted place
in the roster of the Choshu Clan and sent abroad on a scholarly mission, reduced unmercifully to the status of lowly seamen.
The physical toils were somehow bearable, but the affront to

their dignity, which the samurai invariably contemplated with the deepest resentment, was beyond endurance. To protest by way of the sword, as all upstanding warriors were expected to do when their dignity had been violated, would have been pure and unadulterated mutiny. It would have ended disastrously for themselves, and the purpose of their mission would have been defeated. Yet they were tempted, on more than one occasion, to end it all by resorting to violence. It was only after exercising the greatest self-restraint that they were able finally to abandon this vengeful procedure. But it did considerable good to their soul, for their lives so far had been crowded with the vain and arbitrary rewards of a privileged warrior. It was their first taste of practical democracy. It was bitter but none the less edifying.

Added to this humiliating treatment at the hands of the ship's master was the feeling of nausea and exhaustion caused by a life in the odoriferous forecastle and the erratic behavior of the sea along the southern coast of Africa. But on clear nights the moon shed her benevolent beams upon the scene of misery. Nostalgia descended upon them. The fond recollections of their native country revivified their dwindling hopes. Thenceforward they were constantly reminded of the supreme importance of their mission. Their bruised hearts were measurably appeased. It was thus, with a feeling of intense gratification, that they experienced their first magic glimpse of the city of London, where they arrived after four months and eleven days of sea life.

London! A glimpse of this Mecca of the West, and the scales were lifted from Ito's eyes. The magnificent scene of the harbor, bristling with the slender masts of countless ships of war, of titanic steamships, of sailing vessels of every description, was pregnant with testimony as to the marvellous achievements of the outer world in matters of war, of commerce, of transportation. What lay beyond this fascinating epitome of the West—for here the merchant princes of Europe and America had come to barter—was not difficult to surmise. It reflected science, progress, vision, power. Above all, power! This was the measure of the foreigner's mental capacity, of the blonde entrepreneur on whom the haughty somnambulist, Japan, had been loading with contempt, with abuse, with defiance! What fools had his people been to have slept through the centuries, fatuously content with their meagre lot, and grossly ignorant of the prodigious possibilities existing in this and other progressive spheres whence those ships had come! Yet they had blabbed intolerantly of expelling the white man, of reverting to the ancient modes and codes of life; and he himself had until but recently been one of the most intolerant, the most impenetrable, of fools!

Happily, he was no longer a fool. Now that he had achieved the right perspective with regard to the future developments of his country, his mission to Europe seemed vested with a far greater significance than he had ever imagined.

Through the kindness of Jardine, Matheson & Company's officials in London, negotiations were at once started with certain philanthropic gentlemen identified with educational work, as a result of which Ito was placed in the home of a Dr. Williamson, a college professor. In this fashion Ito became a student in the city of London, a student with a mind already enriched with the venerable classics of the East but ready to absorb the magic wonders of Western modernity.

2

Only six months of this incredible, intensive life of an amazed student, and Ito became aware, from a perusal of the London "Times," of disquieting developments at home—developments which induced him to return hurriedly to Japan. Well might he have done so, for his country, worldly-ignorant, cantankerous, intransigent, had plunged at last into the maelstrom of war; and it had need of him. It had need of anyone with sufficient knowledge of the outer world gained through actual contact and observation to advise its leaders of their colossal mistake; and none was more signally qualified than Ito.

With the close of May 10, 1863, the day on which all foreigners were to have been driven off from Japanese soil, Ito's extremist comrades had burst forth with a booming crescendo of martial activities, only to precipitate powerful retaliatory bombardments from foreign warships which spelled disaster, not only to his own bellicose Clan, but to the whole of dissension-ridden Japan. Hostilities were first centered in the Straits of Shimonoseki, Choshu's maritime gateway guarding the southwestern entrance to the Inland Sea, which in turn protected the seat of the Imperial Court. Two armed Choshu vessels, emerging suddenly from their sheltered nooks, opened fire on the "Pembroke," a lone American merchant vessel innocent of any warlike armaments, which was descried dropping her anchor apparently to await the receding of the tide. On May 23 a French vessel arriving from Yokohama was next fired upon by the shore batteries. Three days later a Netherlands merchant ship was likewise attacked. Thereafter Shimonoseki was closed to foreign shipping.

Robert H. Pruyn, the American Minister succeeding Townsend Harris, when advised of the attack on the "Pembroke," dispatched the U. S. S. "Wyoming," Captain McDougal commanding, to secure redress from Choshu. On June 1 the "Wyoming" entered the Straits and fired the first shot in what was designed to be a forcible assertion of American treaty rights. On June 5 two French war vessels arrived in the wake of the "Wyoming" to avenge the attack of May 23, exchanged belligerent salutations with the shore batteries, and landed a strong detachment of marines.

Meanwhile the British squadron, Admiral Kuper commanding, in a vain effort to apprehend the murderers of a Mr. Richardson, who had committed a grave offense at Namamugi against the Lord of Satsuma, bombarded Kagoshima, the Clan's stronghold, and the bursting shells, aided by a strong gale, reduced a part of the town to a flaming mass of wreckage.

But this was not all. In Kyoto rivalry among the royalists themselves had brought about a most unfortunate cleavage. Lord Shimazu (Satsuma), the most powerful of the royalist backers, accepted the offer of Lord Matsudaira of Aizu, a pro-Shogunate Clan, to conclude an entente for the purpose of ridding the Imperial Court of the Choshu ascendancy; and civil war broke out with all its malignant consequences. The Choshu extremists, defeated and ousted from Kyoto, made elaborate

preparations to regain their lost hegemony. The Shogunate
forces, reinforced by Saigo, the peerless general from Satsuma,
repulsed their attack, and proceeded, with Imperial approval,
to undertake a punitive expedition into their very stronghold.

The foreigners also prepared to settle their score with Choshu. Under the aggressive leadership of Alcock, the British
Minister, a combined punitive expedition to force the opening
of the Straits of Shimonoseki and to prostrate the bellicose will
of Choshu was finally agreed upon by the Ministers of the
United States, France, and Holland.

Thus Choshu, ousted from Kyoto, was threatened with the
horrors of a dual invasion: by the resurrected Shogunate army
over the land route, and by the formidable foreign fleets from
the sea.

How Ito, a lone individual, and a mere youth, however
much he was armed with facts invincible and however ambitious his plan of action, could save his Clan from utter demoli-
tion and dishonor, was something which defied speculation.
But Ito, because of his very youth, was determined to risk
everything in the attempt. In that brief sojourn in London
he had learned enough of the conditions in the outer world to
perceive the indubitable error in Japan's policy of exclusion,
enough to deplore the brazen stupidity with which Choshu had
defied the great Western Powers. Though he did not trouble
himself with thoughts of repelling the Shogunate attack, he
was convinced that the foreign punitive expedition must at all
hazards be stayed. His objective was conciliation. He would
appeal to the foreign Ministers and to the Lord of Choshu and
attempt to settle the differences without recourse to war. Obviously the difficulty lay not so much in soothing the outraged
temper of the foreigners as in seeking to break down the stupid
pride and refractory will of his clansmen. He was not destined
to undertake this mission alone, however, for Inouye, who had
by now become his inseparable pal, chose to accompany him.

The two departed from London in March, 1864, landing at
Yokohama barely in time to carry out their plans. Here, however, Ito and his companion were compelled to travel incognito,
as their trip abroad had been made in defiance of the seclusion

law and a public discovery of this fact would lead to their arrest and execution. Their adoption of Western attire and Western habits rendered it comparatively easy for them to disguise themselves as foreigners, more particularly as Portuguese traders. These pseudo-Portuguese with a distinctly Japanese physiognomy spoke a very intriguing English!

After engaging temporary lodgings in a hostelry at Yokohama which catered to foreigners, they interviewed Alcock and started negotiations.

3

Eighteen foreign warships, all of forbidding aspect, were at the time anchored off Yokohama preparatory to launching that punitive expedition to Shimonoseki. Ito appealed to Alcock. He asked for a temporary reprieve in order that he and Inouye might proceed to Choshu to secure the audience of the daimyo and endeavor to bring about a peaceful settlement of the quarrel. In view, moreover, of the obvious hazards which would necessarily have to be encountered in an attempt to reach Choshu by land, he requested that he and his companion be conveyed on a British vessel as far as Shimonoseki. He cited his visit to London, which had revolutionized his own opinion, and he assured the British Minister that if the truth were actually known in Choshu, the attitude of its people toward the foreigners would be certain to be metamorphosed into one of friendliness and cooperation.

Here we are indebted to his "Memoirs" for relating what followed. Alcock, it appears, did not at first seem impressed. "He told us," the "Memoirs" state, "that it was impossible to accede to our wishes. He said that it had already been definitely decided that the eighteen battleships which we could observe in the harbor should proceed to Shimonoseki to commence the bombardment." But Ito was insistent. "Here," he informs us, "we argued exhaustively, assuring him emphatically that we could put a stop to the impending war if only we were given the opportunity to intercede." Alcock then relented: "He called the Ministers of France, of Holland, and of the United States, and the admirals of the British and French fleets, to a conference, which proved favorable, and wherein it was decided that we be employed as bearers of letters of admonition from the Powers to the Lord of Choshu."

Summoned to the British legation at four o'clock the following afternoon, Ito and his companion were informed of this decision—that their request would be granted only on condition that they consented to deliver those letters of admonition. Ito agreed, and the pact was concluded. "We did not, however," he writes, "deliver those letters. To do so would have given the impression to our people that we were mere hirelings in the employ of the foreigners. It was clearly a breach of faith but under the circumstances unavoidable."

The question now arose as to where they should seek to land: "Spreading out a map of the seas, it was observed that the shores near the Choshu capital were fraught with danger, particularly as it was impossible to ascertain where the forts were located. We felt that Himejima would serve our purpose, and it was decided that the vessel should convey us there."

Transported to Himejima on a British battleship, Ito and Inouye were given twelve days in which to accomplish their mission. From thence they rowed across the unfrequented seas to a little seaport village, walked to the town of Mitajiri, where, with the aid of a friend, they reverted to the use of native attire. Thus from Mitajiri to Yamaguchi, the Choshu capital, they traveled unmolested.

Lord Mori received them graciously. Ito, ably assisted by his companion, recounted the amazing experiences he had gained on his recent sojourn in London. He presented a vivid description of the stupendous material achievements of the countries whose pioneers had come to trade with Japan. He explained the futility of Choshu's warlike attempts to resist their peaceful penetration. He revealed the imminence of the four-Power punitive attack upon Shimonoseki. He pleaded for reconciliation as the only hope of preserving the independence of Japan.

Lord Mori was favorably impressed. For three hours, with all the exalted Councillors in attendance and with a map of the world spread before them, Ito's impassioned pleas were deliberated upon with the utmost gravity. History was in the making, with Japan's reawakening—her destiny itself—coming to life through the bold efforts of this youth and his companion who had broken the barriers of seclusion and seen the world's power for themselves......At the end of this memorable session the Councillors were unanimously agreed: a truce with the foreigners must be effected.

But when the truth about Ito's mission reached the public ear, a rabid extremist organization started to denounce him as a betrayer of Japan. A sinister movement to prevent the contemplated truce was immediately set afoot, bringing a disquieting dissension to the Choshu capital. At this Ito, knowing that the extremists—all former comrades of his—would not permit him to live much longer, left for Hagi on a farewell visit with his parents. Returning to Yamaguchi the following day, he found that mob violence had at last broken out. His companion, Inouye, suggested hara-kiri—the prompting of a high official—as being a decidedly more honorable finale to their mission than decapitation at the hands of their foes. Ito replied: "That won't do at all. If death be our reward, I should prefer to die fighting by attempting to cut down as many as possible of those who would dare to draw their swords on me!" A finished swordsman with the courage of his convictions, he was neither a physical nor a moral coward. Fortunately, the Choshu council took effective measures to suppress the hostile movement. "The upshot of it all," writes Ito, "was that neither homicide nor hara-kiri was found necessary."

But when the official reply was drafted, Choshu, it was revealed, considered it proper to refer the question of concluding peace with the foreigners to the Imperial Court, whence the expulsion decree had originated; and for this a three-month reprieve was requested. Furthermore, it was the sense of the council, the reply stated—with more bravado than discretion —that if these terms were not acceptable, Choshu was quite prepared to defend its honor against all comers!

Inouye, heartily disgusted, refused to be the purveyor of so provocative a reply. But Ito, realizing the futility of request-

ing a more conciliatory wording, again decided to settle the
matter in his own way. So the two set out for Himejima,
where the British warship awaited them, and Ito reported the
results of their negotiations verbally in his own words. When
asked about a written reply to the letters of the four Powers,
he explained that considering the nature of his reception he
was exceedingly fortunate in having escaped with his life.

The reprieve was granted. The British vessel returned to
Yokohama, while Ito and his companion remained in Choshu.
Thus did the youthful peacemaker, by using his own judgment
and his own tactics of diplomacy, save the day for Choshu.

4

Its relief, however, was only temporary. Time literally
flew. The three months' truce drew rapidly to a close. From
the east the Shogun's army, bent upon conquest and revenge,
moved menacingly toward the Choshu frontier. The dual
catastrophe to which its leaders had but recently awakened,
became an imminent reality. The Shogunate invasion was
unavoidable, but the naval assault of the foreigners, they decided, must be prevented. Admitting finally that they had
erred lamentably in their arrogant reply to the four-Power
ultimatum, and unaware of Ito's avoidance of the use of the
text, they made feverish efforts to retrieve their blunder.
They now voluntarily sought Ito's services and made preparations to send him to Yokohama to renew the negotiations with
the foreign Ministers, with permanent peace as the objective.
But their demoralized army had retreated as far back as Mitajiri and was no longer capable of escorting him to his destination. Since the foreign vessels avoided Shimonoseki, the only
alternative was for him to go to Nagasaki and there board one
of these ships for Yokohama. But the Shogunate and Satsuma
forces were in control everywhere; not even Nagasaki was a
safe spot for Choshu samurai. This just about exhausted the
last possibility of salvation. Obviously Choshu had reached
an impasse.

The foreign Ministers construed Choshu's inevitable silence
as a refusal to make peace. A fleet of seventeen warships, in-

cluding one American, nine British, four Dutch, and three French vessels, therefore lifted anchor at Yokohama and set sail for Shimonoseki. When news of the fleet's arrival off Himejima reached Ito at Yamaguchi, he hastened to Mitajiri to intercept its passage in order to commence peace negotiations before it started bombarding Shimonoseki. Inouye meanwhile proceeded straight to the scene of the impending assault. But neither Ito nor Inouye reached the fleet in time to talk peace. The bombardment was begun in real earnest. The Maeda batteries returned the fire. For three days the battle raged. Then Shimonoseki fell.

When Ito arrived at the stricken port, he saw that the fleet was beginning to open fire upon the town itself. Confusion reigned. Disagreement among Choshu's leaders prolonged the tragedy. Finally Ito, bearing a white flag, rowed over to the flagship and pleaded for a cessation of hostilities. Peace negotiations were soon made. Ito agreed, on behalf of Choshu, to pay the indemnity of three million dollars demanded and to permit free passage through the Straits to foreign ships.

The attack from the sea, at least, had thus been checked before any irreparable losses were sustained. But at what a price! Further complications loomed ahead, for there was not enough money in the Choshu exchequer with which to indemnify the foreigners. Ito had promised to pay the three million dollars because peace at any price seemed infinitely more desirable than a possible annihilation of Choshu. Since it was obviously impossible to raise the requisite sum within a reasonable length of time to satisfy the foreigners, it became apparent that an appeal must be made either for a mitigation or for some other suitable procedure to alleviate the difficulty of payment. Ito accordingly headed a mission to Yokohama on board a British vessel. But there he learned, to his great relief, that the Shogunate, acting as the central government upon which devolved the responsibility of assuming all such obligations, had already agreed to pay the indemnity out of its own meagre funds.

His mission over, Ito started out on his homeward journey with considerable hopes for the future. But when he reached Choshu he found, to his amazement, that a disagreement over

the adoption of defensive measures to meet the impending
Shogunate invasion had caused a split in the council, and civil
war had broken out within the Clan, with every indication of
developing into a most virulent and a most devastating medium
for committing Clannish suicide.

CHAPTER VI
RESTORATION

I

Ito was now on the threshold of a significant decision. A one-time rabid extremist whose miraculous journey to Europe had transformed him into a decided friend and admirer of the foreigners, he found himself confronted with a peculiarly paradoxical situation inevitable in a change so fraught with conflicting passions and beliefs. Since it was a cardinal principle in Choshu that to be anti-foreign was synonymous with being anti-Shogunate, it followed logically that to become pro-foreign, as did Ito, was to concede the justice of the Shogunate's historic stand and, therefore, to vindicate its foreign and domestic policies. Over and above all this was the change of front of the Emperor himself, who had sanctioned the Shogunate's punitive expedition to Choshu. Choshu was now in the throes of an internal upheaval. A multitude of dissenters who had come to entertain a growing distaste for war since the recent defeats at Kyoto and Shimonoseki, had banded themselves together under the pacifist name of the "Party of Submission." These pacifists had, after a successful coup d'etat, usurped the power long held by the extremists and halted the Shogunate invasion by offering peace terms which were satisfactory to Takamori Saigo, the mainstay of the invading forces, regardless of the ignominy which might be Choshu's unenviable lot. To be consistent, it behooved Ito to take cognizance of these facts, to rally himself on the side of the pacifists, hence in favor of submission to the Yedo avengers.

But here Ito's penetrating mind delved beyond the superficial aspects of a groping, changing Japan. He took occasion to weigh the fundamentals, the venerable ideals of a race dedicated to something essentially higher and nobler—the spirit of Yamato. In this he was sustained by Sho-in's immaculate example. Sho-in had disclosed during his brief but exemplary career, this higher and nobler objective, this indispensable spiritual essence of a true patriot of Dai Nippon, in all its pristine brilliance. He had shown that the struggles for supremacy between the Imperial Court and the Shogunate having *antedated* the coming of the foreigners, one could very properly advocate pro-foreignism and still remain consistently true to the cause of Imperial sanctity! In the end Ito was convinced that his duty, as he perceived it, must consist in continuing to aid in the overthrow of the Shogunate and in spreading at the same time the gospel of peace and good-will toward all foreigners.

At this point, however, with war clouds still brooding menacingly over the battle-scarred Clan—with the extremists maneuvering a counter attack to dislodge the pacifist hegemony —he found that his prospects for launching his particular propaganda were dismal indeed. According, when Takasugi, one of the more adventurous of the extremist leaders who had himself once made a visit to Shanghai, urged him to accompany him on a sojourn abroad, he at once assented.

The two set out together from Choshu with mingled feelings of regret and hopeful expectations. When they went as far as Nagasaki they met a former friend, a well-meaning Englishman who led them into believing that the new British Minister, Sir Harry Parkes, being masterful, independent, and aggressive, might, if reasonable inducements were offered, be persuaded to swing his support over to the side of the royalist factions and thereby strengthen immeasurably the extremists' movement to overthrow the Shogunate. This opened new vistas of possibilities. The Choshu clansmen were already familiar, through their own rash experiences and to a degree painful to contemplate, with the peculiar potency of the foreigner's methods of warfare. The idea of having the British at least assist them in reviving their frustrated conspiracies against the Shogunate must, therefore, be sufficiently tempting, Ito believed, to elicit universal approbation. It fitted into his own prospective schemes. It would destroy the ancient prejudice against the foreigners and facilitate, in particular, an understanding between Choshu and the British. As far as the British themselves were concerned, they would support Sir Harry, Ito was assured, for they were being secretly alienated from the French, who chose to remain consistently friendly to the Shogunate. And the principal inducement for this clandestine alliance might conceivably be the opening of the port of Shimonoseki to British trade.

Armed with this ingenious idea, Ito and Takasugi returned to Choshu, where they labored ever so cautiously to win converts. But everywhere they met with a hostile rebuff. The vast majority of the extremists could not forgive the foreigners for the dismantling of Shimonoseki. Although they had betrayed a distinct sign of relenting during those hectic days following the expiration of the three months' truce when they attempted to send Ito to Yokohama to renew negotiations with the four-Power combine, even that had proved short-lived. Instead of teaching them an object lesson, it had created an entirely opposite effect. Only bitterness and hate and vengeful outbursts had risen in its wake. When the full import of Ito's new propaganda became known to the extremist authorities, he was characterized as a pernicious culprit. His life was again threatened. Nor was his past usefulness to the Clan remembered with the least gratitude.

In order to elude arrest Ito decided not only to take a pseudonym, but also and more particularly to disguise his outward appearance, a task at which he was a past master. He traveled extensively, from hamlet to town, from town to village, playing incessantly and with infinite caution the dangerous game of hide and seek with his pursuers. He must have remembered with bitter irony those halcyon days before the fall of Choshu when the conditions had been reversed and he had crossed mountains and dales to seek the life of the diplomat, Uta Nagai. Finally he attempted to seek refuge in Korea. But Shimonoseki, the only port of egress to foreign lands, was being closely watched; and he was as effectually trapped as a fox in the woods, with the hounds encircling it in close pursuit.

2

Such was his plight when something happened with a sweeping suddenness which completely overturned the councils of Choshu. Kido, one-time leader of the extremists, whose dis-

appearance apparently from the face of the earth following
Choshu's defeat at Kyoto had been a thing of mystery to both
friends and foe, suddenly put in an appearance at Yamaguchi.
Like Ito, he had tramped in ragged disguise across hundreds
of miles of hostile territory, suffering innumerable hardships.
He had thus endeavored, through a silence made necessary by
the exigence of flight, to escape the Shogunate's avenging
sword. His reappearance at this time was charged with a profound significance because it came about almost simultaneously
with the announcement that the Shogunate's second punitive
expedition to Choshu to cripple the extremists who had overthrown the pacifists was about to be launched; because General
Saigo, formerly the offensive threat of the Shogunate forces
(though under compulsion from his Lord), now adopted an
about-face policy by making known his desire to unite his forces
with those of Choshu to overthrow the Yedo Government;
because Satsuma, of which Saigo was supreme military commander, having voluntarily paid over to the British the Richardson penalty of £25,000, had since developed an increasingly
friendly relationship with them, even to the extent of bidding
secretly for their assistance in purchasing foreign battleships
and firearms. All this meant that Choshu, by accepting Saigo's
proffered aid and by soliciting the friendly connivance of the
British, was favored with an unprecedented opportunity to
administer that long-planned, long-heralded coup de grace upon
the Shogunate regime. It meant that Kido had returned from
his self-inflicted exile to resume Choshu's leadership in this
emergency. Finally, it meant that Ito's own ambitious schemes,
precisely as he had devised, were about to be realized.

The meeting of Ito and his former chief was soon effected.
Kido, too, had changed considerably since the two parted on
the occasion of Ito's visit to London. His policy was thenceforward to lift the ban of intolerance from all resident foreigners simultaneously with the restoration of the Emperor. The
Shogunate army must be repulsed, annihilated, and its government once and for all forcibly dissolved. This fact, with war
again looming, served once more to mitigate the rash animosities surrounding the issue of the foreigners. The extremists

agreed to support Kido.

Sustained by Kido's masterful leadership, Ito proceeded with his work under circumstances less perilous to life and limb. The immediate task at hand, a task upon which rested the structure of all future success, was the consummation of the proposed Choshu-Satsuma coalition. Kido still spoke of Saigo with scorching hostility because of the part the latter played in forcing Choshu's humiliating exit from Kyoto. Yet he could not resist a feeling of admiration for the peerless fighter from Satsuma. So, too, did Saigo feel toward Kido, but his pride prevented him from making the initial overtures for an understanding. Ito's particular task lay in counselling Kido to overlook the past for the sake of the more significant future. Saigo was likewise persuaded by his bosom friend, Toshimichi Okubo —a fellow-clansman who was destined to play an equally distinguished part in the Restoration—to forget his pride. Meanwhile two leaders from Tosa, a Clan actuated by similar aspirations, also regarded the proposed coalition as the only effective means of redeeming the nation from the sorry mess into which it had been plunged. These men acted as friendly intermediaries who brought the two principals and their assistants together, and finally succeeded in bringing about their reconciliation. Choshu and Satsuma were thus united, and their respective armies pledged to the conquest of Yedo.

3

Events moved rapidly thereafter. All the conflicting aspects of the whole revolutionary movement converged toward a grand climax with swift inevitability. The Shogunate, when the truth of Saigo's alignment with Choshu became known, wilted completely, its morale disrupted. The foreign diplomats, sensing their supreme opportunity, proceeded jointly to Osaka Bay in a flotilla of nine ships of war and presented their ultimatum to the Imperial Court. The Emperor, forced at last to choose between the formal ratification of all the foreign treaties and the payment of the $3,000,000 Shimonoseki indemnity which the Shogunate had promised but could not pay, sought through his reactionary Councillors to stall them off, only to be confronted with the further threat that a non-compliance would render them "free to act as they may judge convenient." Faced with the inescapable, the Emperor ratified the treaties. Then the young Shogun, Iemochi, died at Osaka; and Yoshinobu Tokugawa, an experienced official who had served as leading Minister under the regime just past, succeeded by right of heredity to his title. Twenty days later the Emperor, Komei, also died; and his son, Mutsuhito, a lad of fourteen, ascended the throne. Here the crafty Lord of Tosa, fearing that with the fall of the Shogunate, which now seemed imminent, the Choshu-Satsuma coalition might attempt to set up its own dictatorship, endeavored to anticipate all such eventualities by advising the newly-installed Shogun to abdicate. It developed, however, that Yoshinobu—and herein lay the crucial elements of the situation—had himself contemplated renouncing his post long before the question was broached to him. For he felt that only thus —only by voluntarily relinquishing all the powers and privileges vested in the Tokugawa Shogunate so that the office of Shogun could thereafter be abolished and the Emperor reaffirmed in his ancient rights—could he best serve the interests of his country. With this salutary, wholly unselfish declaration, he surrendered his authority to the Emperor. The Shogunate was formally dissolved. But dissolution alone did not satisfy the leaders of Choshu and of Satsuma, notably Kido and Saigo, who became the power behind the Imperial Government. Saigo, backed by the armies at his disposal, demanded that Yoshinobu also renounce his rights to his fief, his revenues, and his soldiery, these to revert to the uses of the Imperial Government. The Tokugawa retainers refused to abide by such drastic confiscatory acts. The young Emperor, advised by his moderate Councillors, authorized a compromise—only a portion of the Tokugawa fief, as decided by "universal verdict," would be absorbed. Saigo relented, but he stipulated that Yoshinobu first present himself at Kyoto to make the renunciation in person, and that his troops be demobilized. Yoshinobu agreed, but his troops, reinforced by a fresh army from Yedo, preferred to resist to the death. Saigo massed his troops at Fushimi and Toba to meet the attack of the rebel army. From the south-west came the

invincible army of Choshu to reinforce him. At last, after all
those years of incessant strife, the issue between the royalists
and the Tokugawa retainers was settled by the "arbitrament
of the sword." The rebel army, numbering fifteen thousand,
collapsed completely. The Shogunate, in substance as well as
in name, was extinguished for all time. The supremacy of
the Imperial Government as the sole ruling unit of the nation
was now a permanent, an irrevocable fact.

A week later Ito, wearing a frock coat and with a sword
dangling from his side, stepped ashore at Kobe from a British
battleship on which he had been assigned for diplomatic duty
directly civil war loomed at Osaka. To his amazement he
found the city in the throes of a fresh outbreak between the
Japanese and the foreigners. "The foreigners," he found, "had
virtually captured Kobe and traffic on the highways was forbidden to Japanese." Confusion prevailed everywhere. Going
straight to the British Minister, Sir Harry Parkes, with whom
he had previously achieved a friendly understanding, he asked
to be enlightened on the whole affair from the foreigner's viewpoint. "On the day before," he wrote, describing the results
of this interview, "a few foreigners had crossed the path of
the procession of Tatewaki Hioki, chief retainer of the Lord
of Bizen, and for this offense (it was a crime punishable by
death) they had been fired upon immediately. Whereupon
they, somehow or other, briskly returned the fire. The Bizen
troops next fired recklessly upon the ensigns of the Ministers
of the various countries which flew at the edge of the foreign
settlement. The foreigners retaliated by landing reinforce-
ments and field guns from their battleships, and secured control
of the city. Then they seized several Japanese steam vessels
in the harbor which had arrived from Chikuzen and Ogura,
confiscated their weapons, and disabled their engines." Sir
Harry was indignant—and not a little confused: "He told me
in vitriolic tones that he had theretofore felt that Bizen, like
Choshu, had become friendly to the foreigners, but that judging
from the late incident he must conclude that all the Japanese,
without any exception, were hostile to foreigners! He next
placed a great sheaf of papers before me. These were all

financial obligations incurred by the daimyo which had been placed in the Minister's hands, and represented purchases of firearms, etc., by their city retainers when the change of government took place. He demanded that they be paid. I told him it could not be done the way he wanted it, but that I should see to it that the whole matter was eventually settled. He retorted by saying that no matter how much I boasted, was it not obvious that the affair was simply impossible of settlement? He was particularly vehement in his denunciation of the new government which, he said, assumed to have wrested the powers of the Shogunate, yet made no official announcement to the foreign diplomats to this effect. He said it was an outrage. Very well, I said, I should be able to settle this matter in three days. Thereupon I left for Osaka."

It happened that Higashikuze, the newly-appointed Vice-Minister of the Bureau of Foreign Affairs, was passing through Osaka; and when Ito, upon arrival there, informed him of the state of affairs in Kobe, an Imperial appointment was forthwith conferred upon him to assist Higashikuze in effecting the necessary negotiations. The two, together with a staff of assistants, proceeded to Kobe. The foreign Ministers were granted a formal interview, at which the belated announcement respecting the Restoration was made. Assurances were given that reparations would be made for the Bizen riot, and that the treaties would be scrupulously respected and foreign lives afforded every protection.

As part of the "reparations," a Bizen retainer named Zenzaburo Taki who confessed that it was he who had given the signal which precipitated the attack, undertook to assume sole responsibility for the riot. "Thereupon it was demanded," Ito writes, "that he commit hara-kiri, and the order was duly given. But it appeared to me really pitiable, and with the hope that I might be able to save his life, I conferred with Parkes. I suggested that to demand his self-destruction for a misdeed committed in such confused circumstances was pitiful. Parkes, however, advanced a sound argument: he would not be moved by sentiment. It was not ethical, he said, for a foreign Minister to interfere with a sentence meted out by order of the Japanese Emperor."

This was the second time Ito had repudiated the idea of hara-kiri. On the first occasion, directed at himself, he had regarded it as cowardly, and had threatened to resort, instead, to combat. Now, pronounced officially upon an offending warrior, he declares it to be "pitiful" and strives to prevent its consummation. A Westerner, known traditionally to abhor such an act, and in this instance privileged to prevent it if he so chose and so requested, turned the table on the Japanese by insisting, inferentially, that it be scrupulously carried out!

Moreover, it was evident that from this period on his inner susceptibilities underwent a distinct softening, of which this incident was an eloquent example, for just prior to his advent in Kobe he had taken unto himself a wife—Umeko—who thereafter shared his trials and tribulations, his glory and his successes.

CHAPTER VII
IMPERIAL COUNCILLOR

I

Thus the successful inauguration of diplomatic relations between the Imperial Government and the Western nations was due in no small measure to Ito's linguistic versatility and his knowledge of the Westerner's points of view. As a fitting recognition of his growing usefulness he was, on January 25, 1868, elevated to the position of Councillor. This meant that he was admitted into the "inner circle," there to assist in guiding the nation's destiny along with its foremost leaders—with men like Saigo and Kido and Okubo. It was a signal triumph for a young man still in his twenties and handicapped by a lowly farmer's lineage to be thus honored. Nevertheless it was a breach of centuries-old traditions, which presumed to recognize talent, or even an approximation of talent, only in those possessed of a knightly heritage. Hence it was subjected to considerable criticism emanating from the ranks of the military bureaucrats. But the Imperial Government was now faced with the task of meeting revolutionary conditions and responsibilities, a task requiring an equally revolutionary method of solution; and Ito was permitted to continue with his duties as Councillor. Choshu, moreover, had contributed not a little to the Restoration: Kido had become advisor to the President of the Council of State, and it was through his assiduous interpositions that Ito was able to survive the widespread stigma respecting his lowly origin.

But an even greater surprise awaited his critics, for the next few months, instead of witnessing the damaging effects of their calumniating diatribes, disclosed that an increasing confidence was being placed in him. The government was still in its embryonic stages of development in so far as the centralizing of its new administrative functions was concerned. Various changes, regarded then as extremely radical, were instituted as the needs were felt. Within a month Ito was appointed Secretary of the

Bureau of Foreign Affairs in addition to his duties as Councillor. Then on April 27, 1868, a complete revision of the government organization was effected. Under the new system the country was divided into two hundred and seventy-three Clans, twenty-one Prefectures, and eight Urban Prefectures. Osaka was designated as one of the Urban Prefectures; and because of its growing importance as a foreign commercial center, Ito was appointed head of its Foreign Department, which included a resident commissionership at Hyogo. On May 6 the lower fifth class of the Junior Court Rank was conferred upon him. The occasion was Emperor Meiji's granting of audience, for the first time, to the foreign diplomats, for which Ito was called upon to serve as interpreter. On May 23 he was commissioned Governor of Hyogo. He was at the time but twenty-eight years of age.

2

By this time Ito had begun to nurse a radical political doctrine—the doctrine of feudal renunciation.

"One day, during the latter part of January, 1868," he wrote, "while I resided in Kobe as Governor of Hyogo, Kido came to me and said: 'Though the Restoration has been effected, the Imperial Court is still far too impotent to maintain a successful government. Hence there is a movement afoot within the Satsuma Clan to make a gift of a hundred thousand *koku* (of land). In this connection I have felt advisable that the House of Mori (Choshu) also make a contribution of a hundred and fifty thousand *koku*—the old Ogura, Ishikawa and Hamada fiefs which have been reclaimed as a result of our recent victories. I have already discussed this proposal confidentially with some of my colleagues. What is your opinion with regard to this matter?' To which I opposed and declared: 'I cannot approve of such temporizing measures. What, generally speaking, is the Restoration but a return to the system of government that existed prior to the advent of the military hegemony of the Middle Ages? It means, in other words, the abolishment of feudalism and the consolidation of the military and economic power in the hands of the Imperial

Court. For without it, and without the re-establishment of prefectural (civil) rule, it would be impossible for Japan to adopt universal reforms which would enable her to attain equality with the Western nations. It therefore behooves us to resort to drastic measures—to abolish the Clans and thus bring the entire country under the direct ruling power of the Imperial Court. This cannot be accomplished by a mere contribution of a hundred thousand or a hundred and fifty thousand *koku.*' "

The Restoration, in other words, was as yet a merely nominal affair, for the sources whence the Imperial Court obtained its material sustenance were meagre indeed. All its wars had hitherto been fought entirely by feudal Lords and clansmen professing loyalty to the Emperors; there had been no military organization of its own to speak of. Its financial support was confined to the negligible income derived from the shrines and temples coming within its jurisdiction and the revenues of the confiscated Tokugawa estates, which comprised barely a sixth of the total wealth of the country. The other five-sixths constituted the feudal fiefs, hence the private possessions, of the two hundred and seventy odd Clans, each of which devoted its revenues to its own exclusive uses. Each maintained its own army and navy. Each was consequently a miniature nation unto itself. Ito's counter-proposal lay in striking at the root of this independence—in reapportioning the feudal fiefs as civil units paying direct taxes to the Imperial Government and administered by men appointed by, and owing direct allegiance to, this central civil authority.

Elaborating the origin of this idea in his own mind, he said: "I have good reasons for advocating this step. Ever since I was a child I have read Rai Sanyo's 'Nihon Seiki' (Political History of Japan) with delight and appreciation. Not only was I deeply impressed by his discourse on royalism; I particularly took note of the fact, deep down in my heart, that the system of government which prevailed at the height of the Imperial regime was the prefectural type now in existence in the modern world, and that this constituted the vital source of the Imperial authority. Later, while studying in Europe, I noted that it was likewise the system that had brought about the success and prosperity of the Western nations; and I became even more convinced that feudalism in our country must be abolished. During the early days of the Restoration I once spoke to Lord Iwakura about this. I have not, therefore, arrived at this conclusion by a sudden, overnight musing."

Kido, after listening intently to this counter-proposal, seemed impressed. He did not, however, believe that the time was ripe for its execution. "Your argument," he said, "is sound. As long as the Restoration has become a reality, what you suggest must inevitably be consummated. But it would mean the virtual ruin of our Lord (Choshu) and of all other daimyo, both great and small, and I should warn you against enunciating such convictions in any too rash a fashion. Were you to profess them publicly now, our hopes of success might end in failure."

Since then Kido, Ito found, had abandoned his own idea of making grants of land to the Imperial Court and had given considerable thought to this suggestion. Meanwhile the Lord of Himeji, by a singular coincidence, offered to do precisely what Ito had secretly advocated—to relinquish his own particular fief to the Emperor. The occasion presented a most timely opportunity for Ito, despite Kido's warning, to publicize his doctrine. He thus, in May, 1868, went forth to Kyoto and presented a memorial to Emperor Meiji, urging not only the acceptance of Himeji's gratuitous offer but also the outright dissolution of all the feudal principalities. His plan, morever, provided sufficiently for the compensation of the Lords who would be dispossessed. He would elevate them to the Peerage, confer upon them an appropriate title, and, in conformity with a contemporary monarchical practice, accord them a seat in the Upper House of the government's future legislative body.

The men at the very helm of the government were hardly averse to giving his memorial the consideration it deserved. But they feared that because of its sweeping implications it would meet with a hostile reception throughout the land. Civil war might result. Eventually some such changes as he suggested must be carried out, but the country, they decided, was as yet unprepared to accept them. His memorial was rejected.

When it became known that Ito had publicly recommended such a bold and ultra-radical step, his own clansmen, curiously enough, turned against him. They branded him as a traitor to his Clan, as the betrayer of his own Lord. Appealing to Kido, they demanded that he be summarily dismissed from the service, while the more violent of his denouncers started a movement to assassinate him. To them loyalty to their Clan was paramount. The end of feudalism would mean the extinction of the samurai, their only source of livelihood. The Restoration concerned only matters of nominal overlordship. The essence of nationalism in all its modern significance which Ito had grasped long ere this had not yet taken root in their imagination.

But Kido had meanwhile secured an understanding with Lord Mori—an understanding which, though it approved of eventual abolishment of feudalism, called for cautious methods in carrying it out. Ito was thus temporarily permitted to resign, only to be reinstated soon afterwards, though in a minor capacity, with the *regular* fifth class of the Junior Court Rank. Once his reinstatement had been publicly, though grudgingly, accepted as proof of the confidence placed in him by the Imperial Government, Ito was appointed head of the Hyogo Bureau of Commerce. This was followed in the next few days by another appointment which placed him in charge of the Finance Bureau.

In July, 1868, Yedo was renamed Tokyo and designated as the future permanent seat of the Imperial Government. Thither the Emperor proceeded in September, establishing his official domicile in the palace formerly occupied by the Tokugawa Shoguns. With the removal of the administrative body to its new quarters, Ito set out for Tokyo in response to a summons requiring his presence there to handle the usual diplomatic work necessitated by the change. On June 20, 1869, he was appointed Vice-Minister of the Department of Finance and of the Department of the People's (Home) Affairs.

This rapidity which characterized Ito's reascendancy to a position of influence in the government carried a significant connotation. It meant that the radical ventures he had urged upon the Emperor had meanwhile been bearing fruit. The very men who had at first rejected his proposal had since, under Kido's leadership, carried on a clandestine movement to persuade four of the most powerful royalist daimyo, namely, those of Choshu, Satsuma, Tosa, and Hizen, to take the initiative in surrendering their fiefs to the national government so that other, and lesser, Lords might follow their example. No difficulties were encountered, for the four Lords, in conformity with their reiterated expressions and demonstrations of loyalty to the Emperor, agreed unconditionally to undertake the incredible sacrifice. When public announcement to this effect was made, other daimyo who perceived its inevitability followed in rapid succession to make voluntary relinquishments, so that the Imperial Councillors were sufficiently encouraged to take the matter into their own hands. On June 17, 1869, a proclamation was issued, announcing the end of feudalism in Japan. By that act the Tokyo Government took possession, in the name of the Emperor, of the right to all the lands, the revenues, the soldiery, and other vital assets of the country.

But the compensations provided for the ex-daimyo differed from Ito's proposal in several essential respects. The Clans were retained as territorial units for the administration of local affairs. The former daimyo were ranked with the nobility and simultaneously appointed Governors of their respective Clans, by virtue of which they were required to acknowledge the authority of the Tokyo Government. Their income was fixed at ten per cent. of the revenues of their Clans. Their retainers were similarly employed under the reorganized local governments as officials and clerks and classified as *shizoku*, which ranked them next to the nobility but above the common level known as *heimin*, which embraced all other, non-military, persons.

But the evils inherent in such an arrangement soon became apparent. Though the power of the national government had become practically unassailable from within, the ex-daimyo, as Governors of their Clans, were still able to exercise their ancient liberties. Devotion among the clansmen to their erstwhile Lords continued in many instances to surpass loyalty to the

Emperor.   Many disadvantages that worked to the detriment
of the government's new commitments became noticeably evident.   Evils of the rankest sort resulting from inefficiency,
petty jealousy, and selfish exploitation increased daily.   Conspiracies became frequent.   Except for the diversion of the
revenues to the national exchequer, the status of the feudal
regime remained in effect unchanged.   Ito had foreseen all this,
for he had suggested the outright abolition of the Clans and
the establishment of prefectural administrations to take their
place.   Two years of desultory experimenting passed before the
dissolution of the Clans was finally contemplated.   On July 14,
1871, it was solemnized by the promulgation of an Imperial
edict, setting forth the creation of Prefectures totaling three
hundred and two (they were later reduced to forty-six) to replace the Clans which were ordered dissolved.   This marked
the final overthrow of the ancient military system throughout
the country and the full realization of Ito's doctrine of civil
hegemony.

3

Ito's activities thus far had initiated him into practically all
the existing phases of the military and political life of the old
and the new Japan.   But he was destined further to enlarge
the scope of his activities, for now that foreign intercourse had
become a definite fact with something of hopeful permanence
breathed into it, there emerged from the welter of blasted
traditions the irrepressible spirit of the new age, seeking to
emulate the West, to achieve a like measure of power and prosperity.   This spirit had become father to a general movement
calling for an immediate expansion along Western economic
lines.   The industrialization of the country, the development
of the latest transportation and communication facilities, the
creation of modern financial institutions—all this must be accomplished literally overnight in order to span the gulf between her antiquated standards and those of the West, between
medievalism and modernity.   And because of Ito's experience
in consummating international negotiations, his proven ability
in diplomacy, and his genius for organization which was begin-

ning to manifest itself, he was required thenceforth to quit
political ventures at home for a while and to divert his energies
to this new field of human endeavor.

To begin with, he was appointed head of a mission created
for the purpose of negotiating with the financiers of Great
Britain for a loan of £ 1,000,000 with which to build the first
railway system in Japan extending from Tokyo to Yokohama.
The loan having been secured, work was soon commenced on
the railroad.   Other enterprises of a similar character but of
greater magnitude were to follow.

In July, 1870, he was promoted to the fourth class of the
Junior Court Rank and appointed to head another mission, this
time to the United States, to make a thorough study of her
financial institutions preparatory to the introduction of similar
systems throughout Japan.   This was his second visit abroad.

He made a supreme effort at mastering the intricate methods
of American taxation, of banking, of creating national budgets,
of operating national mints.   Making excellent use of the opportunity, he permitted himself the luxury of a digression by
attempting a searching study into the constitutional form of
government as exemplified by the Republic of the United
States.   Not content with this, he made a further digression
by studying the vast network of American railways and steamship lines.   Finally he wound up his studies by probing into
the marvellous mechanical and electrical facilities which represented the height of America's engineering skill.

Returning to Japan in May of the next year, he entered at
once upon the prodigious task of laying the foundation for the
country's financial system.   Four months of preparatory work
followed.   The existing coinage system was revised, in which
gold was adopted as the standard unit of value.   A national
mint was created in Osaka out of the machinery made available
by the discontinuance, on the part of the British, of their Hongkong establishment.   The Bureau of Taxation came into being.
Here Ito spent most of his time, while not engaged in directing
the affairs of the mint, in inaugurating a system commensurate
with every modern requirement.   Then he intrusted the work
to other men trained along the requisite lines, for he was now

called upon to devote his energies to those multifarious ventures which came under the general grouping of public works.

His "digressions" while studying in the United States served him in excellent stead. Under his keen and intelligent leadership, public improvements multiplied with extraordinary rapidity. Telegraph lines connecting the principal cities as well as the larger islands through submarine cables were established, first in an experimental way, then on a permanent basis. Additional railroads covering extensive mileage and built cobweb fashion reduced the man-driven "rickshas" and palanquins to infinitesimal proportions in transportation values. Modern docks replaced the ancient improvised wharves. Lighthouses lined the perilous coasts. Mining was improved through the adoption of large-scale facilities and the application of the most recent metallurgical discoveries. A postal system modeled after the American plan was introduced. Printing establishments supplanted the crude and laborious processes of depicting words on paper. It was significant, if only to attest the quality of the leadership thus displayed, that none of these innovations was undertaken without Ito himself mastering with surprising versatility all the essential details, mechanical as well as scientific.

CHAPTER VIII

PRESTIGE VS. RECONSTRUCTION

I

Again Ito was lured back into the political arena, though he retained the office of Minister of Public Works. For two pressing problems of major political importance, long held in a-beyance through the adoption of a policy of discreet waiting, had burst forth with all their pent-up grievances to challenge the ingenuity of Japan's ablest statesmen.

Korea, to begin with—or more particularly the Tai Won Kun, her virtual dictator—had not only repulsed Japan's repeated efforts at resuming friendly intercourse, but had treated her envoys with sovereign contempt. Being entirely unfamiliar with Japan's political vicissitudes, the Tai Won Kun, a reactionary and hater of foreigners, assumed that some rebel chief (the Emperor) had irreverently overthrown the legitimate ruler (the Shogun) and now had the temerity to seek friendly relations with his country. Particularly did he resent those rhetorical embellishments surrounding the term "Imperial Founder," which abounded in the text of Japan's official announcement of the Restoration. For he was given to imaginative excesses arising out of a long and unhappy association with neighboring Chinese Viceroys, and he perceived in them—or thought he did—a veiled intimation calculated to include Korea among the vassal states of Japan. Saigo, heading the dominant military clique of Tokyo, which included such Councillors of note as Soejima, Goto, Itagaki and Eto, clamored for a strong punitive expedition, either to compel Korea to retract her hostile attitude, or to avenge the insult hurled at Japan's honor and dignity.

Opposed to this programme of the militarists was the so-called peace party, to whom the problem of modernization and of attaining equality with the great Western Powers seemed of weightier consequence. Kido, whose position as one of the two prime movers of the Restoration was universally respected; Iwakura, a one-time Court noble who had been exiled for his extremist views; Okubo, Saigo's confidant who had done most of the political maneuvering while the latter did the fighting for Satsuma—these colossal figures stood staunchly for national reconstruction. To them the pressing need of the moment was not war but the doing away, by astute diplomacy matched with commensurable internal progress, of extraterritoriality and the conventional tariff, two dominant evils which had been imposed upon Japan by the Western Powers under treaties concluded by the late Shogun's Government. To this liberal group Ito, through the most natural of inclinations and convictions, lent his whole support.

Specifically, their programme called for an early revision of the unequal treaties. But before doing so it was deemed necessary that a first-hand knowledge of conditions in the treaty-Power countries be obtained; also that they be enlightened regarding Japan's substantial progress thus far achieved, politically, economically, judicially, as well as her future plans for their further expansion, which would justify revision. With the Emperor sanctioning this move, the conquest of Korea was held temporarily in abeyance, and these advocates of peace departed on the first official tour of the world.

Proceeding first to the United States, they carried a letter of credence from the Emperor to President Grant which stated their general purposes. "The period," it read,* "for revising the treaties now existing between ourselves and the United States is less than one year distant. We expect and intend to reform and improve the same so as to stand upon a similar footing with the most enlightened nations, and to attain the full development of public right and interest. The civilization and institutions of Japan are so different from those of other countries, that we cannot expect to reach the desired end at once.

"It is our purpose to select from the various institutions prevailing among enlightened nations such as are best suited to our present condition, and adopt them, in gradual reforms and improvements of our policy and customs, so as to be upon

*From "Leaders of the Meiji Restoration in America," pages 10—11.

an equality with them.

"With this object, we desire to fully disclose to the United States Government the condition of affairs in our Empire, and to consult upon the means of giving greater efficiency to our institutions, at present and in the future; and as soon as the Embassy returns home we will consider about the revision of the treaties, and accomplish what we have expected and intended."

At San Francisco, their first port of call, and at Sacramento, where elaborate banquets were given in their honor, Ito, as one of the Ambassadors, spoke to the assembled throngs, defining Japan's hopes for the future—an advance plea for treaty revision. "Our mission," he said,* at San Francisco, "under special instruction from His Majesty, the Emperor, while seeking to protect the rights and interests of our respective nations, will seek to unite them more closely in the future, convinced that we shall appreciate each other more when we know each other better...... To-day it is the earnest wish of both our Government and people to strive for the highest points of civilization enjoyed by more enlightened countries. Looking to this end, we have adopted their military, naval, scientific, and educational institutions, and knowledge has flowed to us freely in the wake of foreign commerce...... Japan cannot claim originality as yet, but it will aim to exercise practical wisdom by adopting the advantages, and avoiding the errors, taught her by the history of those enlightened nations whose experience is her teacher."

At Sacramento he was more specific. "We come," he said,† "to study your strength, that, by adopting wisely your better ways, we may hereafter be stronger ourselves. We shall require your mechanics to teach our people many things, and the more our intercourse increases the more we shall call upon you. We shall labor to place Japan on an equal basis, in the future, with those countries whose modern civilization is now our guide...... Notwithstanding the various customs, manners, and institutions of the different nations we are all members of

*From "Leaders of the Meiji Restoration in America," page 29.
†From "Leaders of the Meiji Restoration in America," page 19.

one large human family, and under control of the same Almighty Being, and we believe it is our common destiny to reach a yet nobler civilization than the world has yet seen. Now, I am sure that you are the advocates of these principles; and these hospitalities, so generously offered, we receive as a compliment to our nation, and as the public expression of these magnanimous sentiments. With thankful hearts, therefore, let us drink to a closer friendship between our countries—one whose benefits shall be mutual and lasting."

At Washington the members of the embassy were agreeably shocked when Ulysses S. Grant declared that his government was quite prepared to entertain treaty revision. They were thus so happily tempted that preparations were at once made to undertake a *separate* negotiation with the United States. But in their eagerness to achieve their coveted mission with the minimum of delay, they overlooked one inescapable disadvantage inherent in such a move which might later prove a detriment. Conscious only of the grand illusion that America's unselfish attitude would exert a most welcome influence upon the great Powers of Europe and thereby facilitate subsequent negotiations, Ito and Okubo made a hurried trip back to Japan to secure the necessary carte blanche from the Emperor. But it was never used. For, while they were on their way back to Washington, the remaining Ambassadors were informed of the folly of a separate revision, since the most-favored-nation clause in the existing conventions would enable the other Powers which might not consent to revision, while retaining their own unequal treaties, to reap every additional advantage which would necessarily have to be conceded to the United States in exchange for the elimination of extraterritoriality and the conventional tariff. All attempts at revision, for the present at least, were in consequence abandoned.

It was not without its beneficial effects, however. To Ito in particular this condition of affairs constituted his first experience in the treacherous profundities of practical international politics. It proved a valuable guide to his future wrestling with problems of a similar character.

Resuming their tour, the embassy visited seventeen countries,

studying, investigating, drinking in the accumulated wonders
of the Old World. Everywhere they committed the usual
faux pas inevitable on a maiden visit to strange lands overflow-
ing with incredibly strange social conventions.

Returning to Japan somewhat chagrined but considerably
more worldly-wise, they found that Saigo's bloc had completed
every preparation—even to securing the Emperor's tentative
approval—to dispatch that long-deferred punitive expedition
to Korea.

2

Then began those memorable debates in the Tokyo council.
The issue was vibrant with significant potentialities. It concerned not merely the question of war or peace, or the difficulties of the immediate present alone. It involved the whole
future development of the country, beginning with her domestic
anfractuosities and embracing inevitably those foreign entanglements on the Asiatic mainland which were soon to become vital
factors in her existence.

Saigo, a man of few but thunderous words, defended his policy with consummate logic, placing national honor above every
other consideration. Opposed to him again were those Ambassadors lately returned from a world tour—Iwakura and Kido
and Okubo and Ito—who denounced militarism with the expert
conviction of men who understood perfectly the futility of wag-
ing a war of conquest on patriotism alone. They contended
that the time was not yet ripe for Japan to think in terms of
a foreign war. She had but recently emerged from her medieval state; a vast reconstruction work was under way. Though
old in culture, she was still an infant nation when judged by
Western standards; and to go to war in the face of this reality
was sheer madness. Her first duty, now as never before, lay
in accelerating the work of reconstruction—in the building of
factories, of machineries, of railroads, of steamships, of the
thousand and one other creations of modern civilization for the
development of her productive efficiency and the enrichment
of her national resources......

When finally the Emperor gave his decision, it was to re-

verse his earlier one: the conquest of Korea was ordered abandoned. Saigo, greatly incensed, resigned immediately. His
supporters followed him en masse.

This left the victorious peace party in control of the government. Again, however, disruption threatened. The seeds of
dissension now lurked in the Formosan question—the question
of sending a punitive expedition against the natives of Formosa
to avenge the murder of fifty-four Japanese ship-wrecked mari-
ners. Though Formosa was under China's suzerainty, the latter, in defiance of international laws, refused to assume any responsibility for the acts of its inhabitants, nor would she counte-
nance any reprisals against her vassal state—an aspect of her
diplomacy which was later destined to involve the Far East in
endless sanguinary discords.

At Tokyo it was the same old story: national prestige abroad
versus peaceful development at home. Kido and Okubo, the
two remaining members of the Meiji triumverate, now opposed
each other with the same relentless vigor with which they had
together fought and defeated Saigo. Kido had become even
more liberal in his views, pleading for a greater consistency in
carrying out the national policy which gave domestic developments precedence over foreign military ventures. Okubo, on
the other hand, had amended many of his views since his triumphant verbal duel with Saigo. He stood firmly upon Japan's
rights in the Formosan question, and fought vigorously for a
vindication of those rights. This was tantamount to a belated
gesture retracting his former stand against the conquest of
Korea. The majority of the Ministers supported him. Ito
alone stood staunchly by Kido.

Outvoted in the council, Kido resigned. This placed Ito in
a difficult situation. To assist in carrying out the government's
revised policy would be working against what he conceived to
be the best interests of his country. It would be working
against his own principles. But there were other things that
must also be considered. To quit now would mean obscurity
thereafter so far as his growing power and influence were concerned; whereas to carry on with his work would enable him to
succeed Kido in perpetuating Choshu's leadership in the council

and to endeavor wherever and whenever possible to fight for constructive progress. It was a significant moment in his career, one of those moments when a decision must be rendered which would either make or unmake him. He decided to remain at his post.

3

Once more the nation's leaders turned to domestic affairs, and Ito, because of the peculiar exigency of the situation, became the man of the hour. Saigo, the fiery patriot, had retired permanently from public service, preferring to spend his days in the brooding silence of the woods, the streams, and the sea. Once a month he returned to the private military college he had established in Kagoshima to deliver one of his impassioned lectures on patriotism. As for Kido, however, the Formosan expedition to which he had objected was soon vindicated when China belatedly acknowledged her responsibility by paying an indemnity of 500,000 taels; and the nation saw no good reason why he should continue to hibernate in the seclusion of his prefectural home. Okubo, for his part, made public assurances that he was more than willing to let Kido thereafter take the helm; that he would support any measure or reform instituted by his great colleague from Choshu. And the only man in whom the two had sufficient confidence and who was, therefore, capable of bringing about their reconciliation was Ito. Hence the Council of State looked to Ito for succor in this hour of uncertainty.

In effecting their reunion and insuring their continued cooperation, Ito realized that an agreement on some vital administrative reform as a future working basis was essential. This he set about to accomplish. But at the very outset he was confronted with other difficulties which became inextricably involved in his problem. Any administrative reform, to merit universal approval, must, he saw, embrace features which would be satisfactory, not merely to the two political giants directing the affairs of state, but also to the group of radical leaders headed by Itagaki, who now clamored insistently for the creation of popularly elected institutions.

The spirit of radicalism had arisen and asserted itself as an aftermath of the defeat of Saigo's bloc over the Korean debate. Though Saigo himself took no part in its propagation—for he was essentially a military-minded man—some of the more politically ambitious of his colleagues had assumed the initiative and organized a party of opposition known as the "Aikoku-To" (Party of Patriotism) which petitioned the government as early as January, 1874, for fundamental reforms which were far in advance of the times. In this manner they had abandoned the less successful cause of militaristic righteousness for the more forward-moving principles of democracy. It was a change that betrayed an obvious paradox, but a change nevertheless that was inevitable. Some means had to be devised in order to create an outlet for their pent-up grievances, and the only effective safety valve which would serve their purpose was the advocacy of radical, as opposed to the government's moderate, progress. With the same relentless determination with which they had attempted to foster national prestige abroad, they now devoted their versatile energies to the very ventures against which they had strenuously fought and lost, differing from their erstwhile dissenters only by being several jumps ahead of them in their own sphere of activities. Progress was their watchword: precipitate progress precipitately arrived at! To satisfy them without flouting the policy of slow and steady development, which alone would meet with Kido's and Okubo's approval, and without endangering the stability of the Emperor's power was, Ito knew, well-nigh impossible. Yet a compromise, he decided, must be achieved.

When finally drafted, Ito's reconciliation measure comprised four articles suggesting basic changes which would serve as the functional units of the central government. These included the creation of (1) a Senate to decide upon measures of legislation, (2) an Assembly of Prefectural Governors as a medium through which the policies of the central government might be carried out and the needs of the prefectural regions made known, (3) a Supreme Court to administer justice and define the laws of the land. The 4th article called for the separation of the Council of State, as a distinct unit, from the Administrative

Departments, the former to decide on all questions respecting the affairs of state, and the latter to execute the regular business of the government.

These innovations represented the first attempt to pattern the political institutions of Japan upon those of the West. They constituted the measure of Ito's experiences abroad, not as an ideal machinery of government, but as an experiment based upon the division of the governmental powers among the legislative, judicial, and executive branches. An experiment, so he figured, to apply the first principles of democracy within reasonable limits to the peculiar conditions and requirements of his country. One outstanding defect, as historians have since pointed out, was noticeable. Neither the Senate nor the Assembly of Prefectural Governors possessed any *initiative* powers in matters of legislation. All such powers were vested in the Council of State. This, of course, reflected the fear on Ito's part of delegating too much power in too precipitate a fashion to those who had not yet demonstrated their fitness to exercise this prerogative intelligently. It was believed, however, that these changes embodied improvements conforming as closely as it was wise, practicable and safe to do so, to a compromise between the wishes of the radicals and the conservatives.

After privately submitting the draft to Kido and Okubo, and with both expressing tentative agreement, Ito managed to bring them together at Osaka on January 29, 1875. A working understanding among the three leaders thus reunited was reached. Meanwhile Inouye, Ito's friend and colleague, had been working incessantly and at length succeeded in persuading Itagaki to consider reentering the Council of State as a representative of the radical element. The two, having exchanged mutual assurances in which Itagaki agreed to cooperate with the conservative group in advancing the reconstruction programme with Ito's conciliatory measure as a nucleus, likewise proceeded to Osaka. A joint conference, presided over by Ito, and attended by Kido, Okubo, Itagaki, and Inouye, was next held, at which all past differences were buried and an agreement cementing the views of those present effected. Soon afterwards they returned to Tokyo. The Emperor's approval was secured. Once more the government started to function harmoniously and, it was hoped, without further interruption.

But the malady which had set up a line of demarcation between the radicals and the conservatives, even at this early stage, seemed far too deep-rooted to be amenable to any form of compromise for any appreciable length of time. Within ten months an entirely unexpected clash arose between Kido and Itagaki over the enforcement of the fourth article in Ito's measure, namely, the question as to *when* the separation between the Council of State and the Administrative Departments, as two distinct entities of the executive division, should be put into effect. The Osaka Conference had merely achieved unanimity over the nature and the framework of the changes to be inaugurated; no question had been raised as to the details regarding their enforcement.

Kido sought to delay its enforcement until such time as the duties and responsibilities of the respective divisions over questions of legislation and administration had been defined with greater clarity. He would consent to the separation only after experience fully warranted it—when the spectacle of transferring some of the oligarchic powers of the Councillors to men of lesser magnitude and abilities became less fraught with apprehensive concern. Itagaki, being a radical, saw no convincing reason why once the principle had been approved it should not be enforced at once. This impasse placed Ito in an embarrassing situation. Being principally concerned with the reinstatement of Kido as the active head of the government, he was morally pledged to whatever steps the latter elected to take. Yet Itagaki, for his part, was merely attempting to carry out, with the utmost assiduity, one of the reforms which Ito himself had proposed.

In the midst of this wrangle word came that the Japanese gunboat "Unyo," while conducting marine surveys in the Yellow Sea, had been fired upon by Korean shore batteries at the entrance to the river Han. This not only revived the Korean question; it precipitated a decision over the reform issue. Pending negotiations looking toward what had now become an unavoidable show-down with Korea, the Council of State voted to postpone all domestic reforms. Itagaki, stoutly dissenting to the end, resigned. Thus the militaristic policy of Saigo, so ably enunciated in the stormy debates of 1873, was at last vindicated, not by his supporters, but by the very men who had opposed him!

4

The show-down with Korea began a momentous chapter in Ito's life. "As Councillor," he said, years later, "I was commissioned, along with M. Boisonnade and Ki Inouye, to conduct an investigation into the attack on the gunboat 'Unyo.' The crux of our difficulty lay in determining whether to single out Korea or China as the object of our indictment. This was due to the fact that Korea at the time declared herself to be a vassal state of China. Still, though it was true that she actually, and of her own volition, paid tribute to China in acknowledgment of her vassalage, it appeared to me that the ties which bound the two countries together were nominal only and that it would be quite in order to regard her as an independent country. As to China, she had always made it a practice when dealing with other countries to confirm her overlordship whenever the circumstances seemed likely to redound to her advantage, and to eschew its responsibilities whenever she found that it would react against her interests. When she found, in this particular instance, that she was about to become involved in some difficulty, she flatly denied that Korea was under her suzerainty. Hence Japan, availing herself of this opportunity, proceeded to characterize Korea as 'Dai-Kankoku' and her ruler as the King of 'Dai-Kankoku.' Furthermore, there had been no official calendar in existence in Korea which indicated the period of her alleged vassalage to China, and we therefore dated the event as the year 500, basing it on the founding of the Ri dynasty.

"It was thus that Korea was for the first time in her history recognized as an independent country. In other words, it was Japan that first proclaimed this independence, for the Koreans themselves had been unable to do so."

The result of this recognition, as sponsored by Ito and his two associates, was a commercial treaty between the two countries, the first of its kind ever to be concluded by Korea as an independent government. This implied, as Ito maintained throughout his subsequent career, that *Japan, having placed Korea on this footing, had become obligated to assist her in preserving her independence against the encroachments of other neighboring Powers*—an attitude of mind which must be fully comprehended in order to grasp the significance of Ito's future dealings with this country's destiny.

5

He was meanwhile, on July 3, 1875, appointed Director of the Bureau of Legislation, this in addition to his duties as Councillor and as Minister of Public Works. For four years thereafter, with the collaboration of M. Boissonade, he was to labor with meticulous zeal in preparing and examining drafts for a revision of the existing laws, most of which were a relic of the old feudal regime. Always adhering to a middle course, with the interests of the radicals and the conservatives constantly before him, he showed a broad sympathy and a precision of mind which proved that he was a worthy legislator as well as a sound administrator.

While on a visit to Kyoto as a member of the Emperor's retinue to participate in the inaugural ceremonies of the newly-constructed Kyoto-Kobe railway, he received the first intimations of a smouldering discontent in Satsuma. Then suddenly, like a furious thunder-clap, the open assault of Saigo's fifteen thousand student-warriors against the government's strongholds, arsenals and navy yards broke out in the city of Kagoshima with all the pent-up fury of a lost cause. It was the climax of a series of insurrections that had occurred spasmodically in various parts of the country as an expression of protest, not merely against the abolition of feudalism and hence the extinction of the samurai status as a means of livelihood, but also against the momentous decision of 1873 repudiating Saigo's policy toward Korea.

Saigo, when the news of this outbreak reached him in the

wilds of Osumi, was struck dumb with mortification. During all the recent outbursts he had remained immovably loyal to the government by refusing to sanction, to aid, or to exploit in any manner whatever the armed demonstrations in defense of his principles. To rebel against the government, no matter what the provocation, was the very antithesis of his teachings, his ideals, his personality. But, alas, the flaming tide of resentment which swept through the hearts of his pupils, forcing them to disregard entirely his familiar precepts, was something which not even he could now control or suppress. It was now impossible to dissociate himself from their ghastly work.

Before the work of suppressing the rebellion progressed very far Kido became seriously ill and died. Okubo, knowing full well that the fundamental cause of this sorry mess confronting the nation was in great measure attributable to his own defiant attitude toward Saigo and his foreign policy, one day bared his soul to Ito—his only remaining associate and equal. He would proceed alone to the scene of battle and there seek a personal reconciliation with Saigo. It was the only way, he felt, in which the rebellion could be peacefully terminated and a future understanding and cooperation with Saigo assured. It was a beautiful thought, a touching denouement to the bloody uprising in which the fate of a whole nation was dramatically intertwined with the lives of two bosom friends temporarily estranged by conflicting political principles. But it was also a manifestly unwise move, for the hazards involved were great indeed; and Ito promptly advised against it.

In September, 1877, the rebellion was effectually suppressed. What remained of Saigo then ceased to exist. He died as one in his tragic situation was expected to die—by falling upon his own sword.

In May of the next year Okubo himself was assassinated by a group of disgruntled samurai who chose to see in him a tyrant, a foe of liberalism, and the cause of Saigo's death and defeat.

Thus did the careers of the Meiji triumvirate—Kido and Saigo and Okubo—come to a swift and dramatic end, leaving Ito alone to carry on the leadership in the work of national readjustment and reconstruction which had but barely begun amid so many stormy dissensions and upheavals.

BOOK III

THE BUILDER

CHAPTER IX
MODERATION

I

Ito's sudden emergence as the preeminent Councillor of the nation was accompanied by the shouldering of a Herculean responsibility—that of maintaining a healthy equilibrium between the masses who now agitated tempestuously for a parliamentary form of government and the Emperor whose confidence he must at all times strive to justify. The time-honored custom of characterizing the Emperor as "heaven-descended, divine and sacred" constituted the bedrock of the latter's power, which it was Ito's duty to sustain. Politically, this sacrosanct being represented that "absolute, supreme, indivisible, and self-determining will of the State," which it was likewise his duty to enforce. But the radicals who, by this time, had come to embrace a vast multitude of people nursing innumerable grievances against the government, had been reading with intense zeal and obvious promiscuity such European authorities on political philosophy as Rousseau, Montesquieu, Marx, and others. These expounded the theory that the power of sovereignty should reside, not in the individual ruler, but in the people who consented to his rule.

In the spring of 1880 the long-heralded separation between the Council of State and the Administrative Departments was finally put into effect, thus affording the radicals the first distinct victory in their fight for political liberty. This was followed by the filing of voluminous petitions demanding unconditional emancipation which literally flooded the Council chamber. The movement gained momentum with astonishing celerity. Itagaki, twice at grips with the conservative Council, now espoused the extreme, idealistic principles of the French socialist writers. Okuma, representing the left wing of the Council, advocated the less radical views typified by the English constitutional government. But his demands were definite and concrete. He carried the fight for popular sovereignty to the very doors of the Imperial Household. He sought the Emperor's approval for the *immediate* creation of a parliamentary body, through which the people could exercise their inalienable rights.

Against this ever-increasing barrage of the popular will Ito found himself compelled to shield the Emperor. Knowing as he did that the time had not yet come for the adoption of out-and-out liberal measures, he adhered to the only safe policy commensurate with constructive progress—the policy of moderation. He knew that the revolutionary demands of the people were based primarily upon a half-baked knowledge of Western democracy. He realized that to transfer the ruler's prerogative to a people who as yet had no conception of political liberty except as a means of redressing their grievances and who for twenty-five centuries had been ruled with no knowledge or experience in self-government, would be disastrous without first giving them sufficient time in which to prepare themselves. He saw that only evils and corruption and a sudden collapse of good government as a result of an irreverent abuse of the power which they insisted upon arrogating to themselves, would follow. Liberalism as they conceived it bore only a remote resemblance to the progressive principle by which its Western prototype was known. It was essentially a refuge for the disgruntled masses, a refuge and a medium of attack through which the former defeated militarists and reactionaries combined with the remnants of the old feudal factions to plague the Emperor with vengeful demands.

Neither, however, did Ito lose sight of the fact that a persistent indifference to their demands would also be likely to breed innumerable social evils. Disruption would follow. This would be equally disastrous, particularly as the government was then striving valiantly to seek equality with other nations through a revision of Japan's unequal treaties.

Partly, therefore, as a means of appeasing the dissatisfied elements, and partly to institute a great reform which would so strengthen the social and political foundations of the country as to command the respect of the Western Powers, he advised the Emperor to bestow upon the people a national legislative assembly *at the end of a reasonable period devoted to preparations,* said period to be determined by the Emperor and proclaimed in unequivocal terms as an incentive to greater efforts at self-enlightenment. This was in line with one of the five articles enunciated in the Emperor's oath sworn to at the time of his accession, namely, that "a deliberative assembly shall be formed and all measures decided by public opinion."

The Emperor, after giving due consideration to the two opposing suggestions as revealed in Okuma's "demands" and as propounded by Ito's "advice," decided to adopt the course of moderate progress. He promised to summon a Diet in 1890. This gave the people nine years in which to prepare themselves to meet its requirements and responsibilities. Okuma, thus defeated, resigned from the Council to form the Progressive faction through which to fight Ito's regime and to create, in the meantime, a formidable following with which to control the first session of the Diet.

2

But though the radicals fumed with discontent, the Emperor kept faith with his people. He who was the embodiment of absolutism had also been a close and sympathetic observer of the extraordinary achievements of his people passing with almost incredible rapidity from the level of worldly ignorance to the giddy heights of modernity. First he had promised to provide them with a parliament; now he was prepared to grant them a constitution. With that just appreciation of the aspirations of his subjects which was remarkable for its rarity in an Asiatic monarch, he decided to give them, of his own free will, a charter limiting his own sovereign powers and conferring upon them for all time what he would thus strip off from his mantle of authority. It was a spontaneous expression of his deep and abiding love for his people. The countless vicissitudes of transient fortunes and sorrowful tribulations which constituted the lot of his dynasty had not, it would seem, quite dimmed the consciousness of that immemorial trust which his forefathers had bequeathed to him down the unbroken line.

Furthermore, he was determined that Japan should have the best possible, the most appropriate, constitution—one embracing every modern feature compatible with the historical and structural individuality of the nation. To this end he instructed Ito to proceed at once to Europe with a staff of capable assistants to make the necessary preliminary research, and to prepare a draft based upon a thorough study of the various constitutional governments then in operation.

Ito left Japan on March 14, 1882. His staff of assistants included men of such exceptional talents—young scholars who later became closely identified with the political fortunes of Japan—as Kentaro Kaneko, Kimmochi Saionji, Miyoji Ito, Miyoshi, Ujitomo, Toda, Yamazaki, Kawashima, Yoshida and others. His first objective was the German Empire which Bismarck's political genius had helped to create out of militaristic Prussia and the lesser German States barely eleven years previously. This was a natural, rather than a wise, choice. No other country in the world presented a closer similarity to Japan, both with respect to political organization and national sentiment. Both, moreover, were revitalized ancient countries starting afresh under brilliant auspices. The choice was unfortunate because the German Government, with all the notable achievements to its credit, was precisely what a searcher after principles in evolutionary democracy should have avoided—a model bureaucracy.

For three intensive months, with headquarters established in Berlin, Ito concentrated his energy upon a study of this pompous bureaucracy as it functioned before his very eyes. Never was the time more ironically opportune. Bismarck was at the peak of his brilliant career. Himself a bureaucrat of the first magnitude, this hot-blooded Chancellor from the ancient forests of Pomerania was directing Germany's destiny on the political chessboard of Europe with an implacable mastery over men and kings. Surrounded on the north by Russia, the stupendous riddle of Europe; on the east by Austria, denied an outlet to the sea; on the west, across the North Sea, by Great Britain, aloof and inscrutable; Germany under Bismarck sought that peace which was vital to her interests in the only feasible manner compatible with her ambitious aspirations — might through calculated intrigues and alliances. In a modern demo-

cratic state Bismarck's unbridled political peregrinations would
have been an utter impossibility. Hence the bold impressive-
ness and the seeming superiority of the bureaucratic form of
government. Just across Germany's border in the south lay
France, defeated in 1870, and making a feeble effort under the
rule of a republican government to wipe off that humiliating
stain. Viewing these unmistakable manifestations of political
contrasts and their respective strength and weaknesses, Ito was
unfortunately led to believe that the German bureaucracy represented the type of government best suited to the peculiar
needs of his own country.

During the latter part of August he visited Vienna, where
he attended the lectures of that eminent authority on political
philosophy, Lorenz von Stein. Returning to Berlin, he remained there until February of the next year. He next went
to Brussels, and thence to London. While preparing to wind
up his studies at the British metropolis he received a telegraphic
message from his Emperor requesting him to proceed to St.
Petersburg as Envoy Extraordinary and Minister Plenipotenti-
ary representing Japan at the coronation ceremonies of Tsar
Alexander III. Fulfilling this mission, he returned to Japan
on August 4, 1883, after an absence abroad of a year and a
half.

3

When he stepped ashore at Nagasaki, with the native background of his political consciousness profoundly saturated with
multitudinous impressions of European monarchical institutions, Ito had already formulated a decision as to precisely what
lines he should follow in drafting the constitution of Japan.
The work in itself would be a colossal one. It would engage
his constant attention and that of his assistants for a considerable length of time, perhaps several years. Meanwhile, during
his absence abroad, the spirit of radicalism had encouraged the
masses to venture far into the realm of free thought and free
speech. Drunk with the newfangled liberty, these promiscuous
converts of Marx and of John Stuart Mill were making all
manner of attempts, with a fearful crescendo of sacrilegious

utterances, for the immediate attainment of what they conceived to be their just political rights. Ito, viewing these extremist tendencies, became convinced that a bulwark to the Throne must be set up, some bureaucratic unit that would stand between the Throne and the populace as well as check the rampant growth of "dangerous" ideas.

In pursuance of this policy he instituted several fundamental changes. First of all, he created the Department of the Imperial Household, of which he himself was appointed Minister, thus establishing a separate administrative body to guard the Emperor's personal interests and placing them beyond the possible encroachment of irreverent radicals. His next act was the drafting of the Peerage Ordinance, reviving the ancient nobility with hereditary titles equivalent to the European ranks of Prince, Marquis, Count, Viscount, and Baron. The new Peerage thus formed embraced what remained of the old Court nobles, the ex-daimyo, and those ranking civilian and military officials who, by virtue of distinguished service rendered in the name of the Emperor, made up the dominant ruling class of Japan. This group of Peers, numbering five hundred and five, was made the basis for the organization of the Upper House in the forthcoming Diet.

Thus did Ito reveal the first indications of launching a bureaucratic regime. Much of this change must be attributed to the German influence. But to one charged with the responsibility of preserving an even tempo in the march for political reforms in a nation that was as yet totally unfitted for self-government, it was also an inevitable one. Yet he was not a foe of true liberalism. He was, in fact, fundamentally inclined toward liberal principles, as attested by his various contributions to the political, social, and economic development of his country since returning from his first London journey. He differed from Itagaki, Okuma, and others *professing* liberalism merely in the application of its principles—in his adherence to sane and moderate, as opposed to precipitate, progress.

And for his particular services rendered since the Restoration, he was rewarded by the Emperor with the title of Count.

4

Foreign complications in 1884 again assumed an aspect of major importance in the nation's councils. Korea, divided against herself, continued to be a source of friction and turmoil. After a series of insurrections wherein the reactionary natives, first under the resurrected leadership of the Tai Won Kun, then with the connivance of the Queen herself, and always with the backing of the Chinese, sought vainly to retain their supremacy, the impotent King, now a virtual figurehead taking orders from Kim Ok Kiun, the Progressives' leader, invited the Japanese Minister, Takezoe, to help create a new Cabinet and, in the meantime, to secure the assistance of Japanese troops to guard the palace against rebellious plotters. The Japanese, for reasons best known to themselves, responded readily enough, but were forthwith attacked by two thousand Chinese troops who had entered Seoul to restore to power the defeated pro-Chinese reactionary regime. The assault, in which the Korean insurgents joined forces with the Chinese, resulted in the massacre of some thirty Japanese, the burning of the Japanese legation, and the wilful confiscation of their property. What remained of them escaped to the coast under constant fire and thence to a safe retreat.

All this pointed to but one obvious conclusion. It meant that Korea had become a coveted prize, to be wooed, to be fought for, to be exploited by two ambitious rivals, each for reasons as diametrically at variance as the poles. China, still maneuvering to exact fabulous tributes from her one-time vassal, was at the height of her aggrandizing orgies. Japan, far-seeing but fundamentally selfish, saw with shrewd clarity that Korea, because of her strategic geographical situation, must be made into a buffer between herself and her continental neighbors. To achieve this end Korea's ruling classes and her disorganized masses must be welded together into a strong and unified nation, free from all foreign entanglements and domination. Both the Japanese and the Chinese, however, were equally culpable in that they had given aid to opposing factions in Korea to foist upon this country the kind of government which they respectively believed would be for the best interests, not only of the Koreans, but also of their own national aspirations. Both had aligned themselves with movements in which conspiracy and intrigue had been freely indulged. The Koreans themselves, who were most vitally affected by this struggle for hegemony, seemed incapable of working out their own destiny. Torn by rival factions to whom patriotism meant practically nothing and the spoils of victory everything, they had no public opinion to speak of, no national consciousness which would save their country from disruption. Over and above all these conflicting circumstances was the belief,conceived by Ito and deeply imbedded in the minds of many Japanese, that—let the phrase be repeated—*Japan, having placed Korea on an independent footing, had become obligated to assist her in preserving this independence against the encroachments of other neighboring Powers.*

Thus the issue, which at first concerned itself with Korean domestic reforms, now necessitated, as far as the Japanese chose to view it, a positive show-down with China. Owing to the extraordinary nature of the problem and the character of the people whom Japan had to deal with, Ito himself proceeded to China to achieve this understanding.

At Tientsin he was met by Li Hung Chang, the Chinese Viceroy who was delegated with full plenary powers to set forth China's claims. Thus occurred for the first time the meeting between two of the most brilliant diplomatists of the Far East. Li, the politician *par excellence*, the man who was known far and wide for his shrewdness and sagacity and his egregious skill in Machiavellian statecraft, was not a little contemptuous of his lesser-known opponent from Dai Nippon. Blinded by the iridescent mist of his own omnipotency, he miscalculated by several mental kilometers the measure of Ito's aptitude for driving hard bargains.

With all his reputed skill, Li's diplomatic vocabulary seemed singularly limited. His only defense was the conventional one, long since repudiated, wherein he sought justification for the acts of his countrymen in Korea on the oft-repeated pretext that China had merely striven to protect the interests of her vassal state. She had, in other words, done no more than fulfill her natural responsibilities. If Japan wished to avoid hostilities with China, she must, he said in effect, respect those ties and cease her meddlesome trickeries at the Seoul Court. He could conceive of no other solution. The Mikado must be advised of it.

Ito was vaguely disappointed. He had expected a far clever-er alibi from one so indubitably eminent; but this was child's talk. He was forcibly reminded of a previous clash with China when Korea, for the first time, tasted the wine of freedom from his proffered cup:

> " ......she (China) had always made it a practice when dealing with other countries to affirm her overlordship (over Korea) whenever the circumstances seemed likely to redound to her advantage, and to eschew its responsibili-ties whenever she found that it would react against her interests. When she found, in this particular instance (the attack on the Japanese gunboat 'Unyo'), that she was about to become involved in some difficulty, she flatly de-nied that Korea was under her suzerainty."

The same naive drama was being re-enacted before him, only the circumstances were now reversed. There was the question of indemnity for the murdered Japanese, for the confiscation of their property, for the burning of their legation; and only by a categorical affirmation by China of her rights of suzerainty, supporting her claim that these unfortunate occurrences had been inevitable in the performance of her duty to her vassal, could she hope to claim immunity therefrom. Ito saw through it all. Only one retort, to him, seemed to suffice; an equally conventional one. All that he had come to demand, he said in effect, was peace with China, but that peace must be based upon *a mutual respect for Korea's independence.*

Through five intransigent meetings the two came to grips with the same obvious question, unwilling to seek any other way out of the impasse. Finally, biding his time, Ito attempted a ruse. He had been grievously hurt, he as much as let it be known, by Li's repeated "obstinacy," and he threatened that unless Li agreed to compromise Japan would feel justified in taking whatever steps she deemed appropriate in enforcing her will upon Korea. His terms were threefold: first, China and Japan must recall their respective armies of occupation from Korea; secondly, both countries must refrain from sending any military instructors to Korea; thirdly, a mutual consent must first be obtained in the event it became necessary in the future for either China or Japan to dispatch troops to Korea to protect their respective nationals.

Thus adroitly he eschewed any mention of suzerain rights, though it was clear that an acceptance of these terms on the part of China would be tantamount to waiving them irrevocably. But Li evidently failed to grasp its significance. His mind, moreover, was now distracted by the aggressive inroads of the French in Annam; and the hostile front assumed on two sides by forceful antagonists seriously impaired his equanimity. He had schemed to force Ito by a process of slow diplomatic torture into an abject submission to his own arbitrary terms, but had himself, he saw, been precipitated, very suddenly, into an embarrassing situation, to emerge honorably from which he must either accept Ito's terms or invite a serious impairment of China's prestige. "Face" must be saved. Believing that the proposed compromise in no way compelled China to renounce her immemorial claims over Korea, he yielded. And this delusion—for delusion it was—did not altogether vanish from Li's mind until it brought disaster in its wake ten years later.

5

With the Sino-Japanese imbroglio of 1884 thus brought to a close, Ito plunged at once into the task of resuming his work on the constitution. He was now concerned with that provision dealing with the reorganization of the Ministry along modern lines. The existing government was a curious improvisation consisting of a hodge-podge of both ancient and modern institutions. These included a Chancellor, a Vice-Chancellor of the Left, and a Vice-Chancellor of the Right, together with a group of Councillors who performed the regular duties of a modern Cabinet Minister. The Chancellors functioned merely as administrative overseers, with the power to decide on all measures submitted by the Councillors before securing the Emperor's approval. This singular creation, which was begotten by a union of the old and the new regimes, and which was the result of several changes following the altercation between Kido and Itagaki over the oligarchic functions of the Councillor, Ito proposed to replace with a modern Cabinet consisting of a Premier and the Ministers of Foreign Affairs, of Home Affairs, of the Army, of the Navy, of the Treasury, of Justice, of Education, of Communications and of Agriculture and Commerce. In the new Cabinet the Premier would receive his appointment from the Emperor and become the supreme administrative head of the government. He would not only replace the Chancellor and the two Vice-Chancellors, but would also appoint his own Cabinet Ministers, thereby assuming the entire responsibility of his administration. He would himself be responsible to no one but the Emperor. The Emperor would retain his prerogative of creating new governments by making fresh appointments to the office of Premier in accordance with the trend of public thought.

When Prince Sanjo, the Chancellor incumbent, was made aware of this contemplated change, he became so enamored of its possibilities that he recommended to the Emperor its immediate adoption, without waiting for the formal promulgation of the constitution. To this end he submitted his resignation, leaving no doubt that the man who deserved the distinction of becoming the first Premier of Japan was none other than Ito himself. Sanjo's proposal was duly approved by the Emperor, and Ito received his appointment on December 22, 1885.

CHAPTER X

EMANCIPATION

I

The success of Ito's first Cabinet depended in great measure
upon the outcome of Foreign Minister Inouye's work on treaty
revision. Although no further effort had been made after the
return of the traveling Ambassadors in 1873 to eliminate from
Japan's commercial treaties the two humiliating clauses dealing
with extraterritoriality and the conventional tariff, work had
nevertheless been progressing steadily, under Ito's direction, in
connection with the compilation of a criminal code which would
conform more closely to those of the Western nations and which
would justify at least the abolishment of consular jurisdiction.
The displeasure of the masses with regard to these inequalities
was considerable, but instead of evincing itself in impotent ful-
minations against the Westerners' selfishness or of blinding the
nation to its own shortcomings and imperfections, it served,
singularly enough, to spur the government on to greater efforts
and greater attainments. The criminal code, with M. Boisson-
nade's able collaboration, was in due course completed and
solemnly promulgated. The time to discuss treaty revision
with the Western Powers, Ito decided, had arrived at last. He
accordingly directed Inouye to call a conference of the foreign
diplomats at Tokyo, admittedly to secure complete autonomy
for Japan; and with what tact and shrewdness and political
perspicacity his Foreign Minister could muster, the negotiations
were started on their historic course.

But the Western Powers, with the exception of the United
States, would not yield so readily to the sweeping curtailments
proposed by Inouye. After a series of unfruitful meetings, a
compromise was drafted by the dissenting diplomats, to which
Inouye was compelled to acquiesce for want of a more desirable
revision. Extraterritoriality was to be relinquished, not at
once, but gradually. Two foreign judges were to be placed in
the Japanese courts until 1903 to offset whatever disadvantages

this might incur against the Treaty Power nationals. Tariff autonomy was withheld, but the duties were increased from five to ten per cent.

When these unfavorable developments reached the public ear, a stormy outburst of popular disapprobation greeted the luckless Inouye. The nation, apparently, felt that it had stood long enough for the dilatory tyranny of the Western Powers. It was now no longer regarded as a question merely of judicial incompatibility, or of commercial disadvantages, but of national self-respect. All the pent-up grievances of a down-trodden race, which hitherto had been patiently held in check, were bared with savage indignation. Ito's Government was besieged with scathing denunciations. The opposition, or non-government, faction at once seized this opportunity to cast vengeful aspersions upon his administration. Swayed by the mounting success of its crusade against the bureaucrats, it clamored with increasing boisterousness for the resignation, not only of Inouye, but of the entire Cabinet; and its supporters were legion. They comprised now all those elements which grouped themselves under the ambiguous nomenclature of liberals and progressives.

Inouye finally bowed to the will of the opposition. He brought the treaty conference to an abrupt close and submitted his resignation. Ito thereafter attempted to save the life of his administration from the vitriolic attacks of the opposition by himself assuming the vacated portfolio of Foreign Affairs. But the opposition continued, with even louder exacerbations, to plague his government. Its onslaughts assumed all manner of shapes and forms, of viper-thrusts and torrential anathema. It knew nothing of the insurmountable difficulties involved in dealing with the Western nations. It was concerned more particularly with avenging a wounded pride than with the grappling of monumental realities which it but imperfectly visioned.

To silence these wrangling disturbances, Ito caused the issuance of the "Hoän Joretsu," an ordinance designed to effect a more rigorous surveillance over the radical utterances in the daily newspapers. He sought justification for this ordinance on the ground that it was for the "maintenance of public peace." But the opposition characterized it as a deliberate attempt to suppress free speech. Ito maintained that no guarantees respecting free speech had ever yet been made by the rulers of Japan. The ordinance, moreover, was intended merely as a temporary measure, to relieve a temporary strain. It was to be supplanted by the constitution which was now in the course of completion, and which would provide fully for similar contingencies. Nevertheless it was a patently unwise move, for it served rather to add fuel to the fierce flame of popular protest.

Finally Ito swung to the opposite extreme: he attempted a remedy through conciliation. He invited Okuma, leader of the Progressives, to become Foreign Minister in his Cabinet. But it was another untoward move, for it disclosed the obvious hint that the administration was becoming slowly vulnerable. Thus did Ito, though his move was conscientiously motivated, play inevitably into the opposition's hands. The latter took full advantage of this precious opportunity. It clamored, more insistently and more vociferously than ever before, for the dissolution of Ito's Cabinet. In the end Ito perceived that further resistance, no matter how undeserved the popular rebuke, would breed incalculable mischief, perhaps sanguinary dissension. So he yielded at last and dissolved his government in favor of one created by Kiyotaka Kuroda.

But in yielding the reins of government to the opposition, he took immediate steps to provide for the creation of the Privy Council. This was made an integral part of the constitution on which he was meanwhile engaged.

The Privy Council became the highest advisory body of the Emperor. Because it was vested with that rare privilege of dictating the policies of the government through *adverse* counsel, it represented the most powerful organ of the State. And having been rewarded by the Emperor to head this body, Ito rose from the precarious rôle of Premier to the more substantial one of President of the Privy Council.

In this manner Ito became the Emperor's most trusted, most assiduous servant. In the eyes of the masses, he became, conversely, a most pronounced bureaucrat, a foe of popular rights. The truth, however, was that he was a cautious realist, progressive but far-seeing, who chose to carry out whatever policies he felt were most appropriate from the standpoint of national stability to the conditions peculiar to his country and age. He was now striving to devise effective instruments for insuring the blessings of moderation—a vital move in preserving the necessary equilibrium between a magnanimous ruler and his impatient subjects. At a later date, when the political state of the nation justifies a more liberal orientation of policy, he will support the people's aspirations with unequivocal firmness and zeal.

2

Ito's attention was now concentrated wholly on the final touches of the constitution. The Imperial Household Law was also being simultaneously drawn up. The Privy Council deliberated upon these drafts and conferred daily with the Emperor at the Akasaka palace. Here Ito reviewed for the Emperor's information and approval all the salient points respecting each and every article, their varying purposes and relative merits in comparison with those prevailing under slightly different conditions in contemporary monarchical governments. The Emperor, in suggesting changes and rendering the ultimate decision, revealed an extraordinarily liberal mind, broad, sympathetic, paternal. At length the constitution was completed.

In its completed form, this fundamental law of the land was neither Japanese nor yet Western in its essential concept but a curious welding of the two. It was a unique human document, a masterpiece of discrimination, assimilation, and conciseness, reaffirming in irrevocable form some of the most profound theocratic-patriarchal convictions that had been bequeathed to the race from the very beginning of time, as time is calculated in that land of legends and ancestor-worship, and instituting other changes more closely attuned to the forward-moving creed of the times, including the most enlightened social and political innovations of the West.

It provided for the creation of the Ministry, the Diet, the Judicature, and the Privy Council in accordance with those modern ideals of government as prescribed by the monarchical system. These formed the basis for the division of the administrative powers among the executive, legislative, and judicial branches, with a separate body to serve the Emperor in an advisory capacity.

It defined the Emperor's rights of sovereignty, these being to give sanction to laws; to convoke, open, close, and prorogue the Diet and to dissolve the House of Representatives; to issue ordinances in place of law when public safety demanded it; to decide upon the organization of the different branches of the administration and to appoint, dismiss, and determine the salaries of all civil and military officers; to assume the supreme command of the army and navy and to determine their respective peace standing; to declare war, proclaim the law of siege, make peace, and conclude treaties; to confer titles of nobility, rank, orders, and other marks of honor; and to order amnesty, pardon, commutation of punishment and rehabilitation.

To the people it guaranteed the right to hold civil and military offices; liberty of abode; immunity from entry and search of homes, from arrest, detention, trial or punishment, except according to law; the inviolability of the secrecy of letters and the right of property; freedom of religious belief; liberty of speech, writing, publication, public meetings and associations; and the right to present petitions.

These provisions dealt only with fundamentals, leaving the details to be enacted by law. They still, it is clear, reserved for the Emperor such powers as enabled him to exercise the autocrat's prerogatives. But for over two thousand years the Emperors of Japan, though absolute rulers in theory, were never known to have assumed the rôle of a despot. In fact, the very contrary was true; and none among his subjects stooped to such irreverence as to believe that the constitution, in so far as the provisions defining the ruler's rights of sovereignty were concerned, would be prejudicial to the interests of the people.

Although this Magna Carta of Japan obviously was not intended as a means of achieving, overnight, that quintessence of democracy which exists in certain Western commonwealths today, it nevertheless represented a notable stride in that direction. Moreover, it was a voluntary gift of the Emperor to his subjects, and considering that barely twenty years previously Japan had still been in a state of medieval ignorance and turmoil, it represented a significant milestone in her political life.

Then came the day of all days—February 11, 1889—when, under the most brilliant auspices in the nation's history, the constitution was proclaimed. Thus it was that the essence of Imperial absolutism came to its voluntary end in Japan; and the dawn of human liberty, which had already crept into the Western firmament amid the horrid shrieks and groans of sanguinary revolutions, flashed its streaks, not of starkly blood-red hues, but of resplendent benevolent gold, upon this young-old race of the East. Emperor Meiji had fulfilled the solemn pledges of his dynasty. The supreme mission of Ito's political life had been accomplished. But in truth it was, for him, merely the beginning of a yet more tempestuous life, a life made worthy by glorious deeds but besieged by the inexorable demands of an existence continually consecrated to the service of the State, honored, hated, misunderstood, invariably without repose, always undaunted.

3

The straining effects of overwork began to tell on Ito's once vigorous constitution. That delicious relaxation from a life crowded with arduous strife and achieved in a simple villa by the sea, with the restful majesty of Fuji's sacrosanct peak burgeoning into the measureless grey of autumn twilights, beckoned him with a lure that became increasingly irresistible. Moreover, with the foundations of the national government now made permanently secure by the constitution, he felt it was high time the veterans stepped aside and gave the younger statesmen an opportunity to work out the many problems with which the nation was faced. Sooner or later the efficacy of constitutional government in a country where, for twenty-five centuries, political liberty had been an entirely unknown factor must be tested; and the time, he decided, might just as well be

now.   So on October 30, 1889, he resigned from the presidency
of the Privy Council and retired, for recuperative purposes, to
his seaside home at Odawara.   The Emperor was extremely
loath to accept his resignation, and his consent was given only
on condition that Ito would constantly be at the beck and call
of the monarch; that he would come to the latter's aid immediately whenever the country was faced with problems of
national import and national urgency.   But the well-earned rest
to which Ito had looked forward with such pleasurable antici-
pations was suddenly cut short, for early the next year he received a summons from the Emperor to report at once for duty
in Tokyo.

The reasons were not particularly urgent but were none the
less, in the opinion of the Emperor, of sufficient weight to render Ito's presence at the seat of the government imperative.
He cited the need of effective supervision over the preparations
for the first session of the Diet and the nationwide perturbation
resulting from repeated failures of Foreign Ministers to secure
a revision of the treaties in a manner that "comported with
the national dignity of Japan."   The laws governing the election of members to both Houses of the Diet were in the meantime promulgated; and when the dark clouds which hovered
over the first general election had cleared away, Ito, it was revealed, had been elected, as a Count, to a seat in the House
of Peers.   And when that body finally convened, the added
responsibility of acting as its first presiding officer was heaped
upon his shoulders.

But the zest for work, for service to his Emperor and country, again gripped him and spurred him on.   In the labyrinthine
depths of his seemingly endless work he found that peace which
comes to a man who is happiest in the consciousness of a duty
well performed.

4

Soon afterwards he encountered one of his most difficult
tasks—difficult not so much because of its complexities as because of its extreme delicacy—on the outcome of which seemed
to depend the very existence of his country.

The national unrest to which the Emperor had alluded in summoning him from his retirement at Odawara assumed serious proportions, culminating in a series of public blunders and public scandals. Okuma, student of Bentham and of Austin and of John Stuart Mill, and the Progressives' pillar in Kuroda's Cabinet, had taken up the work of treaty revision where Inouye had left off, only to discover, to his extreme embarrassment and misfortune, that not even intransigence in diplomacy could avail against the studied tactics of the Western diplomats. But the masses, impatient and severely critical, ascribed his failure rather to gross ineptitude (an assassin hurled a bomb at him, depriving him of one of his legs) and precipitated the early overthrow of the government. This brought General Yamagata, the veteran organizer of the Japanese military system, to power. Yamagata, however, soon sensed that if the temper displayed by the Lower House were any criterion of the feelings of the people, then his chances of securing their public support were precisely nil; and he retired, directly after the Diet's adjournment, in favor of Matsukata, bureaucrat from Satsuma. Matsukata, giving no heed to the continued agitation of the people for renewed attempts at treaty revision, steered clear of this dubious undertaking, knowing as he did that only futility and his own ignominious defeat would follow inevitably in its wake.

Suddenly the whole nation was transfixed with horror when the Crown Prince of Russia, who was then visiting in Japan, was reported as having been seriously wounded in an attempted assassination in the town of Ohtsu, about an hour's ride from Kyoto. The perpetrator of this crime, astonishing as it may seem, turned out to be an officer of the law who had sworn to protect the lives of the people. He freely confessed, when questioned by his superiors, that he had attempted to slay the Prince for those long-suffering grievances that had been rankling in the breasts of his loyal countrymen. Russia, he charged, had along with other Western Powers persistently withheld autonomy from Japan; and Prince Nicholas must pay for it with his life. Had she not also, as part of her perennial scheme of seeking a strategic seaport free from ice floes, been encroaching with sedulous insidiousness upon spheres regarded by Japan as vital to her interests? The early raids on the northern Japanese islands, the virtual theft of Saghalin—were not these proofs of her sinister purposes? Then the present mission of the Crown Prince—was not this also a part of Russia's treacherous plots? Else why should he come to Japan in eight ships of war? Why had the admiral of the fleet defied the order of the Japanese Government and sought freedom of access to all the ports of Japan?

Whether, however, there was any basis of truth in these allegations was obviously not important. The point which every true patriot should have considered—which Tsuda, the would-be assassin himself, should have pondered over if he had been half the patriot he imagined himself to be—was that no nation could afford to permit such an assault upon a foreign royalty within its dominions without seriously endangering its prestige and integrity. And for this stupid act of a chauvinist a terrible retribution awaited Japan. For Tsarist Russia could not be so easily propitiated.

Ito was first made aware of this unfortunate affair at a hot-spring resort near Odawara, where the news had been relayed by telegraph from the Premier's office. He at once set out for Tokyo to confer with Matsukata and his Cabinet. The Emperor entrained the next morning for Kyoto, where the Russian Prince had gone, to convey the nation's regret. The Government found itself in a quandary. The spectre of Russian reprisals, assuming divers forms, loomed portentously on the official horizon.

In this moment of crisis Ito, in his unique capacity as Japan's Elder Statesman, took the lead in deliberating upon measures for making amends. He knew that only a summary execution of the Prince's assailant would satisfy the Russian Government. But under the existing Japanese laws this could not be done. There was no provision in Japan's criminal code which contemplated this form of punishment for an attempt upon the life of a royal personage other than that of Japan; and Nicholas was a Russian. To execute Tsuda in spite of the unmistakable provisions of the law would be serving merely

the ends of expediency.   It would, on that account, constitute
a deliberate undermining of the judicial system of Japan.   This,
in turn, would react with a thunderous force against the government.   The radicals would triumph.   For a country just
beginning to test whether or not constitutional government
was a blessing to humanity, such perversions of the written
code were indeed inadvisable in the extreme.   Yet to forego
this swift and seemingly necessary means of settlement was
certain to bring forth, not only the wrath of Russia's millions,
but the condemnation and mistrust of the whole Western world
as well.   And this, too, at a time when Japan was clamoring
insistently for the abolishment of extraterritoriality!

Two Cabinet Ministers, Goto and Mutsu, proposed that a
secret hireling be employed to "destroy" the Prince's assailant.
This, they contended, ought to be satisfactory to both Russia
and Japan—Russia, because the crime against her Crown Prince
would be avenged; and Japan, because it would release her
from the obligation of executing a criminal against the provisions of her own laws.   But Ito immediately counselled against
any such unlawful procedures.   It was at best, he said, a shame-
ful exhibition of clandestine state murder, an even more virulent form of conspiracy, which was the most dangerous thing
that could happen in a civilized community.   He would consent
to nothing save the most honorable means within the power
and the jurisdiction of the government.

Five hours after the Emperor's departure Ito also entrained
for Kyoto to confer with the Russian Minister, who was now
in attendance upon the injured Prince.   Meanwhile the Tsar
instructed the latter to have the Prince removed to his battleship.   This was regarded in diplomatic circles as a serious re-
flection upon the vigilance and integrity of the Japanese Government.   The Prince himself expressed a desire to proceed to
Tokyo to return the Emperor's visit before leaving Japan.   To
avoid a possible repetition of the attack, the Emperor offered
the use of his official coach on the Kyoto-Kobe railway and
escorted the Prince in person to his destination.   Ito accompanied the royal personages as far as Kobe and returned to
Kyoto, where Ministers Aoki, Inouye and Enomoto were also

present, to resume the deliberations pending the availability of the Russian Minister's attention.

The rest of the Cabinet, meeting in Tokyo, decided with the Premier's support to meet the situation by drafting a rescript, to be endorsed by the Emperor, authorizing the execution of Nicholas's assailant on the ground that an attack upon the life of a foreign royalty was equivalent to an attack upon Japan's own royalty. This decision was relayed to Ito in Kyoto. Ito realized the imperativeness of gambling the nation's destiny on this alternative if none other could conceivably be devised which would do justice to Russia without jeopardizing Japan's judicial integrity. Everything now depended upon his own decision in the matter, for whatever he suggested the Emperor would approve as a matter of course. The Privy Council was consulted. Opposition was at once expressed there. A Supreme Court judge upheld the opposition.

Ito then interviewed the Russian Minister, who had in the meantime returned to Kyoto, and questioned him as to what he had to say in the matter. He had nothing to say. Was this, Ito desired to know, to be interpreted as approving tacitly whatever measures Japan chose to take in effecting a just settlement? The impossibility of pronouncing the death sentence was explained. When it was further made known to him that life imprisonment was the maximum sentence which could legally be imposed upon the Prince's assailant, his facial expression underwent a visible change. It was obvious that, though he refused to commit himself, only the death sentence would satisfy his government. If Japan failed to fulfill her inevitable mission in the manner desired by Russia, to what lengths would the Russian Government go in obtaining satisfaction? He did not know. Finally Ito decided to let the law take its limited course, come what may. The judges, sitting at Ohtsu, interpreted that law as making an indubitable distinction between a crime committed against the Japanese Emperor and against any other individual, be he commoner, prince or king.

Fortunately for Japan, there was no sequel to this perilous mishap. The extraordinary sympathy which the Emperor himself showed in safeguarding the Prince's life after the attack alone softened the temper of the Russian Government. Tsuda was sentenced to serve his maximum term, and the episode became in due course a closed chapter in the history of Japan.

But national perturbation continued on its devastating course. The upshot of all these disturbances was that the Emperor once more summoned Ito to head the Privy Council.

Then came the inevitable aftermath. The affair had given rise to innumerable criticisms and indiscreet utterances in the public press designed with undisguised malice to embarrass and overthrow the government. When the Diet convened in the fall of that year, Home Minister Shinagawa introduced an Administration bill providing for the censorship of all newspapers, magazines, and other publications devoted to subjects dealing with diplomatic affairs. This was the first attempt on the part of the government since the promulgation of the constitution guaranteeing free speech to muzzle the press. Not only was it unconstitutional; it aroused public indignation and gave the Lower House an invincible weapon with which to renew its attacks upon the bureaucratic Ministers. The bill was promptly thrown out. Early the following year, when the general elections were held, the Home Minister next attempted with what proved to be a gesture of studied defiance to precipitate the seating of a pro-Administration Diet by maneuvering a nation-wide interference with the work of the provincial election machinery. Ito, from his exalted post at the head of the Privy Council, at once protested against this Ministerial conspiracy, for conspiracy it was. The government refused to heed his protest. There was great commotion everywhere, wordy battles, fist-fights, and sudden death. Twenty-five people were reported dead, while three hundred and eighty-eight more were seriously injured. Ito threatened to resign. The Emperor refused to consider his resignation. This conveyed the obvious implication that if anyone must resign in consequence of the Administration's opprobrious conduct, certainly the fair-minded Privy Councillor should be the very last to leave his post. This was as it should be. Public scorn pointed its accusing finger at the Ministerial offender; and the scheming Shinagawa, with his mischievous designs partially accomplished, retired in ignominy from the Cabinet. Soon afterwards the Diet and the Ministry came to grips on the subject with a malicious exchange of impeachment threats and recriminations. Premier Matsukata came to the end of his tether.

CHAPTER XI

WAR

For the second time, with the fall of the Matsukata Government, Ito was called upon to accept the premiership.   But his choice of Ministers was necessarily confined to a very narrow field of executives of proved ability and loyalty, on whom the Emperor could place his ultimate confidence.   Again it was a government of veterans, that is to say, of bureaucrats—a tendency which was becoming increasingly intolerable to those espousing liberal penchants.   Nevertheless, Ito had revealed himself during the last election scandal as a staunch supporter of justice and good government without presuming to draw any political line of demarcation between the opposing factions; and it was believed by the veterans that he could obtain sufficient support from the Lower House on the strength of this meritorious record alone to insure a continuance of bureaucratic leadership.

But on the morning of November 27, 1892, two days before the opening of the fourth session of the Diet, Ito was seriously injured in a collision which occurred at Marunouchi in Tokyo between the *jinrikisha* in which he was proceeding to a conference at the Imperial palace and a speeding carriage which belonged to Prince Arisugawa.   While he was thus disabled and prevented from executing his all-important duties at this critical period, Home Minister Inouye was chosen to assume temporary leadership of the government.   During the two-month interval which lasted until February 7 following, the day on which Ito was able to resume his work as Premier, the Administration budget for 1893 became, as was expected, the subject of a bitter controversy in the Diet; and the parliamentary dissension of the previous years was renewed.   But with this difference, namely, that the budget included, among other essential things, the so-called national defense fund—a gigantic appropriation for the building of expensive modern battleships.

To Ito it was a supremely necessary item, despite the sacrifices it would inevitably entail, considering the fact that Japan was surrounded on every hand by hostile nations, and the only effective way of compelling their respect was through the maintenance of an adequate navy sufficient for all defensive purposes. To the people at large, however, the nation was already over-burdened with taxation and could not positively support such a huge programme without passing through another decade of poverty and suffering. Thus the issue—preparedness versus economy—constituted the axis on which revolved the ever-recurring question as to whether Japan should become a mighty influence in shaping the future of the Far East, or whether she should be condemned to eternal mediocrity.

It is extremely problematical whether Ito's presence in the Diet woud have aided, even so much as by the winning of a single doubtful vote, in strengthening the Administration's cause against the vilifications of the opposition. A deadlock ensued, and the Lower House, uncompromisingly insisting upon economy, voluntarily recessed, only to threaten the Administration upon resitting with the drafting of a strange memorial to the Emperor—a strange record of accumulated factional grievances against not only the existing Ministry but against all previous Ministries, rather than a pertinent request for Imperial intercession in this particular controversy. Here Acting Premier Inouye resorted to the customary defense when confronted with such a dilemma—the Diet's sitting was hastily suspended and prevented, at least for the time being, from having recourse to its supremely opprobrious measure.

When it met again on February 7, 1893, to take a vote on the memorial, Ito mounted the rostrum of the Lower House and made his first parliamentary speech as Premier. "Since you have decided to appeal to the Emperor," he said, "I feel it is hardly necessary for me to add my arguments in defense of the Administration. I can only say that with both the Government and the House of Representatives refusing to yield a single step, I perceive no hope of effecting a solution, and that at this moment when you are about to secure the passage of this memorial the Government has no other recourse but to

voice its complete disapproval." He charged that the memorial, constituting as it did an obvious pretext for articulating
factional grievances arising out of the overthrow of feudalism,
it possessed little merit as an indictment against his Administration. "Our constitutional form of goverment," he continued, apropos of the budget controversy, "does not consist, as
you apparently seem to feel, in administering the affairs of the
nation through the joint decisions of the Diet and the Government alone, but through the approval of the Emperor in whom
is vested the rights of sovereignty." He thus endeavored to
show that whatever the Government proposed to do—in this
instance the passing of the appropriation for the building of
modern battleships—should not be construed as arbitrary and
suggestive of autocratic finality until the Emperor had expressed his approval or disapproval, which, it was clear, he had not
yet had the opportunity of doing. To prefer charges against
his Government at this premature stage was, therefore, he said,
patently anachronistic.

But his logic was wasted on unhearing ears, for the opposition was in no mood to be lectured. It served rather to intensi-
fy the feelings of factional antagonism. The memorial bill was
speedily voted on, passed with unmistakable unanimity, and
presented to the Emperor on the following day.

In order to forestall a victory for the memorialists and the
consequent subversion of his preparedness programme, Ito besought the Emperor—as Premier, not as Elder Statesman—to
have the Diet dissolved. The Emperor, however, had other
plans. He issued, instead, a rescript embodying a remedial
measure which fulfilled the aspirations of the Administration
and the Diet at one and the same time. His remedy consisted
in providing for the battleship fund by transferring 300,000
yen annually from the Imperial Privy Purse for six consecutive
years and ten per cent. of the annual stipend of the civil and
military officials. He would thus provide for the nation's defense armaments out of his own private resources and out o
the funds made available through retrenchment in overhead.
Thus was the crisis averted.

It was, however, soon forgotten. When the Diet met again,

fresh disagreements arose over the wounds of the old. Denunciations, recriminations, and sibilant epithets flew like red-
hot chips across the assembled throng of cantankerous law-
makers. The ubiquitous budget was again subjected to the
pruning knife. The old subject of treaty revision was again,
despite the obviously unfavorable outlook, made the basis of
attack upon the Ministry. Ito made his second, third and
fourth speeches in the Diet, beseeching patience and counselling
moderation. Then Tooru Hoshi, the speaker of the Lower
House and the leading opposition light, was implicated in a
scandal involving the Tokyo Stock Exchange and forced by
the government to leave the Diet. Threats of impeachment
were in consequence hurled by his supporters at the Ministry.
Memorials upon memorials were drafted with a vengeance.
But Ito stoutly refused to resign. For two consecutive sessions
the Diet was adjourned, prorogued, dissolved. Parliamentary
strife, with all its haranguing vicissitudes, went on noisily
apace.

2

All this, moreover, was welcome news to China, which she
digested with a particularly fine relish. Dissension at home
meant impotency abroad, and China was quick to take advantage of Japan's domestic ailments to bring Korea more completely under her control.

Since the signing of the Tientsin Treaty Korea had again
reverted to the rule of the Queen and her conservative, pro-
Chinese associates. The King was merely an animated figurehead now carrying out the Queen's wishes, or those of his
Chinese advisers. The Tai Won Kun, the erstwhile reactionary leader, had become a negligible factor: political principles
meant nothing to him without the power to sway the ignorant
masses and the prejudiced intelligentsia. Kim Ok Kiun, the
liberals' standard-bearer, had sought refuge in Japan, only to
be later enticed to Shanghai by the Queen's indefatigable plotters and there reduced to so much mince meat and returned to
Korea in his post-mortem state as a warning and a threat to
other designing liberals. Then, like a flash, the Tong Hak

rebellion broke out among a group of rabid Koreans to whom hatred of the foreigners had translated itself into a mystical cult of Oriental fanaticism. China acted swiftly to exploit the situation. She secured, through Yuan Shih Kai, her resident representative at Seoul, an agreement with Korea, as a result of which Chinese troops in great number were at once dispatched to assist in quelling the disturbance. This assistance was rendered, Yuan assured the Korean King, as a demonstration of those ancient ties of political kinship which, he insisted, still bound Korea to China, despite previous official disavowals of such ties. It was patently intended, with Li Hung Chang still laboring under his monstrous delusion respecting the effects of the Tientsin Treaty, as an irrefutable proof for the benefit of other interested Powers, especially Japan, of Korea's acceptance of China's promiscuous overlordship.

Ito, sensing that China was again up to some subtle mischief, likewise authorized the dispatch of Japanese troops to Korea. This was ostensibly to protect the lives and property of Japanese nationals during the pending crisis, and China was duly notified in accordance with the agreement reached at Tientsin. In reality, however, it was designed more particularly to sustain, with force if necessary, the status of independence which he had persistently assured for Korea.

Meanwhile the Tong Hak rebels were subdued by native forces without outside assistance. But the trouble was only begun, for here the question of the evacuation of the Chinese and Japanese troops precipitated an uncompromising attitude on both sides which renewed the ancient animosity with fatal swiftness. China insisted upon her repeatedly expressed contention that inasmuch as she was merely extending aid to her "vassal" state, she was under no obligation to evacuate her troops in compliance with the wishes of a third Power. Japan attempted to demolish this hollow intransigence by proposing joint action for the reorganization of Korea's internal administration, specifically to rehabilitate her and thus to obviate future interventions in her affairs. This was a course which, if accepted, would have bound the two countries to assume a joint responsibility for Korea's independence. Had China agreed to this compromise, hostilities would have been then and there avoided. But she perceived in it a magnificent opportunity to brand Japan as a meddlesome hypocrite, a government which presumed to compel respect for Korea's integrity, yet undertook to propose external action interfering with her internal affairs. What she omitted to observe was the fact that this sudden championing of Korea's sovereignty constituted a categorical denial on her own part of her own claims of suzerainty.

Events moved rapidly thereafter. China dispatched a fresh army of eight thousand men. Japanese troops in Seoul, anticipating this move, accomplished a coup d'état. The palace was seized. The Korean King and his Councillors were rendered powerless. The reins of government thereupon fell into the hands of the Japanese Minister and his military advisers. The Tai Won Kun, a former foe of Japan but the only available member of the Korean royalty who was in conflict with the deposed administration, was placed at the head of the new government to carry out the reforms proposed by Japan. The Sino-Korean treaty was forthwith abrogated. The Chinese troops were ousted from Korea.

Thus Japan, the boasted upholder of Korean independence, committed an amazing about-face: she herself reduced Korea's sovereignty to smithereens, though it was admittedly an emergency measure necessitated by the war. And for this Ito, who as Premier sanctioned the whole course of events, must be held for strict accountability. How can this warlike commitment be reconciled with his principles of peace, of moderation, of respect for Korea's integrity? The answer will not be found in any superficial manifestations which become immediately observable and which do not embrace the totality of the problems involved. It will be found, instead, in his lifetime of determined struggles on behalf of Korea, which had but barely begun. With Korea so woefully disorganized, so hostile to progress, so utterly impotent, it was impossible to render any such assistance on terms of equality as between this country and Japan. Ito's interest was therefore necessarily, at the moment, protective and hence paternal. He was merely fulfilling his oft-repeated pledge to assist the Koreans in preserving their

independence against the encroachment of other neighboring
Powers whose object seemed predatory, but he would reserve
for Japan, for her own protection, the right to enforce whatever
precautionary measures she deemed imperative in the circumstances. Moreover, the time, to a realist of his calibre, was
far too hazardous to indulge in lofty preoccupations in abstract
idealisms and idealogies, though he was, when the occasion
properly evinced itself, an essentially liberal-minded statesman.
The test of his sincerity must be measured by the fruits of his
efforts.

Nor did he labor under any delusions respecting the war
with China. In common with other leading statesmen of Japan,
he had come to entertain a genuine apprehension of the "perils
of propinquity" arising out of the dominance of any hostile
Power within the territorial confines of Korea and to feel entirely justified in having recourse, in the interests of self-defense,
to any conceivable means for the prevention of such an eventuality. This had become a preponderant part of Japan's Far
Eastern policy. It had had its stirring beginnings in the debates of 1873 when Saigo attempted to discipline the Tai Won
Kun. Ito had opposed it then because of the greater need of
domestic rehabilitation. But China's repeated attempts to utilize questionable means of expediency in retaining her hold on
Korea made it necessary that Japan resort to desperate measures of defense. Thus the paramount question, as Ito perceived it then, was whether China should be permitted to absorb
Korea, or whether Japan, for her own security, should expend
millions in men and money to prevent this danger and at the
same time demand of Korea that she be guided by her efforts
at reform if she were to be protected as a sovereign and independent state.

Summing up the course of events up to the time war was
declared, he said, addressing the Diet: "China's insolence became increasingly intolerable. On the one hand, she asserted
her claims of overlordship over Korea; yet, on the other, she
insisted upon scrupulously respecting the latter's sovereign
rights. She herself schemed to interfere, yet decried all efforts
proceeding from other sources. She alone presumed to exercise

complete control. Her purpose has been clearly revealed. When the Korean insurrection broke out, she first proceeded to extend her own powers in that country; and rather than entertain any thought whatever for the restoration of public order and for the support of Korea's independence, she betrayed a desire to infringe upon the latter's sovereign rights and to absorb her nationals. Long before the Tong Hak rebellion had completely subsided, she insisted that order had been restored and clamored for the withdrawal of our troops. Yet she seized the opportunity to increase her own troops, and to attempt further acts of aggression. While thus violating the spirit of the Tientsin Treaty, she secretly strove to coerce Korea into rejecting our well-meant counsels. Offers of mediation were made, but China would not listen. Our Acting Minister, distrusting her motives, issued a manifesto, holding her responsible for any future disturbances which might arise. Not only did she repulse our well-meant proposals for cooperative action and threatened the peace of the Far East; she quickly resorted to warlike measures. There was no other recourse for us but to take up the challenge."

3

After all those stormy squabbles between the Administration and the Diet, between the bureaucrats and the spokesmen of the masses, peace again settled vicariously over Japan—peace through war! The consciousness of a common menace engendered by the outbreak of hostilities with China brought about a complete reconciliation—a complete vindication of Ito's realistic policy.

The war proved to be an egregious farce. That Japan, the as yet pathetically insignificant David of the Far East, prostrated this flabby Goliath within eight months, was not at all surprising, though it was considered then as an amazing feat. The incredible thing was that Li Hung Chang, who should have been fully cognizant of China's weakness, repeated his erstwhile blunders by continuing, on the one hand, to overestimate her strength, and, on the other, to underestimate the power and the temper of the Japanese.

Even after viewing the dual tragedy of the disastrous naval defeat off the mouth of the Yalu, which gave Japan complete control of the sea, and the fall of Port Arthur within a single day, Li persisted in treating Japan with disdainful disrespect. He knew full well by then that China's hopes of averting her doom were slight indeed. He knew that were he to bungle this little affair with Japan his own position in the Peking Court would become precarious. Yet, instead of making overtures of peace in the only legitimate fashion, he sent a Mr. Detring, a German, with a letter to Ito, presumably to sound him on China's possibilities of securing peace without ignominy. Ito was not averse to discussing peace, but a mere agent of Li's, coming as he did without a carte blanche from the Chinese Government, could not be received. Detring was peremptorily refused a hearing.

Li next sent an American, John W. Foster, former American Secretary of State, to do the thinking and the talking, with two Chinese officials of doubtful rank but possessed of the proper credentials, to lend official weight to the negotiations. Ito was about to recognize this mission—even the customary preliminaries were completed—when he thought twice about discussing so grave a question as that of war or peace with a group of vicarious representatives whose decisions and commitments he was not at all sure the Peking Government would accept with finality. For the second time Li's artful gestures—gestures designed to belittle as well as to escape responsibilities—were repulsed.

Meanwhile two Japanese divisions under Generals Yamagata and Oyama had invaded Manchuria. Weihaiwei fell. Newchang and Yingkow followed in rapid succession. Peking came within striking distance of the Japanese offensive. For the first time Li bestirred himself with desperate seriousness. China's defeat was obvious and complete. Further indiscretions on his part were certain to precipitate a disaster at Peking. He decided that he would himself head a peace mission to Japan.

When this information was transmitted to Tokyo, Ito made public the text of the Japanese terms upon which peace might be had by China. These terms included, among other things, the recognition of the independence of Korea, the payment of an indemnity of 300,000,000 taels, and the cession of the Liao-tung peninsula, Formosa, and the Pescadores.

Li was thoroughly displeased. It was annoying enough to have to contemplate the dishonor of a great country such as China, physically prodigious and possessed of an ancient civilization, going down to defeat before the insufferable pygmies from Dai Nippon. But to face the consequences of an ignominious peace treaty was even more annoying still. He decided to lessen the ignominy, to outwit his ancient rival, if not in the fortunes and calculations of war, at least in diplomacy. He submitted the Japanese terms to the Ministers of Russia, Germany, and France, and asked for the support of their respective governments to demand from Japan a mitigation of the terms, especially with regard to the cession of Manchurian territory. This marked the first secret step in China's long and devious attempts at revenge—attempts which, with her own force of arms proving unavailing, were calculated to pit other nations more powerfully situated but unmindful of her designs, against her foe. Conditions, fortunately for Li, were peculiarly favorable. He received a most encouraging response. Russia in particular was inclined to regard with jealous interest any indication of a too precipitate rise and expansion of a Far Eastern Power among spheres which she herself was bent upon exploiting. France was an ally of Russia; no hesitation was expected from her, nor shown, in agreeing to Li's request. Germany was now seeking to obviate the constant threat on her eastern frontier by befriending the great Russian bear. She also became a willing accomplice in this international conspiracy.

With this little understanding tucked away in the back of his cerebral repository, Li started out for Japan. Ito went forth to meet him at Shimonoseki.

4

Ten tumultuous years had passed into history since their last meeting at Tientsin. They were met now under circumstances far different from those which had dominated the deliberations of that futile conference. The years had brought travail and wounded vanity to China; much of Li's patronizing propensities had worn off. Ito had changed but little. There was nothing conspicuous about the development of his political life, save that of a courageous and perspicacious plodder. He knew nothing of Li's machinations. He had no inkling as yet of the silent menace which was soon to swoop down upon him and conjure up a terrible anti-climax to what rightfully should have been a brilliant disposition of a brilliant victory.

Li opened the negotiations by asking, first, for an armistice. Ito agreed to grant it, but stipulated that China must turn over to the Japanese troops, as guarantees of her sincerity, her fortresses at Taku, Tientsin, and Shanhaikwan; her railroad between Tientsin and Shanhaikwan; her supplies of arms and ammunition. She must also reimburse Japan for the expenses of her army of occupation.

These were the customary terms to which any vanquished nation must submit in order to secure a suspension of hostilities pending the conclusion of a treaty of peace. Li, however, expressed considerable amazement. Amazement turned to incredulity—or perhaps it was a clever affectation, for no one could begin to explore the depths of a Chinaman's mind, particularly that of a diplomatist of Li's sinuous calibre, without emerging with even greater confusion than when he had started out. But Ito had long since learned that to quibble over terms with a Celestial gentleman was a decidedly futile affair. Peace, he said in effect, ought to be worth the price to China.

Li, rather than yield to Ito's terms, withdrew his request. Subsequently he signified his intention of negotiating for a treaty of peace without concluding an armistice. Then at the close of the second session a Japanese gun-toting fanatic, who had become obsessed with the mad notion that Li was personally responsible for the war and for the sorry mess in Korea, intervened. Li was painfully wounded in the face. But China was immeasurably benefited thereby. As an expression of his sincere sympathy and that of the Japanese nation, Ito granted the armistice without any provisos whatever.

But when Li recovered sufficiently from his wound to proceed with the negotiations, Ito was to learn that stern measures must again be resorted to. Li not only objected to the cession of Formosa and the Liaotung peninsula as specified in the original Japanese terms, but also demanded that the indemnity be reduced from 300,000,000 taels to 10,000,000 taels. Ito gave him four days in which to withdraw his objections. Li continued to file voluminous protests. He received, in the meantime, renewed assurances from Van Brandt at Berlin that the three Powers would later intervene. In the end he capitulated. The treaty, as finally drafted and signed, carried substantially the original Japanese terms, with the exception of the amount of the indemnity which was reduced to 200,000,000 taels.

Li obviously had few regrets. It was some comfort to him to feel that this business of concluding a peace treaty with Japan, so far as it affected China's ultimate fortunes, had not yet ended—not by a long shot—though Ito was blissfully unaware of it.

5

Precisely six days after Li and Ito had affixed their signatures to the Treaty of Shimonoseki, the silent menace behind the Three-Power conspiracy instigated by Li suddenly burst forth, creating consternation throughout Japan. It materialized in the form of a diplomatic note presented by the Russian Minister to the Japanese Foreign Office, reading:

"The Government of His Majesty the Emperor of all the Russias, in examining the conditions of peace which Japan has imposed on China, finds that the possession of the peninsula of Liaotung, claimed by Japan, would be a constant menace to the capital of China, would at the same time render illusory the independence of Korea, and would henceforth be a perpetual obstacle to the permanent peace of the Far East. Consequently the Government of His Majesty the Emperor would give a new proof of their sincere friendliness for the Government of His Majesty the Emperor of Japan by advising them to renounce the definitive possession of the peninsula of Liaotung."

This note was reinforced by identic threats from the Ministers of Germany and France.

The Liaotung peninsula constituted a little strip of Manchurian territory which jutted out into the sea between the Bay of Korea and the Gulf of Chihli. Bounded on the west by China proper, on the east by Korea, and on the south by the sea, it held the key to the situation in the Far East. The fortress at Port Arthur reared its menacing bulk in Kwantung, a diminutive neck of land lying at its southwesterly tip. This ancient citadel, the most strategic stronghold in China, difficult of approach by sea, and steep in ascent, was virtually impregnable. The whole of Liaotung represented a portion of the territory actually conquered by Japan. Her right to claim it as part of her spoils of war was thus upheld by every international military consideration receiving the indubitable sanction of history since the beginning of time. To Japan, particularly the military leaders who had persuaded Ito against his better judgment to demand the cession of this peninsula, it moreover appeared in perspective as something enormously important and, for that reason, superlatively desirable. It could be developed into an excellent barrier for the defense of Korea against the future exploitations of China. More than that, it could be made to serve as the first effectual bulwark for the preservation of Japan's own security. To renounce it now, after China had lawfully ceded it to her under the most legitimate conditions, was in itself, let alone the conspiracy which forced it, a matter provocative of the most excruciating national agony. History records that there was, inevitably, a considerable gnashing of teeth and the shedding of "tears of blood." Japan was to learn, aside from China's desire for revenge, that the motive behind this treachery was something vastly more significant than the feigned altruism on behalf of China and Korea, which appeared in the text of the Three-Power notes of intervention.

As Ito viewed it, only three obvious courses lay open to Japan to meet this situation. First, she could refuse outright to abide by the demands of the European coalition, which meant that she must prepare for another war, this time against the combined navies of three of the leading Powers of the world. Secondly, she could appeal to the rest of the Western nations

with a view to determining the issue by arbitration.   Thirdly,
she could swallow her pride and accept the mandate of the
coalition.

Ito elected to take the second course.   It occurred to him
that the other Powers might possess sufficient interest in justice
and fair play to deprecate this unwarrantable gesture of the
coalition.   But he quickly discovered, through the Japanese
diplomats stationed abroad, that the whole world presented an
aspect either of utter indifference or of fear of the three con-
spiring governments.   The chances under the circumstances of
securing a favorable hearing were indeed remote.   Nor did he
relish the idea of stampeding the nation on another military
rampage, even if dishonor could be avoided in the attempt,
for in that direction lay national suicide.   The inevitable
must therefore be faced, and he came out unhesitatingly, with
the approval of Emperor Meiji, to inform the Ministers of
Russia, Germany and France, that Japan would renounce her
claims to Liaotung, as demanded, in favor of China.   A supplementary treaty embodying this modification was thereupon
concluded with the collaboration of the three Ministers, and
signed at Peking.

Then the people of Japan awoke as from a terrible nightmare.   The nightmare became a seething reality.   The full
import of the renunciation of Liaotung, the overwhelming
shame attendant upon this act, turned the nation into a writh-
ing, cursing mob.   It spat venom and hate and irreverent
diatribes, not at Li, the principal conniver, nor at the uncon-
scionable members of the coalition, but at Ito whom they conceived, by some distorted view of the whole situation, to have
been responsible for all the humiliating consequences.   That
Ito had taken the only possible course without plunging Japan
into a still greater predicament from which she was bound to
emerge with immeasurable losses out of all proportion to the
value of the territory renounced or the humiliation involved,
failed to impress his critics.   Never was a more terrible exhibition of mob imbecility shown.

In the midst of this nationwide uproar the Emperor decorat-
ed Ito with the Grand Cordon of the Chrysanthemum and made

him a Marquis to boot. The effect was immediate and im-
pressive. The dissension was stilled, as if by some mesmeric
power. Ito's vindication was magnificent in its completeness!

One thing was certain: Korea's independence from China was
definitely recognized by the world at large. For this the war,
from Japan's viewpoint, seems to have been well worth the
effort. How will Ito render this independence complete by
conforming Japan's policy to the letter of its implications?
That will depend upon how steadfastly the neighboring Powers respect its inviolability. Until Korea completes her national development and until she demonstrates her capacity to resist
all foreign exploitations successfully, he will continue—for the
sake of his country's security no less than for the freedom of
the Koreans—to maintain that eternal vigilance which is the
price of independence. That at least must be retained as a
right and privilege for the sacrifices made in consequence of the
war. The ultimate responsibility must rest on the shoulders
of the Koreans themselves.

CHAPTER XII

POLITICAL PARTIES

I

Ito's Administration survived the 9th session of the Diet, despite the efforts of the opposition to bring about impeachment proceedings over the Liaotung issue. The war with China had served as an eloquent testimonial to the necessity of developing an impregnable defensive fleet. Hence the consummation of the war was followed immediately by the inception of a prodigious battleship-building programme. In addition, a vast colonization scheme was formulated for the development of Formosa, which China had grudgingly ceded to Japan. A similar enterprise in Hokkaido, which had had an early beginning, was subsidized anew.

To all these ambitious projects Ito gave his unqualified support, to the exclusion of the more pressing domestic problems arising out of post-war economic evils. The Chinese indemnity was thus almost wholly consumed in paying for improvements which concerned only remotely the suffering millions who clamored for financial relief.

The opposition, headed now by Okuma and Matsukata, quickly seized this opportunity to concoct an issue over which to bring about the dissolution of Ito's Government. Ito strove to prevent the collapse by seeking the cooperation of the two leaders. He invited them to fill the portfolios of Foreign Affairs and of Home Affairs respectively. To yield to the opposition now without devising some means of curbing its attack would have been tantamount to a revocation of his preparedness programme. But the personnel of his reorganized Cabinet suffered severely from the effects of incompatibility. His scheme fell through.

In this manner Ito's second Administration, which successfully prosecuted the first foreign war of modern Japan, came to an end. But the Okuma-Matsukata Ministry which then took up the reins of government disclosed glaring weaknesses. A

stiff retrenchment programme was introduced to counterbalance
the enormous expenditures incurred during Ito's regime, but a
snag was soon encountered. A sharp disagreement arose between the two standard-bearers over the bill increasing the land
tax—a subject which was certain to contribute vitally to the
problem of national economy. Okuma expressed unalterable
opposition to the increase but was outvoted in the councils, and
resigned. In doing so he took with him the support of the
Progressive wing. This showed conclusively that the agreement originally reached by the combination had been centered
merely on breaking down the structure of Ito's Administration;
that beyond this destructive purpose there was nothing fundamentally harmonious about the joint policies its principals espoused. Matsukata, for his part, succeeded in bringing about
a premature dissolution of the 11th Diet in order to obviate
the vengeful thrust of the Progressive insurgents. The following day he also submitted his resignation.

For the third time Ito was summoned to create a Ministry.
At first he sought to reconcile the various factions by inviting
Okuma and Itagaki, leaders respectively of the Progressives
and the Liberals, to share the responsibility of his Cabinet.
But both insisted with equal firmness that their acceptance of
a portfolio would be contingent upon securing control of the
Home Department, where bills appertaining to domestic improvements originated. Thus the impracticability of this
course became manifest. Thereupon Ito switched over to the
other extreme. Factional considerations were eschewed, and
his choice of Ministers was effected along strictly non-partisan
lines. But factional politics had become too deeply imbedded
in the minds of the people to enable a "transcendent" Cabinet
to function successfully. Sensing its futility, Ito altered his
plans by concluding an entente with Itagaki and his Liberal
followers. Opposition to this move, however, was voiced by
Finance Minister Inouye. The entente was called off. The
Liberals became incensed. The result was a grand amalgama-
tion of the Liberals and the Progressives, who now called
themselves the "Kensei-To," or Constitutional Party. The
measure of this consolidated opposition was revealed in the

defeat, in the 12th session of the Diet, of the land tax bill, a controversial relic of the previous Administration which Ito revived in order to meet the deficit in the national budget. Thus the party system of government emerged from its experimental stages and at last became a factor that must be seriously reckoned with.

Ito, for patriotic reasons, was opposed to the party system, but he was fully cognizant of its potency and he had the wisdom to welcome it and to calculate its possibilities. As he conceived it, one of three courses now lay open to him to meet this extraordinary situation. The first was that he might himself create a political party, while retaining the office of Premier, with his incumbent non-factional Ministers as a nucleus. Through this party he could bid for support of his Administration from the people. The second course was to resign and support a government headed by a member of the party which he would thus create. The third was the alternative: to turn the government over to the Constitutionalists. His ultimate choice was determined, not by his personal desires or inclination, but by judicious planning after gauging the popular will. He decided to take the last course—to respect the position of the Constitutionalists.

In his letter of resignation to the Emperor, composed in classic phrases, Ito asked that his title of Marquis be also stripped from him. Why he did so is perhaps beyond the understanding of the modernist. Suffice it to say that to him it seemed the most natural thing for one in his circumstances to do. It revealed perhaps more clearly than any other of his acts his fine sensibilities as a patriot and as a man. During the last decade he had striven with a typically Rooseveltian perspicacity to develop the basic power of his country in the only way in which it could possibly command the world's respect. Moreover, the recent developments in the Far East had made it imperative that Japan adopt radical changes in her foreign and domestic policies, changes in which considerations of national defense must take precedence over domestic issues. But it was evident, from the attitude of the opposition, that the enforcement of such a programme was wholly incompatible with the wishes of the people. The people, meanwhile, had become sufficiently united in spirit since the war with China, burying as they did the ancient animosities resulting from the over-throw of feudalism. They had become sufficiently schooled in their responsibilities under the constitution and they had waited long enough to deserve a greater measure of trust from above. So far his own activities had been confined almost entirely to the advancement of the interests of the State and his reward had been a Marquisate. Henceforth he would work for the people, for their further edification, to the end that they might more assiduously and more intelligently inter-pret and execute their duties and responsibilities to the State. Such a policy would necessarily be in opposition to all those forces which constituted the essence of oligarchic authority. Hence his decision to renounce the Marquisate—a final and conclusive proof that he was, at heart, essentially a democrat. But the Emperor saw no convincing reason why Ito should not serve the people in his existing status, nor would he consider stripping a public servant of his reward for past services simply because of a change in his future policies; and the title remain-ed with him.

This of course marked Ito's formal renunciation of bureau-cratic principles. It was a change that presaged the shattering of age-old alignments, the doom of oligarchism, and the begin-ning of the triumph of the masses. It was unprecedented and it was incredible and it aroused nationwide conjectures as to what his ultimate intentions might be. The militarists, ob-serving as they did his past decisions and commitments with the fixed notions of their particular creed, could not perceive the motive in a man who would spare the "insulting" Koreans for the sake of peace and progress, but who would fight the "insolent" Chinese in the name of self-defense, and who would now adopt a line of action yet more completely at variance. The bureaucrats, who had begun their careers with him as heroes of the Restoration, could not understand the inner work-ings of the mind of a man who had done so much to strengthen the position of the oligarchs, yet who now undertook to re-nounce his title and proceeded to serve the masses. The radicals, incurably impatient with regard to questions of political progress, were mystified by this man who was so confessedly enamored of Western institutions, yet who, in the name of moderation, kept a constant check upon their sweeping aspirations—only to break away from the citadel of conservatism in this precipitate about-face fashion.

2

The next two years Ito spent in travel. His rôle was that of an unofficial observer endeavoring to combine whatever pleasure it was possible for a man of his rank and associations to secure with the serious business of garnering facts and information wherewith to start his new career as an avowed champion of the masses. Furthermore, it was high time he paused in the midst of his labors at the helm of the government to conduct a personal survey in the far corners of the Empire of the measure of his handiwork, to view the trend of progress.

He visited China and Korea, where an intimate acquaintance with the recent post-war developments was formed. This was particularly important in view of the unfortunate turn events had taken in that troublesome region where one costly war had already been fought out and another was swiftly brewing. At Seoul, in the course of a speech delivered at a dinner given in his honor by the Korean Foreign Office, he made the following declarations:*

"Japan's policy toward Korea has since (the crisis of 1873) been unchanged; in other words, her object has always been to assist and befriend this country. It is true that at times incidents of an unpleasant nature unfortunately interfered with the maintenance of unsuspecting cordiality between the two nations. But I may conscientiously assure you that the real object of the Japanese Government has always been to render assistance to Korea in her noble endeavors to be a civilized and independent state.

"I am sincerely gratified to see that today Korea is independent and sovereign. Henceforth it will be Japan's

*From "Makers of Modern Japan," by J. Morris.

wish to see Korea's independence further strengthened and consolidated; no other motive shall influence Japan's conduct toward this country. On this point you need not entertain the slightest doubt.

"Japan's good wishes for Korean independence are all the more sincere and reliable because her vital interests are bound up with those of your country. A danger to Korean independence will be a danger to Japan's safety. So you will easily recognize that the strongest of human motives, namely, self-interest, combines with neighborly feelings to make Japan a sincere well-wisher and friend of Korean independence."

These were significant utterances, particularly in the light of subsequent developments which brought international upheavals in their wake, and in which Ito remained faithful to his principles as a "well-wisher" of the Koreans.

He next toured the interior of Japan, inspecting the various governmental units as they functioned away from the great centers of national political turmoil. What he found in the core of this maze of provincial politics was not at all reassuring. A malignant growth in the form of a shameless abuse of political privileges was spreading with disquieting persistency. The new experiment in local self-government which was supposed, under the powers granted by the constitution, to have supplanted an oligarchy of some twenty-five centuries' standing, was proving, not a blessing, but a breeder of baser evils—of even more intolerable oligarchies. Bellicose factions and miniature Tammany Halls were wreaking havoc on the prefectural institutions and depriving the people of every legitimate opportunity to govern themselves. Corruption was rampant.

When he returned to his seaside home at Oiso it was to proceed with the projected preparations for the formation of a mammoth political party. This was in line with the decision he made at the time he resigned from the premiership. It would also be the only practical remedy for the eradication of the evils he had witnessed in the provinces. He would thus attempt to unite as many of the contending factions as possible under the leadership of one central organization, where disciplinary regulations governing the conduct of public officials as well as platforms defining the concerted policies of its members could be formulated and vigorously enforced.

Men like Saionji, Kaneko, Hara, Suematsu, Watanabe, who had either flourished under Ito's regime or approved of his political views, flocked to his standard. With that scholarly devotion to the ideals of Japanese constitutional government which had so often been misconstrued by the radicals, he drafted a nine-plank platform, summarizing the salient points of these ideals. It required those who would pledge themselves to its fulfilment (1) to support the constitution, (2) to respect the principles of the Meiji Restoration, (3) to maintain the purity of the election system, (4) to foster friendly relations with foreign countries, (5) to promote the national interests in conformity with conditions prevailing abroad as well as within, (6) to encourage education as a means of enhancing national progress, (7) to support the industries and the commerce of the nation, (8) to create local organizations for the attainment of social and economic cooperation, (9) to fulfill the responsibilities inseparable from political parties solely for the public welfare.

With this platform as a basis, the first *genuine* political party of Japan, the "Seiyukai," emerged from the welter of factional strife on August 25, 1900.

3

The reaction of the people to this singularly forward-moving development in the interest of good government was indeed profound. It seemed to radiate every promise of achieving something of that harmonious progress in political circles which hitherto had been distinguished particularly by its absence. The Constitutional Party, which was in reality hardly any more than a mere consolidation of two inimical factions—the Liberals and the Progressives—for the overthrow of Ito's third Administration, and which suffered a collapse precisely four months after its joint standard-bearers assumed the helm, now formally disbanded in order to enable its members to affiliate themselves with this newly-created party. Among those who thus encamped under Ito's political tent were Hoshi, Ozaki, Matsuda, Haseba, Oh-oka, all men with an outstanding record, either of achievement or of notoriety, whose stars were destined further to scintillate in the dark political firmament of Japan. Okuma, the incorrigible dissenter, alone among the veterans adhered to his principles by keeping himself conspicuously aloof. When the next election came along, the party seated 156 members in the House of Representatives. Thus was its new-born strength revealed.

Premier Yamagata, who succeeded to the Constitutional Administration, accepted this as an irrefutable testimony of the popular will, for it was clearly evident that under the circumstances there was no possibility of his securing the Diet's support. He thus informed the Emperor of his desire to retire in favor of a Seiyukai Government created by Ito, the party's founder and leader.

Ito strongly opposed this move. He was fully conscious of the unwisdom of foisting the reins of government upon a newly-organized party at so early a period in its career. He preferred to give its members the opportunity of acquiring a more thorough knowledge of the responsibilities of party government if ever he were to accept this trust on behalf of the Seiyukai. But the complexion of the forthcoming Diet had brought about a situation wherein no one else, obviously, would care to have it thrust upon his shoulders. The Emperor, perceiving this difficulty, urged him repeatedly to accept the premiership on the new basis. His friends, particularly Inouye, prevailed upon him to abide by the Emperor's request. He was thus confronted with a responsibility resulting from his own creative efforts which could not be evaded. With the greatest of misgivings he consented. It was his fourth, and his last, venture as Premier of Japan.

True to Ito's suspicions, the Seiyukai ministerial enterprise proved to be a decidedly premature affair. The rise of the party was too superficially meteoric to enable it to make much headway in a country where the power of the conservative element was so solidly entrenched. Nor was it conducive to a salutary effect upon the political consciousness of its lesser stars, whose sole interest in the party's success was centered on the quest for individual prestige.

Watanabe, the man who had served as organization chairman, first started to stir up dissension within the party with a malicious cannonade of invectives when it became known that the post of Finance Minister, which he coveted, was to be conferred upon Inouye, who was Ito's choice. Inouye had been indefatigable in his efforts on behalf of the Emperor to bring about Ito's acceptance of the premiership. His appointment was not a reward but one of the major conditions upon which Ito had agreed, against his better judgment, to take over the reins of government. But out of sheer desire for party harmony, Ito was finally compelled to silence this vicious attack by gratifying Watanabe's great ambition. To resist it by holding fast to his habitual "transcendent" principles would have wrecked the party. Now that he had become inextricably involved in party politics, the question of adhering to the rules of the game, no matter how odious, was not only a necessary consideration in the perpetuation of its usefulness, but a vital one as well.

Thus the evils of partisanship dominated the fate of the Seiyukai from its initial advent into national politics. Verily, the Westernization of Japan was proceeding along truly Jacksonian lines. Yet the process would not have been complete had not the vices been assimilated along with the virtues with equal assiduity!

Nor was this all. Watanabe's unseemly conduct was the cause of considerable resentment among the other Cabinet Ministers, particularly on the part of Hoshi, the Communications chief, who proceeded to express his own petty grievances by voicing opposition, chiefly for spite's sake, to all of Watanabe's financial measures. Thus the selfishness inseparable from party wrangles now developed a serious dissension within the Ministry itself. Hoshi himself was not immune from the scathing diatribes of his critics. The *Mainichi Shimbun*, a Tokyo daily headed by Saburo Shimada, took elaborate pains to unearth a notorious scandal in which the Communications Minister had played the leading rôle. Hoshi, the *Mai-*

nichi exposé revealed, had brought about corruption in the administration of the city of Tokyo through the establishment of a system of municipal control very much akin to the tactics traditionally imputed to the Tammany clique in New York.

For all these unsavory manifestations emanating from the Ministry the charge of autocracy and corruption was hurled unmercifully at Ito. The charge, singularly enough, originated in the House of Peers and was contained in a memorial signed by 187 members. This was indeed suprising news to Ito, for the Peers had always held themselves consistently aloof from all the boisterous conflicts in the Diet. Furthermore, Ito was himself a Peer. He had always been their leader and adviser whenever the duties of Premier did not take him away from the Upper House. His principles, his qualities of leadership, were among them a matter of common knowledge. This sudden change in their attitude was therefore something which, obviously, connoted a greater significance than that which appeared on the surface of the memorial. The truth, though Ito was as yet unaware of it, was that the Peers had begun to maneuver an organized hostility against him because they believed he was scheming to become a virtual dictator by concentrating the power of the government in the House of Representatives, where he could always control, through his party, the majority vote. The charge against him was consequently more of a pretext under which to dismantle this alleged dictatorship. Even the Peers had thus become involved in the meshes of party strife.

This truth was borne out when the 15th session of the Diet convened in December, 1900. Two Administration bills of vital importance were introduced, one for the passage of the national budget for 1901, the other providing for an increase in the tax on säké, beer, sugar, and tobacco. Included in the budget was an item for the maintenance of the Japanese army in China, which had been engaged for some time, along with those of the leading Western nations, in putting an end to the Boxer uprising. The tax increase on the four articles of luxury was designed to meet the obvious indebtedness which this additional item would necessarily incur. Both bills passed the

House of Representatives with a minimum of argumentative discussion, for the Seiyukai members were in control there now. But when they reached the House of Peers, the committee on taxation to which they were referred forthwith voted for their rejection. Ito then appeared in person before the committee to elicit its view on what might be proposed in lieu of the tax increase, for the money had to be raised. But he received no encouraging response.

The members of the committee insisted that perhaps bonds might be issued, or that old securities in the possession of the government might be sold, or, still further, that there ought to be something available in the Chinese indemnity. None of these suggestions Ito deemed practicable or advisable. Bonds, he pointed out, could not be issued unless there was something tangibly certain on which the government could depend to redeem them at maturity. The contemplated tax increase was to provide for just such a contingency, the only difference being that the revenue thus made available would be applied directly to the equalization of the budget. Neither the floating of new bonds, nor the selling of old securities could be effected for such purposes, he explained, without throwing the markets into dire confusion. As to the Chinese indemnity, it was simply not available.

The fear was then expressed by the Peers that the government might convert the revenue obtained from increased taxes to uses other than those specifically designated in the bills. This, Ito contended, was the height of absurdity, for it was a plain and incontrovertible fact of which not even the Peers could pretend to be ignorant, that the government was particularly enjoined from committing such an arbitrary act by constitutional limitations which it was impossible to override.

When the vote was finally taken the bills were as a matter of course defeated. Thereupon Ito caused the sitting of the Diet to be suspended for ten days, hoping that in the interval a compromise measure might be drafted to save the situation. He should have known that the Peers, in this crisis, were determined merely to be stubborn; that a compromise was the last thing to which they would hold themselves amenable. He even went so far as to summon a special session of the Seiyukai representatives in order to wrest from them the promise not to oppose any compromise proceeding from the House of Peers. When, at the expiration of the ten-day truce, he found the Peers were still adamant, he besought the Emperor to postpone the re-sitting of the Diet for another five days. He still had faith in their sincerity; he still refused to believe that their actions were guided by anything save the most exalted considerations for the nation's welfare.

The five days were soon up. The Peers were as incorrigible as ever. Ito had reached the end of his rope. There remained absolutely no other legal recourse to which he could now turn to relieve the government from this impasse. But at this juncture, when everything seemed so dark and hopeless, the Emperor quietly interceded. He had been carefully observing the trend of these developments in the Diet. His convictions were those of an impartial judge, capable of viewing the case with the precision of a detached mind. His decision was rendered in the form of a gentle rebuke. The rebuke was contained in a rescript addressed to the members of the House of Peers. Its effect was electrical. Again a vote was taken. Not a single dissenting voice was raised. The bills were passed.

It was a signal triumph for Ito. Yet he believed otherwise. Regardless of whether he was to blame for the whole incident, or whether he was not, he nevertheless, as the responsible Councillor, had brought upon the Emperor the burden of interceding between hostile factions in the affairs of the government —an imposition which, according to the code of the Nipponese, made his position, his continuance in office, both morally and spiritually untenable. He thus addressed a note to the Emperor, seeking his views as to the advisability of his, Ito's, relinquishing his post of Premier. His Ministers did likewise. The Emperor's reply was reassuring. It dismissed the suggestion of a self-reproachful resignation with the statement that it was entirely undeserving of serious consideration.

But the non-Seiyukai minority in the Lower House, who had hitherto kept up a silent vigil, knowing as they did the futility of attempting to overcome the odds against them, suddenly seized this opportunity—a most unseemly procedure—to air their grievances. A resolution of non-confidence with a view to impeaching the government was introduced, charging Ito in particular with having—of all things—"violated the constitution." The charge was based upon the assumption that Ito had *deliberately influenced* the Emperor in an effort to seek his intercession on the government's behalf. To support this accusation, Ito's self-reproachful note to the Emperor was cited as being tantamount to a confession of guilt!

The whole thing was a trumped-up affair, for the circumstances in the case were too obvious to admit of any possibility of misapprehension. When Ito mounted the rostrum of the Lower House to answer this charge, his voice shook with indignation, and his choice of phrases to characterize the parliamentary vagaries of his accusers was none too mild. "I do not," he said, in part, "concede to the House of Representatives the right to intrude upon the affairs of the government in its relation to the House of Peers, for it is unquestionably outside the pale of consideration. The present controversy concerns only the government and the House of Peers. Furthermore, this is not the place to render an interpretation of the constitution. Nor is there any necessity for so doing." He had no patience with those who, like his accusers, would place political expediency above the considerations of the state. "I stand here before you," he said, "as Prime Minister of this Empire, and I speak purely from the point of view of the government. And to me the complexion of your political affiliations makes not the slightest difference." This was a sarcastic thrust: "You speak of the constitution as having been demolished by my actions. But the constitution still exists today in a healthy state, in consequence of which both Houses of the Diet are, as you observe, still intact and functioning!" He denied that his note to the Emperor was influenced by any such motive as he was charged with having entertained, but refused to reiterate the sentiment which had inspired his act. He dismissed it with the peremptory remark that the Emperor had already rendered a statement which constituted a decision requiring no further elucidation. "From what I have observed in your arguments," he continued, " you seem to be determined to force the resignation of my government in the event your impeachment resolution should pass. But inasmuch as I still have the confidence of the Emperor, I could not possibly relinquish my post on account of a mere resolution. Rather would I suggest to those of you who are supporting this resolution that if such be your intention, why don't you memorialize the Emperor with respect to this non-confidence bogey? It seems to me you ought to have the power to do that. If it is all the same to you, I should recommend this step!" It was evident, from the drift of the buzzing remarks which interrupted this speech, that his accusers were smarting painfully under the sting of his relentless sarcasm. "Those of you who are scheming to oust me from this House in order to prevent my speech-making here are welcome to do so," he challenged. "I feel that the passing of a paltry resolution does not clearly enough express your feelings in the matter anyhow. But you may as well understand that under our constitutional form of government you had better reveal your utmost strength when attempting to oust anyone from public office. A mere tickling affair, such as you are now indulging, has no effect whatever......"

The impeachment resolution was finally put to a vote. With the Seiyukai representatives voting en bloc, there was no possibility of its passing. It was defeated by a majority of twenty-seven.

But if Ito hoped to find peace after the conclusion of this parliamentary farce, he was doomed to a crushing disappointment. No sooner had the adjournment of both Houses taken place than the petty dissension within the Ministry centering on the policies and personality of Finance Minister Watanabe was renewed with undiminished vigor. Hoshi, the erstwhile leader of the opposition with a black record of his own, had resigned following the *Mainichi* exposé, but his place was now taken by Hara, who, together with Kaneko, Suematsu, Hayashi and Matsuda, proceeded to reject all the financial plans submitted by Watanabe for the rehabilitation of the nation's productive scheme preparatory to the completion of the 1902 budget. It was one continuous wrangle after another. Personalities and policies were so hopelessly confused in the issue that harmony was impossible. Ito, though he was willing to sacrifice much in the interest of the state, nevertheless became weary of all this show of Ministerial dissension. On May 2, 1901, he submitted his resignation to the Emperor, after which he demanded of his Ministers to prepare to quit the Cabinet. Eight days later the Emperor's consent was handed down.

CHAPTER XIII
ALLIANCES AND AGREEMENTS

I

On September 18, 1901, Ito left Yokohama on a trip to Europe. It had originally been intended as a pleasure jaunt to the Pacific coast states to recuperate from the effects of overwork, but a last minute decision over impending international complications rendered it suddenly necessary that he change his destination and overlook, for the time being, the considerations of his own health. Passing through the United States, he tarried on the Atlantic coast barely long enough to enable him to pay his respects to President Theodore Roosevelt at Washington, and to attend the Yale centenary at New Haven, where he received the honorary degree of Doctor of Laws. Then he proceeded to St. Petersburg by way of France.

This visit to the Russian capital was invested with a grave significance. It was the result of six years of astounding developments in the Far East following the conclusion of the Sino-Japanese war. During this period Russia had assumed the rôle of an aggressor, utilizing every available pretext for effecting a steady penetration into Manchuria and Korea. It constituted the climactic efforts of her eastward movement, so prominently disclosed of late in the feverish haste attendant upon the completion of the Trans-Siberian and the Chinese Eastern Railways—a movement which meant for the people of Russia an escape from the frozen wastes of Siberia, but of which the ultimate purpose of the Tsarist regime was to connect St. Petersburg with a number of naval bases in the ice-free waters of Manchuria and Korea.

Japan's difficulties with Russia antedated the coming of Commodore Perry. The early raids on the northern islands, Admiral Poutiatine's unwelcome visits, the boundary disputes in the beginning of the Meiji era, the Saghalin deal—all these gestures in which the Russian penchant for exploitation was evinced in unequivocal fashion, implanted a mingled fear and distrust in the Japanese breast for the wiles of Russian diplomacy. The war with China was fought admittedly to obviate the "perils of propinquity" arising out of a Korea controlled by a hostile foreign Power; but the peace negotiations were hardly over when Russia prepared to step in where China had been obliged to quit, to perpetuate the work of exploiting the Hermit Kingdom.

In October, 1895, the Queen of Korea was finally murdered in one of those sporadic revolutions in the palace at Seoul, in which the Tai Won Kun, now an obsequious accomplice of Japan, played the part of the conquering insurgent. Japan's position, no matter who headed her government, was invariably the same. She was now opposed, even as Ito had demonstrated at the outbreak of hostilities with China, to the dominance of any ruling clique which, with the connivance of foreign exploiters, betrayed any evidence of antagonism to her suggested measures of reform. To carry out such a policy was in itself an infringement of Korea's rights of sovereignty. But her contention was that she had a vital stake in Korea—so vital that it amounted virtually to her lifeline—and that she must consequently, in sheer self-defense, have recourse from time to time to such action as the exigencies of the situation made imperative. Her programme was declared to be two-fold. First, she must protect her own lawful and vested rights there; and, second, in order effectually to realize this, she must assist Korea—even against her will if need be—in strengthening her defenses, political as well as military, so that in the end she could repel unaided all gestures of exploitation proceeding from neighboring Powers possessing no vital interest in her destiny. For an impotent Korea, Japan insisted, was a perpetual menace to her own security.

Russia, refusing to concede the right of Japan to dictate Korea's internal policies, reinforced her legation in Seoul with a fresh force of seven hundred marines, thus to commence the strengthening of her own position there in opposition to Japanese dominance. The Korean King, deprived of his able consort and fearful of the bellicose insurgents, fled to the protection of the Russian legation. For this singular act of confidence in, and preference for, Russian support on the part of the King, committed obviously through the friendly connivance of Russian officials, the Russian Government subsequently dubbed him Emperor of Korea, a title which was thereafter assumed with sedulous suavity.

Korea thus definitely passed under the control of Russian influence. Russian officers supplanted the Japanese instructors in the Korean army. This gave Russia the opportunity to mould and to dictate Korea's military development. Timber concessions on the Korean border along the Tumen and Yalu rivers were then secured, nominally on behalf of a Vladivostock merchant. This marked the beginning of Russian exploitation of Korea's economic resources. She then set about to establish a naval base at Masampo on the southeasterly tip of the Korean peninsula. The significance of Masampo lay in the fact that it constituted a strategic link for the Russian fleet between Vladivostock and Port Arthur, and it was situated in dangerous proximity to the unprotected shores of Japan.

Twice Japan attempted—first through General Yamagata at St. Petersburg and later at Tokyo through the Nishi-Rosen negotiations—to effect an arrangement whereby intervention in Korea's domestic affairs on the part of Russia and Japan would be strictly regulated in future by mutual agreement. But the best she could obtain was a convention based upon parity of interests, which left Russia free to act in whatever manner she desired within the limits of this ambiguous category.

Russia meanwhile spread out her imperialistic tentacles into Manchuria. In May, 1896, her Foreign Minister, Prince Lobanoff, together with her Finance Minister, Sergius Witte, concluded with Li Hung Chang a secret alliance against Japan. With this clandestine agreement as a bait Russia obtained from China, through the Russo-Chinese Bank, the right to build the Chinese Eastern Railway across Manchuria. Li believed, apparently in all sincerity, that this railway would greatly facilitate the movement of Russian troops into China, there to join the Chinese army in repelling the common enemy—Japan. It was to be a part of his futile scheme of revenge for that defeat suffered at the hands of Japan in 1895. Witte, however, was concerned primarily with the establishment of a short-cut across Manchuria to Vladivostok for the Trans-Siberian Railway, both for purposes of aggression as well as of economy—aggression against China and economy at China's expense. China now began to reap what she had sowed—to pay off at an enormous sacrifice her debt of gratitude to Russia, Germany and France for having forced Japan into returning the forfeited peninsula of Liaotung in 1895. Russia, revealing shamelessly her sleek hypocrisy, seized Port Arthur on the peninsula. This was to be her share of the spoils. When China protested, she resorted to bribery. Li, who now saw that the situation had developed beyond his control, accepted from Witte a handsome gift of five hundred thousand taels in exchange for a twenty-five year lease on Port Arthur. The Boxer Rebellion next furnished an excellent pretext for Russian occupation of Manchuria. Though she agreed to the protocol terminating the allied march on Peking, she refused to evacuate her troops pending a separate agreement with China involving the dismantling of the Manchurian forts, the disbandment of the Manchurian army, the appointment of a Russian political resident at Mukden, and the exclusive right vested in the Russian veto respecting the building of railways and the development of mines in Manchuria.

All this, to Japan, meant but one thing. It meant that Russia was headed for conquest, for the gobbling up of Korea and Manchuria—a grave menace to her existence.

The policy of the Katsura Ministry, which came into power following the resignation of Ito's Seiyukai Administration, crystallized, inevitably, on a closer cooperation with Great Britain, for she alone among the Western Powers seemed sufficiently affected by Russia's movements to view them with apprehensive concern. The result was the renewal of negotiations on the part of the Katsura Government for the formation of an Anglo-Japanese alliance—negotiations which had been started by Takaaki Kato and Joseph Chamberlain in 1898, but which had since been held in abeyance through subsequent British apathy

Ito, being a realist, was not averse to such an alliance, but he favored it only as a last resort. Its essential purpose was conceived in a spirit of challenge, of returning threat for threat. In the end, he perceived, it would lead to war with Russia. Japan was as yet a relatively parvenu member of the family of nations, existing in the doubtful security of its outer fringes. For such a nation to engage one of the greatest Powers of the earth in a military combat was, he felt, little short of madness. Should Russia refuse to listen to reason, some such course might become unavoidable, but until both countries had placed their cards on the table, face up, Japan must act with extreme caution. His visit to St. Petersburg was, therefore, to make a supreme effort on behalf of peace.

2

When it became known in London that Ito's destination was St. Petersburg, the customary British insouciance underwent a distinct change. Speculations became rife. Could it be possible that Great Britain's continued indifference toward an alliance with Japan had compelled the latter to contemplate an about-face policy and to seek, instead, an alliance with Russia? Though ordinarily protected by a solid armor compounded of a powerful admixture of an impenetrable shrewdness, an inflexible pride, and an invincible self-assurance respecting her own naval prowess, Great Britain now saw in a possible Russo-Japanese entente the spectacle of another hostile combination organizing against her interests. For she was admittedly in the midst of one of the most difficult situations in her history.

Russia was her most dreaded foe, whose eastward movement had long since been looked upon as threatening eventually her colonial frontiers in southern Asia. She had, in addition, France's attachment to Russia, by treaty as well as by a traditional defensive policy, to reckon with. Germany, ambitious, portentous, was threatening her supremacy on the seas with a formidable naval programme. All three of these unfriendly Powers were now indefatigably at work in a network of intrigues and alliances, at home and abroad, in Europe as well as in the Far East, to imperil her interests. The Boer War in South Africa had proved disastrous in men, money, and morale. Her "glorious isolation" had become, not an object of pride and prestige, but a dangerous misnomer.

Ito, upon reaching as far as Paris, was made aware that Great Britain had at last considered seriously an alliance with Japan. He was further apprised of the fact that negotiations in London between Lord Lansdowne and Baron Hayashi, Minister to the Court of St. James, were progressing favorably. In a meassage from Premier Katsura he was urgently requested to remain in the French capital pending further advices, for it was felt in Tokyo that his visit to St. Petersburg at this critical period might produce an unfortunate effect upon the London negotiations. Baron Hayashi was meanwhile instructed to proceed at once to Paris and submit to Ito for his consideration, and particularly for his approval, the terms of the alliance thus far agreed upon, together with the telegraphic messages exchanged on the subject between the Tokyo Foreign Office and the Japanese embassy in London.

Premier Katsura saw no hope for a Russo-Japanese understanding. He was avowedly an advocate of the alliance. He was striving desperately for its consummation. He would risk a war with Russia rather than permit this opportunity of joining forces with Great Britain slip by.

Ito reiterated his opposition to the alliance if it must arbitrarily supplant all efforts at a peaceful understanding with Russia. Nor would he heed the Premier's request to call off his visit to the Russian capital. "It appears to me," he telegraphed the Premier from Paris on November 15, "that the wisest policy would be to postpone final action on the present negotiations until I have first sounded the Russian Government. Meanwhile I should particularly urge that you undertake a most careful and a most thorough study, not only of the phraseology from the most significant to the minutest detail, but also as to the probable effects upon our future." He made, in addition, several precautionary suggestions respecting the terms of the proposed alliance—suggestions which indicated that his opposition was not based upon political prejudice, or upon personal obstinacy, but upon an intelligent desire for caution. Should he fail in his mission vis-à-vis Russia—and he was not at all certain he would succeed—there was no doubt he would favor the alliance as the ultimate defensive scheme, and as such

. it must be made to serve every major contingency in the most effective fashion to which the signatories might be able to agree. But his saner judgment decreed that the way of peace, though sore beset, was the better way and that it must have precedence over all other methods of solution.

Meanwhile, in a series of meetings with Foreign Minister Delcassé of France held on November 13-14, he received the assurances of the French Government that its policy in the Far East was one of sincere and disinterested friendliness toward Japan. This policy, Delcassé explained, was necessarily conservative. It would strive in particular to preserve the status quo in China, especially with reference to vested interests. It contemplated no movements against Japan as there were no existing problems on which the interests of the two countries were likely to clash. When reminded that Russo-Japanese aspirations in Korea were in conflict and constituted a source of future danger which Ito desired to forestall by means of a revision of the existing convention between the two countries, Delcassé assured him that the French Government, because of its friendship for Russia, would be glad to offer its services in arriving at a just agreement which would be satisfactory to all concerned. Russia, he believed, was not unmindful of Japan's commercial and industrial stake in Korea. Delcassé, in brief, hoped for a Franco-Russian-Japanese understanding, and it was evidently his hope that this entente would assume the forefront in Far Eastern affairs.

Soon afterwards Ito left Paris and resumed his journey to St. Petersburg by way of Berlin. From London Baron Hayashi hastened to explain that Ito's decision to proceed on his mission to Russia, despite the excellent progress of the Anglo-Japanese negotiations, was leading the British to entertain grave doubts as to Japan's sincerity. Premier Katsura also telegraphed Ito at Berlin, reminding him that it was impossible for Japan to defer action on the matter. Ito denied vigorously that whatever he undertook to accomplish at St. Petersburg would in any way be inimical to an Anglo-Japanese understanding. An alliance with Great Britain, on the other hand, might conceivably prevent an understanding with Russia. He arrived in St.

Petersburg late in November and prepared at once to secure an audience with the Tsar and to interview Foreign Minister Lamsdorff.

It was with the greatest difficulty, in which every reasonable dissimulation and prevarication was resorted to, that Premier Katsura and Baron Hayashi were able to suspend final action on the British proposal. The Premier, in a last desperate message to Ito before the interview with Lamsdorff, besought him to confine his efforts to "conversations for an exchange of opinions."

3

Early in the afternoon of November 28, 1901, Ito was received in audience by the Russian Emperor, Nicholas II, at Tsarskoe Selo. He was accompanied by his interpreter, Mr. Tsuzuki, and the medium of communication was the German tongue. When, however, the Tsar discovered at the outset that Ito spoke English well, the conversation was thereafter, at his request, carried on sans interpreter in that language.

ITO:* I feel very grateful for this opportunity to pay my respects to Your Majesty.

NICHOLAS II: I have so often had reports concerning you that your visit to St. Petersburg and the fact that it has been possible to meet you here are a source of great happiness to me, especially as I know that you are a statesman with a friendly regard for Russia.

ITO: I appreciate your Majesty's sentiments.

NICHOLAS II: I wonder if I met you during my visit in Japan.......

ITO: I was received in audience at Kyoto. Then I had the honor of accompanying Your Majesty to Kobe.

NICHOLAS II: Oh yes, I recall it now. I remember it very clearly. My impression of that visit is linked with only the most pleasant associations. I am very glad to say that the relations between your country and mine have been particularly

*The conversations with the Tsar and with Lamsdorff, Witte and Lord Lansdowne, as given in this chapter, are translations from the official Japanese text which was published as an appendix to the 1st volume of Ito's Secret Memoirs—" Ito Hirobumi Hiroku." See Bibliographical Note.

friendly in the past. I hope that the future will bring increased friendliness and good will. I feel that harmony between the two countries is not impossible. Not only will it be for their mutual benefit but it will also contribute to the peace of the Far East and perhaps to the fulfilment of a greater purpose.

ITO: I feel precisely as Your Majesty does. I can assure Your Majesty that it is also the conviction of my Emperor, who values very highly the cordial relations with Russia and sincerely hopes that this cordiality will continue throughout the future.

NICHOLAS II: I am happy to hear you say so.

ITO: I shall convey Your Majesty's words to my Emperor directly upon my return to Japan. I am sure they will be a source of great satisfaction to him.

NICHOLAS II: What I have just said is not a mere passing statement; it represents something which I strongly believe and which reflects the true sentiment of the people of my country. I should especially request that you transmit this to your Emperor.

ITO: I shall most certainly do so.

Here the political aspect of the conversation ceased, and until the audience was terminated the two indulged in informal chats concerning the health of the Japanese Imperial family and Ito's future itinerary. The Tsar invited Ito to return to Japan by way of the Trans-Siberian Railway. This was declined with regret owing to the inclement weather which prevailed along the railway at this time of the year and consequently necessitated prolonging Ito's visit, which could not be done. At parting the Tsar presented him with the highest Imperial Russian decoration bestowed upon foreigners.

4

The interview with Foregn Minister Lamsdorff, held at the latter's official residence in the afternoon of December 2, was carried on exclusively in the German tongue with Mr. Tsuzuki interpreting. An exchange of greetings, in which Ito thanked Lamsdorff for the magnificent reception tendered him a few days previous, preceded the principal topic of conversation.

ITO: I am here on this visit, not as an official carrying out the instructions of my government, but merely as an individual who, being fortunately out of office, has undertaken this pleasure trip. I consider it a great good fortune that I have thus secured the opportunity to meet you today and to exchange our opinions with reference to the problems of the Far East. Of course, I intend to bare my thoughts to you and to express myself fully, and I hope you will likewise divest yourself of diplomatic formalities and express yourself with the utmost candor.

LAMSDORFF: I feel the same way about it myself. Let us speak without any reservation whatever.

ITO: I have always felt the necessity of cultivating friendly relations with Russia. The Tsar assured me the other day that such was also his feelings in the matter and that harmony was not only possible if the two countries were to approach each other with sincerity, but that it would conduce to the fulfilment of a greater purpose than the mere fact of peace in the Far East. I replied that the Emperor of my country would be greatly pleased with these words. When the Tsar further declared that such was not only his feelings but his strong belief as well, and that it was not merely his belief alone but that of the whole people of Russia, I felt particularly gratified. My own convictions have since been greatly fortified.

LAMSDORFF: Yes, the Tsar has spoken to me about it, and I, too, am of the same opinion.

ITO: It is indeed satisfying to hear that from one who holds the important portfolio of Foreign Affairs. If we are to hope for a continuance of this friendly state, it behooves us to rid ourselves of the causes which constantly create misunderstandings. Needless to say, the problem of Korea is one of these. What are your views concerning this problem?

LAMSDORFF: What you say is only too true. Still, the Russian Government some years back proposed a new agreement looking toward a solution, and the Japanese Government refused to consider it then on the ground that such a proposal was unnecessary as the existing agreement was quite satisfactory. This ought to show that the sincerity of the Russian Government regarding the Korean problem has been clearly indicated. It seems to me that, properly speaking, Japan ought to make the next move for an understanding. If you have any proposal to make in this connection, I should like to hear it.

ITO: Regarding that proposal of the Russian Government, it was broached during the Boxer Rebellion, and we felt it was unnecessary to involve a third party in an agreement which concerned only Japan and Russia. Hence we thought that the existing agreement, though inadequate, would serve a better purpose than the one proposed.

LAMSDORFF: I see. Yes, I agree with you on that point: that it is unnecessary to involve a third party. But what plans have you under consideration to take its place?

ITO: It goes without my saying that the problem of Korea is almost a matter of life and death to Japan. The Japanese, moreover, are constantly entertaining the fear that Korea might some day be absorbed by Russia. Of course, at the present time there is a clear agreement between Japan and Russia concerning Korea, but we cannot accept it as final. The situation today is such that, unless a more conclusive agreement is established, there might arise an endless series of misunderstandings in the future between the two countries. The fact that Japan possesses a paramount interest in Korea is something which I presume the Russian Government has always recognized. Korea is so impotent that not only is she unable to protect the lawful rights and interests of the Japanese, but also incapable of suppressing insurrections occurring within her own borders. Therefore, unless she is given advice and assistance, what ought to be Japan's paramount interest will be bereft of its reality. And yet, if both Japan and Russia should jointly render this advice and this assistance, it would be impossible to say that the danger arising from unfortunate clashes would not occur.

LAMSDORFF: What I believe is this. As long as harmony between the governments of Russia and Japan is fully established, and as long as both countries act in concert to bring pressure to bear upon Korea, I do not think that the Korean Government will refuse to heed their counsel. Should Japan insist upon saying white and Russia black whenever an affair crops up in Korea, it would enable Korea rather to take advantage of these opportunities. It would then be somewhat like the case of Persia, Turkey, and other countries similarly situated that are gaining more or less influence in the world in spite of their own lack of power. And so I believe that by providing now for a detailed agreement upon which both countries can rely in the future in the event of disagreement, Korea can be made to discharge faithfully her duties as an independent country.

ITO: If I were allowed to speak frankly, I should say that the plan you have suggested was all the more likely to invite conflicts between the two countries. No matter how well the central governments may cooperate, it cannot be believed that the danger arising from unforeseen misunderstandings will not occur when our respective peoples come in contact with each other out there. The more detailed an agreement, the more sharply would interpretations differ. For instance, if a disturbance of some sort should occur in Korea, what would happen? Both countries would dispatch troops to suppress it. A clash between these troops would be inevitable. I think, therefore, that if either Power should render this assistance alone it would be of greater advantage and convenience. As you well know, the maintenance of Korean independence is a vital problem to Japan, and for that reason the Japanese would not be able to feel at ease were this exclusive right vested in Russia.

LAMSDORFF: You have spoken of advice and assistance. What precisely are you referring to when you speak of rendering assistance?

ITO: To the protection of life and property, of course, and necessary assistance for the maintenance of public order, which Korea is incapable of accomplishing through her own unaided efforts.

LAMSDORFF: In that case, does it include the rendering of military assistance?

ITO: Certainly. I think there is no other way to suppress disturbances whenever they arise than by the dispatch of troops.

LAMSDORFF: Russia heretofore has never entertained any other intention toward Korea, but she must positively refuse to permit the use of Korean territory for strategical purposes.

ITO: That is only natural. Japan does not harbor any design toward Korea which will threaten her independence. Nor does she intend to utilize Korea for strategical purposes against Russia. She would confine the use of her troops to the suppression of disturbances and the restoration of public order. This does not mean, therefore, that she would dispatch them for the purpose of occupying Korea.

LAMSDORFF: The present agreement between Russia and Japan is, as you know, based on parity, so that if Japan should send a hundred soldiers to Korea, Russia might likewise dispatch a hundred, and so on. But if Japan should be entrusted with the affairs of Korea and recognition also given her for the exclusive right to send troops to Korea, it would be necessary for her to guarantee that under no circumstances would she utilize Korean territory for strategical purposes. Besides, if Japan should build fortresses along the Korean coast, it would cut off communication between Vladivostok and Port Arthur, a thing which Russia, for her own protection, cannot overlook. And so, if Russia can secure a positive guarantee that strategical advantages will not be taken by Japan in connection with this channel of communication, I do not believe she will object to entrusting Korea's affairs to Japan. The difficulty lies in determining as to what constitutes a positive guarantee.

ITO: That, I think, is a point which Russia, from the standpoint of her own interests, is quite justified in stressing. Japan would not, therefore, refuse to provide this guarantee should Korea's affairs be entrusted to her. But if Russia should make strategical provisions in the vicinity of the Korean border and threaten the independence of Korea, Japan could not possibly view it with indifference.

LAMSDORFF: What, then, would you offer as a guarantee?

ITO: Well, it seems impossible, does it not, for me to suggest a guarantee here other than to make a pledge?

LAMSDORFF: Just a pledge?

ITO: I feel there is no other recourse.

LAMSDORFF: How would this do: suppose Russia were entrusted with a small district in the south of Korea, and Japan given a free hand throughout the rest of the country?

ITO: There is a report emanating from Russian troops that a small district in southern Korea has already been occupied as a base for military operations as well as for defending Russia's means of communication, but the people of Japan have refused to give credence to such a report.   The southern portion is precisely the most important part of Korea in the maintenance of Japan's security and independence, so that if it should fall into the hands of another country, the Japanese would at once feel as if their own independence had been threatened.   I believe, therefore, that to entrust this portion of Korea to Russia would not only be inconsistent with harmony between Russia and Japan, but would also involve the danger of precipitating conflicts.

LAMSDORFF: As I have said, I am merely expressing my own individual opinion.   I do not know what the Tsar feels about it, nor as to what the Minister of the Navy and other members of the Cabinet believe.   But I should like to suggest that you put yourself, for the moment, in the position of a Russian and consider the situation from his angle.   Do you think that by giving Japan a free hand throughout the whole of Korea, Russia would not be overrun by a feeling of national uneasiness?   Contrast this with the situation in which only a portion of southern Korea, which is extremely narrow and tiny when compared with the whole of that country, is entrusted to Russia.   Even if a measure of uneasiness is felt by the Japanese there, its relative insignificance when compared with the feelings of the Russian people when faced by the spectacle of the whole of Korea dominated by Japan, would not bear argument.

ITO: It may not always turn out to be that way.   Gibraltar certainly comprises a very diminutive area, yet it possesses the power to control the destiny of the seas.   The idea, moreover, of securing harmony between Russia and Japan and of affording peace and satisfaction to the people of Japan, is by no means an unwise policy for Russia to adopt. Take, for instance, the situation in China. Her recent Boxer Rebellion, fortunately, has been settled satisfactorily; but China is the sort of country where there is no telling what might occur, at any time, at whatever place, in her national life. Should there be a repetition of last year's affair, it ought to make a considerable difference to Russia to be able, on the one hand, to proceed without being burdened with doubts as to what Japan's feelings in the matter might be, and to be unable, on the other, to proceed in such a state of mind.

LAMSDORFF: Perhaps it does.

ITO: There is no necessity for me to indulge in further explanations. Russia is a great country. She is so situated that she can develop in any direction. Japan, on the contrary, is a country surrounded by the sea and with a closely limited scope. It seems hardly necessary for Russia, under the circumstances, to be so apprehensive over a little affair like that of Korea, don't you think?

LAMSDORFF: We don't feel apprehensive! And we don't fear anyone!......You might, however, let us have a draft of your suggestions with regard to the solution of this problem. I could then discuss it in detail with the other Ministers and even confidentially secure the Tsar's opinion concerning it. Besides, it would enable us to amend it or to submit a counter proposal.

ITO: I shall do so.

5

The next day Ito, in order to obtain the views of other members of the Tsarist Cabinet, held a lengthy tête-à-tête with Sergius Witte, the man who, above all the younger liberal councillors of the St. Petersburg regime, was instrumental in advancing Russia's programme of expansion beyond Siberia's frozen steppes. Again Ito expressed his deep and unalterable concern over the trend of developments in Korea. Witte, being a seasoned diplomatist, was decidedly more straightforward in his utterances and hence less cautious than Lamsdorff.

"Russia," Witte said, beginning with platitudes, "has no desire for territorial aggrandizement. In fact, she may be said to have the disadvantage of being already much too large."

His own particular interest lay in the field of national finance. "Ours," he continued, "happens to be an era when we must look to her internal requirements and promote the development of her social and economic life."

Nevertheless, despite his innocuous protestations, his achievements thus far, in meeting those needs, had embraced an extensive economic exploitation of regions beyond the periphery of Russia's legitimate frontiers. Having outwitted the wily Li Hung Chang in the matter of building the Chinese Eastern Railway, his objectives lay obviously in the fertile plains of Manchuria. Consequently he did not appear to manifest as much interest as did the timid and hesitant Lamsdorff in the rôle which Korea might be induced to play, his only apparent reservations vis-à-vis Japan being that of using the Hermit Kingdom as a possible bargaining point in his scheme of negotiation and expansion.

"Since Russia," he said, coming to the point, "has promised to evacuate Manchuria, it is hardly the wish of the Imperial Government to occupy that territory permanently. To be sure, we have in our country—in yours, too, for that matter, and in every other nation—men who, especially among the military, aspire to imperialist ambitions. Such, however, is not the policy of our government, nor that of the Tsar. As Finance Minister, I should be the first to oppose any such movement, for Russia, frankly, cannot afford it. However, there is one point I should like to stress, and that is, that Russia possesses a great railway in the East on which she has invested over 300,000,000 roubles. The benefits of this railway will naturally accrue to all the civilized countries of Western Europe as well as the Far East, particularly Japan. And in taking the necessary measures to guard this railway, Russia must devote the full measure of her powers to the task. I should especially wish to have you bear this fact in mind."

Ito was not unsympathetic with Witte's legitimate aims in Manchuria, though he was aware that Russian activities there did not appear to have been confined within such obviously narrow limits. "I fully recognize the necessity," he assured him, "of taking suitable measures to guard the railway." But since he had not come to Russia with the object of bargaining with her Ministers with regard to spheres of interest over which Japan could as yet claim no vital concern in matters of national defense, he made no further allusions to Manchuria, indicating that if any proposal in this connection seemed desirable, it must come from Russia—as did his own proposals concerning Korea—in specific terms. Insisting that "so far as Japan is concerned, she has more at stake in Korea than Russia has in the railway," he repeated what he had expressed to Count Lamsdorff the previous day, namely, that the political, industrial and military affairs of Korea be placed under Japan's sole protection.

"I assure you," he said, "that my country has no intention of exploiting Korean territory for strategical purposes against Russia. Our military intervention will be strictly limited to the work of suppressing disorders within Korea which may disturb the peaceful relations between Korea and Japan and in the Far East generally. In times of peace, as at present, our troops are sent there, not for military purposes, but to preserve order, and our mission there does not, therefore, exceed the limits of performing the necessary functions of the police."

Here he laid down, as he did to Lamsdorff, his proposal of restrictions in concrete terms which Japan would undertake to respect if conceded the sole protective interest in Korea: "In order to set the people of your country at rest, we can guarantee that the independence of Korea will always be protected, that no strategical advantage will be taken against Russia on Korean territory, and that no military projects will be erected in the Korean Strait which will imperil its freedom of communication."

Witte, spurred no doubt by Ito's categorical recognition of Russian interests along the Chinese Eastern Railway in Manchuria, thereupon threw caution to the winds and became suddenly and refreshingly generous. "If you can guarantee those three things," he said, "we have no objection to your handling of Korean affairs in whatever way you see fit.   Vous pourez fairece que vous voulez!" He even committed himself as willing to bind the proposal in the form of an agreement!

6

At the second meeting with Lamsdorff held on December 4, 1901, Ito presented the promised draft, and the discussion was resumed.

ITO: I have brought here with me today, in accordance with the promise made the other day, a draft of the suggestions which I have drawn up as I view the thing. (Hands over the document to Lamsdorff, who reads it, as follows:

1.   Mutual engagement to respect the independence of Korea.

2.   Reciprocal undertaking not to utilize any portion of Korean territory for strategical purposes.

3.   Reciprocal engagement not to make any military provisions along the Korean coast which might imperil freedom of communication in the Strait of Korea.

4.   Recognition on the part of Russia of the exclusive right of Japan to exercise a free hand respecting the political, industrial and commercial relations of Korea, and to give advice and assistance in the interest of good government, including necessary military assistance for the suppression of disturbances bordering on civil war, which might threaten the peaceful relations between Japan and Korea.

5.   This arrangement to supplant all previous agreements.)

LAMSDORFF: Of course, I must give it a close perusal and examine it thoroughly before I can say anything definite. But it appears to me, at a glance, as though it is a little too one-sided to form the basis of an agreement.

ITO: My understanding of what you said the other day was that, provided Japan did not exploit Korea's independence or her territory for strategical purposes, and provided further that Japan refrained from building fortresses along the Korean coast which might threaten communication in the Strait, your country would be inclined to recognize Japan's exclusive right to exercise a free hand in Korea along commercial, industrial, political and military lines. That is why I have submitted the draft as it is.

LAMSDORFF: But, generally speaking, an agreement usually involves mutual concessions. This draft provides merely for the benefits of your country and requires that my country make all the concessions. The agreement now in force is based upon equality, so that if one of the signatories chooses to dispatch five hundred troops, the other may also send a similar number. Were the exclusive military and political rights entrusted to another Power, it would be immediately construed in Russia as a concession. While Japan has everything to gain, Russia, on the contrary, stands to lose everything, which is indeed very embarrassing.

ITO: Nevertheless, as I said the other day, unless Korea's affairs were placed entirely in the hands of Japan, it would be impossible for the Japanese to rest in peace. Besides, as far as the independence of Korea and other such guarantees are concerned, these were not originally proposed by me.

LAMSDORFF: It is exactly as you say. But I should like to have you consider the thing from our point of view. Should we conclude an agreement based upon this proposal, how would the people of Russia feel about it? They are bound to clamor insistently for an explanation as to why Russia has found it profitable or necessary to discard an existing agreement based upon equality merely to secure Japan's good will. Furthermore, you speak of guaranteeing the independence of Korea, but an independence which is subject to political as well as military intervention is, to speak plainly, an independence in name only. If Russia were to concede such a right to Japan, there must be certain advantages which she also might be credited with. No agreement of a practical and permanent nature is possible unless both parties are willing to make concessions or to profit together. I feel that it cannot be consummated on the basis of this proposal.

TSUZUKI (Interpreter) to LAMSDORFF: Do you mean, then, that there is no hope for an agreement based upon this draft?

LAMSDORFF to TSUZUKI: Not at all. Until I have secured

the opinion of the Tsar and of the other members of the Ministry, I cannot say definitely whether there is any hope or whether there is not.

(Tsuzuki conveys this information to Ito.)

ITO: What advantages, then, would your country demand?

LAMSDORFF: That also is a point on which I cannot make a definite reply until I have ascertained the expert opinion of the Tsar and of the various Ministers. But it certainly is a strange proposal which makes no stipulation as to what benefits we may obtain thereby. From what you stated the other day I gathered that as long as Korea's affairs were entrusted to your country, recognition would be given Russia for a full liberty of action in China in the event of trouble.

TSUZUKI to LAMSDORFF: If such has been your impression, it must have been due to the inadequacy of my efforts as interpreter. What the Marquis (Ito) said then did not go beyond intimating that if Russia should entrust Korea's affairs to Japan and harmony between the two countries be thus achieved, Russia would be able to take necessary action in China in the event of a future disturbance without being burdened with doubts as to what Japan might feel towards her.

LAMSDORFF: Is that so? But since our interests in North China are similar to yours in Korea, can't there be an understanding in which recognition is given this fact?

ITO: It may depend upon what you regard as North China. The Chinese seem to include all that portion north of the Yellow River.

LAMSDORFF: Simply that region adjoining our national boundary.

ITO: That seems a little too vague. There is no necessity, of course, to decide now as to what constitutes North China. But since there is no reason why we should have a foreknowledge of what your country's demands might be, how would it be if you made up a tentative list of them?

LAMSDORFF: Yes, I should like to do that. But you are leaving this afternoon, are you not? If so, do you plan to carry on negotiations for this agreement at Tokyo between our representatives and your government?

ITO: If assurances can be given that an understanding is possible on the principal points at issue, which would form the basis of this agreement, I shall telegraph my government to that effect. Otherwise I cannot take such an action. I believe that my government would give a more or less serious consideration to whatever I undertook to propose.

(Here Tsuzuki, the interpreter, tells Lamsdorff, for his information, of the power and influence which Ito commands in Japan, of the Emperor's supreme confidence in him, of the foremost place he occupies among the Elder Statesmen, whose advice on vital international problems determines, in the final analysis, the Emperor's decision in such matters. Everything he says will therefore carry considerable weight with his government. Lamsdorff replies to Tsuzuki that he is well-informed on this point.)

LAMSDORFF: But if you are leaving today, there would not be time enough to do it while you are here.

ITO: I expect to stop over at Berlin for about ten days, or probably two weeks. How would it be if you forwarded the information to me there?

LAMSDORFF: I doubt if that would be possible. A problem such as this requires a thorough investigation and a mature deliberation. I have only one day in the week allotted to me in which to speak to the Tsar; aside from Tuesday I cannot approach him. And so, whether it can be done during your stay in Berlin is a point on which it is impossible for me to make a promise.

ITO: I am not asking for a promise. We have conferred with each other merely as individuals, and aside from considering the possibilities of effecting a new agreement, I should like you to feel that this proposal (the outline which he had prepared) is simply a scrap of paper. And if you are of the opinion that there is no possibility at all of consummating an agreement on the basis of this proposal, perhaps I had better take it with me now.

LAMSDORFF: As a matter of fact, I cannot say that there isn't any possibility. But since what you and I are both striving for are identical, there ought to be a way in which this objective can be attained. The only point on which we must be careful is to see to it that the stipulations do not lean too much on one side. When Mr. Komura was ambassador here, we often indulged in irresponsible discussions on Oriental problems. At that time, merely as one of the problems of study, we spoke on the possibility of giving Japan a free hand in Korea, in return for which Russia would be given a free hand in Manchuria.

ITO: I see.

LAMSDORFF: Of course, we have no intention of occupying Manchuria permanently. The evacuation of our troops, however, must be conducted according to certain stipulations. But regarding that as secondary, there is this to be considered about the present proposal. If we should forward our reply to you in Berlin, and you took occasion to disagree on some of the points raised, and we found it necessary again to submit our reply, the process would assume the nature of a negotiation between Berlin and St. Petersburg and thus incur considerable difficulties. I feel, therefore, that it would be wiser to transfer the negotiations to Tokyo.

ITO: Even if we did transfer the negotiations to Tokyo, the whole affair would be futile unless we did so after it had been definitely established that there was hope for the successful consummation of the agreement. This is what I meant when I made my previous statement.

LAMSDORFF: I understand that you are intending to proceed to Paris afterwards. How would it be if we opened negotiations there?

ITO: I do intend to stop over at Paris again, but I believe it would be too late then.

7

Despite Ito's significant allusion to the necessity of arriving at the earliest possible decision, Lamsdorff's reply embracing the Russian counter proposal was delayed for over a week and did not reach Ito, who awaited its arrival in Berlin, until the thirteenth day after his departure from St. Petersburg.

Meanwhile, on December 6, 1901, Ito telegraphed to Premier Katsura the result of his conversations with Lamsdorff, more particularly the terms upon which he had insisted as the basis for a Russo-Japanese understanding over Korea. Included in this report was Ito's recommendation which savored of a mingled plea and warning: "It is of course to be expected that were we to enter into actual negotiations, the Russians will make counter demands in the nature of a compromise. Judging from the distinctive tenor of our conversations, their proposal, barring for the moment the scope of its limitations, will doubtless involve Russia's liberty of action in the region of Manchuria. Let me tender one word of warning. Russia already has Manchuria under her control, and is actually exercising a free hand. If the Imperial Government decides to adopt the policy of approving negotiations with Russia, I hope to be able to secure in advance the precise nature of her counter proposal, for I am in constant touch with Lamsdorff and Witte through private correspondence. As I perceive it, now is the most opportune time to establish concord with the only other country possessing a vital interest in Korea. I should most sincerely urge upon the Imperial Government to strive for friendly harmony. This, however, would become impossible after the conclusion of an alliance with Great Britain."

In spite of this plea and this warning, the Tokyo Government, unable any longer to bear the intolerable suspense, acted with desperate haste. On the following day the Elder Statesmen, in a secret session attended also by the Premier and Foreign Minister Komura, decided to ignore the Russo-Japanese understanding and to conclude the British alliance. The outcome of the Ito-Lamsdorff "conversations" was still believed uncertain and a further delay, they felt, might influence the British Government to drop the negotiations entirely. On the 9th the Emperor approved the verdict of the Elder Statesmen. The next day Baron Hayashi was instructed to resume the London discussion with Lord Lansdowne and to work for its speedy consummation.

Ito's persistent efforts in the interest of peace were thus administered a most discouraging blow. Those Elder Statesmen, including Inouye, his otherwise faithful friend and co-worker, who had been closely associated with him for nearly a half century as empire builders, turned against him at what he considered a most critical period and in a most distressingly short-sighted manner.

The British alliance, because of its obvious implications, would, so far as he could see, reject as hopeless all peaceful measures without a fair and sufficient trial. It would prepare the way for the use of forcible, destructive means in solving the peculiar difficulties of the Far East. Under its proposed terms, both Japan and Great Britain would commit themselves as being free from any aggressive intentions in China and Korea. The "preponderant" interests of Great Britain were defined as existing in China, while those of Japan were declared to be in Korea.

In the event either of the high contracting parties became involved in a war with another country, the other would "use its efforts to prevent other powers from joining in hostilities against its ally." In plain words, should Japan choose to go to war with Russia, Great Britain would see to it that no other country joined forces with Russia in attacking Japan. To be even more blunt, the Tokyo Government, in concluding this alliance, was deliberately preparing for a war with Russia, and Great Britain was equally determined to take advantage of Japan's difficulties with Russia by goading her on to fight her battles for her; for Russia, be it repeated, was as much a potential foe of Great Britain as of Japan.

Nevertheless Ito refused to abandon his efforts. He still adhered with that invincible tenacity of purpose so characteristic of his public life, to the need of a peaceful, as opposed to a forcible, solution. He believed that this had become even more necessary in securing an understanding with Russia over Korea, for the Tsarist regime could not be daunted by any such threats as the alliance was calculated to serve. He felt that notwithstanding the impending obligations to Great Britain there was nothing inimical about a separate understanding with Russia, particularly as such an understanding was designed merely to remove the cause of Russo-Japanese friction, whereas the alliance would solve no problems; would, in fact, be of no

practical effect except in the event of war between the two countries. He knew that there was still hope for his projected
agreement, although the consummation of the alliance with
Great Britain was bound to offend the Russians and induce them
to stiffen their terms considerably. He continued to strive for
the goal on which he had set his mind. "I regret exceedingly,"
he told Premier Katsura in the course of his telegraphic advice
from Berlin dated December 12, 1901, "that my proposal has
been rejected by the Japanese Government. What I, however, diligently hope for is that at a future favorable opportunity Japan may, in connection with an understanding with
Russia over Korea, securely preserve through this means the
freedom of independent action. Consequently it is my wish
that the alliance be firmly kept a secret by the concluding governments. I urge this because a public disclosure of such an
alliance will have a portentous effect upon the attitude of the
various continental Powers."

Lamsdorff, in his counter proposal approved by the Tsar,
agreed substantially to the first three terms contained in Ito's
draft. Russia would thus respect the independence of Korea.
Russia would abstain from utilizing any portion of Korean territory for strategical purposes. Russia would likewise refrain
from making any military provisions along the Korean coast
which might imperil freedom of communication in the Korean
Strait.

Agreement on Lamsdorff's part to these three articles was
to be expected, inasmuch as they were substantially his own
suggestions which Ito had willingly incorporated into his proposal.

As to Ito's fourth article, however, Lamsdorff proposed to
limit Japan's liberty of action in Korea to industrial and commercial problems only. Politically, Japan would not be allowed
to intervene except after conferring with Russia, presumably in
specific instances, such intervention to include military assistance only in the event of an insurrection.

Further restrictions were placed in a fifth article, wherein
Japan was forbidden to dispatch any more troops in suppressing
such insurrections than were deemed absolutely necessary. Such

troops, moreover, must be recalled immediately upon the restoration of public order and should under no circumstances cross the frontier bordering on Russia.

Lamsdorff added a sixth article in which Japan was required to recognize Russia's exclusive right to exercise a free hand in Manchuria.

Lamsdorff, in brief, *would stipulate minutely respecting restrictions on every phase of Japan's liberty of action in Korea, but would brook no restrictions whatever on Russia's freedom in Manchuria*—a decidedly "one-sided" proposal, such as he had himself particularly desired that Ito should avoid.

Ito, in his reply to Lamsdorff dispatched from Brussels on December 23, 1901, stated that the Russian counter proposal embraced so many provisions which were of such grave importance that he would be compelled to subject it to a "deep and penetrating" scrutiny. Recounting his immediate impression, however, he stated: "Though I do not entertain any doubt as to the desire of the Russian officials for harmony, I must confess that with your draft as the basis for future negotiations, there does not appear to be any hope for concluding an agreement between the two countries which will have a real and lasting effect.......According to this proposal, Russia undertakes to recognize Japan's actions only within specially prescribed limits and to interpose stringent restrictions under articles two, three and five. And yet, on the other hand, it is noted that Japan must recognize every phase of Russia's freedom of action, no matter what the circumstances and however extreme the penetration of its political authority...... The impression I have received is therefore that the suitability of this draft as the basis for proposing future negotiations with the Japanese Government is seriously open to question. As I see it, an understanding which is both practicable and lasting must, as clearly suggested by you in our recent conversations, be impartial in its effects and calculated to bestow equal benefits upon both countries. Such being the case, I must request for an opportunity to delve more thoroughly into this proposal before I can state my position definitely. Moreover, the time alloted for my present itinerary is nearly up, and I believe it would be impossible for me to forward my reply before my return to Tokyo. I wish, however, to hasten to assure you that I appreciate the spirit which has actuated the leading men of your country in desiring an understanding with Japan......"

Though Ito had no prescience as yet of what its ultimate effects might be, this message constituted his farewell to Russia—farewell to his earnest hopes for bridging the gap which was alienating Japan from Russia, farewell to all his efforts toward peace in the Far East. He had done his best, had done it under circumstances of extreme national urgency with shrewdness and discretion. With the imperialists of Russia displaying such rank indifference and the war group in his own country so eager to hurl defiance at the Russian bear, failure was inevitable. No one could have done more, or to better advantage.

Nevertheless he telegraphed Lamsdorff's terms to Tokyo and intimated that he would be able to secure an adjustment satisfactory to Japan if negotiations were started, as Lamsdorff desired, at Tokyo. His colleagues in Japan, however, were now emphatically opposed to an understanding with Russia, not only in principle, but also as to any possible terms regarding Manchuria. Their policy toward Russia was bold and clear-cut. Neither in Manchuria nor in Korea would they concede her a speck of privileges. To recognize Russia's special rights in Manchuria, in however restricted a sense, would constitute an infringement of China's integrity. It would be contrary to the precedent laid down in previous diplomatic gestures in which Japan, Great Britain and the United States jointly urged upon China not to conclude a separate treaty with Russia. It would brand the fair name of Japan with the stigma of inconsistency. It would earn for her the gratuitous suspicion and ill-will of China, of Great Britain, and of the United States. So, at least, Premier Katsura contended. Yet he spoke nothing of the inconsistency involved in Japan's assumption of similar privileges in Korea! Thus, for the second time, Ito's proposal was rejected by the Tokyo Government.

Ito meanwhile proceeded from Brussels to London. Many believed at the time that this visit to the British capital presaged the swinging of his support, in consequence of the collapse of his scheme for a Russo-Japanese understanding, to the British alliance. London regarded him as a formidable question mark. He had been characterized as the principal obstacle to the alliance. There was still a bare possibility that upon his return to Japan he might be able so to influence the Emperor and the other Elder Statesmen as to bring about an eleventh-hour reversal of the verdict favoring the consummation of the alliance. He was suspected of harboring a particularly friendly regard for Russia. Yet he was, in truth, neither pro-Russian, nor pro-British, but simply pro-peace.

In the course of two meetings with Foreign Minister Lansdowne he endeavored to clarify the position he had taken and to sound the views of British officialdom. He made no commitments respecting the proposed alliance inasmuch as negotiations were still pending in diplomatic circles and his visit was essentially unofficial. He showed wherein his proposal for a Russo-Japanese understanding in no wise constituted an obstacle to Anglo-Japanese relations. He pointed out that it was merely intended to alter the status quo in Korea, where the British possessed no vested interests, in connection with the rights of foreign intervention, namely, to dispense with the existing agreement between Russia and Japan based upon parity of interests, and to conclude a new one which would reserve for Japan the sole right to render "advice" and "assistance."

"The first point on which I wish to secure your understanding," Ito said, "is with respect to Great Britain's and Japan's policies vis-à-vis China. Though I do not hold the slightest dissenting view concerning the territorial integrity of the Empire of China and the principle of the open door, Russia, it must be observed, is already in possession of a railroad in Manchuria. I am interested to know what your opinion may be in connection with the natural extension of its influence arising out of this situation." He added: "Needless to say, it is extremely doubtful whether the Government of China, weak as it is, can successfully cope with any oppressive measures coming from that direction."

Lord Lansdowne admitted having signed a convention with Russia the previous year in opposition to the will of Parliament.

"In this convention," he said, "we recognized the railway in Manchuria as coming within the Russian sphere of influence. We did not, however, extend our recognition in connection with any other privileges." Nevertheless he was not unamenable to a conciliatory view of Russia's position: "The situation of Russia differs from that of Japan, or that of Great Britain, in that her territorial boundary is contiguous to that of Manchuria, and her interests there, compared with ours, are consequently correspondingly greater."

"What are your views," Ito inquired, "about Russia's recent demands upon China for more and more privileges in Manchuria as compensation for the evacuation of her troops from that region?"

"Russia," Lansdowne replied, "is confronted with two obstacles in her treaties concerning Manchuria. First, she is enjoined from trampling upon the treaty rights of other Powers there; and, second, she is pledged to respect China's rights of sovereignty." Again he was conciliatory. "Great Britain, however," he said, "has no desire whatever to go to war with Russia merely to protect these rights—and so, I trust, has Japan." He added: "We can only hope that the treaty rights as well as the rightful interests of the various Powers in Manchuria will be preserved with justice and equity."

He inquired, in turn, what the Japanese Government contemplated doing about the problem. Ito insisted that the views he was then expressing were those of himself alone; that he could not say with certainty what precisely constituted the fixed policy of the existing government in Tokyo. "From what I have observed before taking my departure from Japan, however, and from what I have since been informed," he said, "it appears to me that the attitude is one of opposing every move taken by Russia to acquire new privileges and new interests."

The possible entanglements which an alliance would impose jointly upon Great Britain and Japan with respect to Russia's expansion in Manchuria led Lansdowne to reflect upon its probable interrelationship with Japan's problems in Korea, where Great Britain admittedly possessed no vested interests.

"The proposed Anglo-Japanese agreement," he said, "will be a radical departure from the traditional policy of my country, which has been one of taking independent action on all international problems, even to the extent of becoming completely isolated. It is quite possible that Parliament will under the circumstances interpose serious objections, and its opposition will, in all probability, center on the contention that the likelihood of Great Britain being dragged into a war with Russia to support Japan's position in Korea is much greater than that of Japan coming to the aid of Great Britain in a war with Russia over Manchuria, and that, therefore, Japan will stand to profit much more than will Great Britain."

Here Ito took occasion to emphasize the fundamental difference between his own view of the situation and all others. "Before proceeding with a discussion of Korea's problems in this connection, I must first inquire whether you would object to our beginning negotiations with Russia to make a new treaty establishing Japan's paramount interest in Korea, in place of the present Russo-Japanese convention which imposes serious obstacles upon Japan and is consequently one which is neither satisfactory under present conditions nor likely to meet with Japan's permanent approval."

"Do you intend, then, to conclude a separate agreement with Russia on a basis similar to that of the proposed Anglo-Japanese agreement?"

"I should especially wish that there be no misunderstanding on this point," said Ito. "I have no intention of promoting any scheme with respect to Russia and Great Britain which will be in the nature of an intrigue. Nor do I propose to work for a Russo-Japanese alliance. I merely wish, in this connection, to improve upon the existing Russo-Japanese convention, because I feel that only by so doing can the future peace of the Far East be assured."

"Our only point of possible objections," Lansdowne replied, "lies in your sharing with Russia any likely concessions at Great Britain's expense. However, if such, as you assure me, be not your intention, and if, further, you propose to conclude an agreement with both Great Britain and Russia for the purpose of promoting peace, we not only do not object, but, what is more, wholly approve; for ours, too, is a policy of peace."

"I should particularly appreciate your remembering this point," Ito said, "when this aspect of the problem comes up for solution."

The conversation now shifted to the possible attitudes of other Powers toward the proposed Anglo-Japanese set-up. The United States Government, and President Theodore Roosevelt in particular, was certain, Ito felt, to favor this crystallization of policy to oppose Russian ambitions in the Far East. He was doubtful, however, of Germany's ultimate aims, though she had in the beginning made vague commitments to favor Japan's course. The possibility that she might be persuaded to return to the Franco-Russian fold and repeat the triple intrigue of 1895 against Japan did not appeal to him as precisely encouraging.

"The United States," Lansdowne assured him, "will no doubt approve of our course. As to Germany, I was once indirectly informed that in the event of hostilities between Japan and another Power she would not merely refuse to become involved, but as well to induce France to observe a like neutrality. Such a commitment seemed rather far-fetched, and when Great Britain requested for a confirmation, Germany replied that her decision would be one of strict neutrality; that she would accordingly under no circumstances interfere with the alignment of other Powers. This would seem to indicate that Germany's attitude still lacks clarity. But judging from the present state of affairs in Europe, it is extremely likely that she would wish to take an independent course. Consequently, I do not believe she would care to join this alliance. Nevertheless, since she has never manifested any antagonism to Great Britain's and Japan's making common cause on the present question, I am sure there need be no misgivings there."

London entertained Ito with all the pomp and assiduity befitting both the man who had so many achievements to his credit and the occasion which required so much tact. Said the Lord Mayor in a welcoming speech: "The incidents of that career do not only represent the achievements of a great character, of a wonderful brain, an indomitable will and public spirit; but they have carried with them from year to year the destinies of an empire which it is hardly too much to say has been created in a few decades. Whether we look to the growth of civilization, the increase of political and commercial relations, the spread of science, or the establishment of constitutional freedom, we are amazed at the almost fabulous progress of Japan in the last forty years. The promotion of all that may be placed to the credit of our honored guest."

Ito replied: "The progress of Japan in the past has been due entirely to the powerful guidance of her sovereign and the loyal patriotism of her people. All that I have done for my country does not exceed the limits of having served as one of the links in the harmonious cooperation of advancing civilization."

Elaborate functions in his honor were carried out with perfect hospitality. The climax of all these eulogies, in which much was conveyed between the lines, came soon after his departure from London when the King forwarded to him in Paris the Order of Honorary Knight Grand Cross of the Bath.

8

On January 30, 1902, while Ito was proceeding homeward on the high seas somewhere between Naples and Nagasaki, the Anglo-Japanese alliance was finally signed. Public announcement to this effect was made on February 11. When Ito landed in Japan on the 25th, he found public opinion lining up solidly back of the alliance. To press for a Russian understanding in the face of such an overwhelming sentiment in favor of the British, despite the fact that the two problems were in his opinion essentially unrelated, seemed unwise indeed. No one at the helm of the Tokyo Government had rightly understood his purpose, nor supported him during his journey abroad: neither his colleagues, the Elder Statesmen, nor the Privy Councillors, nor the members of the Cabinet. Not even the mass seemed to appreciate the far-reaching aspects of the course to which Japan was now irrevocably committed. There remained one factor, however, upon which he could rely, namely, the Seiyukai Party, which was certain to control the next sitting of the national legislature. But, though he had never given up hope so far as a separate Russian agreement was concerned, he realized that further efforts in that direction at the time would merely serve to breed endless discord; that at no other time in her history as a modern Power was Japan so urgently in need of unity and cooperation. He thus accepted the inevitable but prepared to warn the nation against resorting to unnecessary extremities. At Nagasaki he availed himself of the first opportunity to make a public statement. Addressing a multitude which had turned out to welcome him, he declared:

"The purpose of this alliance is to preserve the peace of the Far East, to promote the orderly development of the commerce of all nations, to extend the benefits derived from such contacts. That you will make every endeavor to cultivate a closer friendship with Great Britain is, naturally, expected; and I have no doubt it will be sedulously carried out. But I earnestly hope that by so doing you will at no time alienate the people of other countries; that you will strive always to improve the friendly relations with all the peoples of the earth, to the end that our commercial and industrial activities may continue to function unimpaired.

"The foreign relations of our country should invariably be free from factional or party strife. They constitute a common problem affecting the whole nation. Should any divergence of opinion arise over this problem and bring about the creation of, say, a British faction, or a Russian faction, or even a French faction, the consequences thereof would breed incalculable evils and indeed demolish the indispensable unity of our nation. Alliances between nations are generally formed through the consecration of the services of such participants to a common cause. Thus the nationals on either side are honor-bound to comply with and uphold the terms throughout the length of the agreement irrespective of factional considerations or the particular complexion of the administration."

9

Here, in evaluating the principles for which Ito had fought

and lost, it seems fitting that we make a final comment. Throughout those hectic negotiations in Europe, the one significant aspect of the problem which ought properly to have been taken
cognizance of, appears to have been ignored most arbitrarily,
namely, Korea's right to self-government.   Nor does she seem
to have been consulted at any time as to her choice of alternatives in the matter of deciding which of the Powers—Russia
or Japan—should exercise a free hand over her affairs.   And
despite Ito's prodigious efforts at playing the rôle of moderator,
one might feel justified, when viewing the problem from this
angle, in ascribing motives of aggression to his insistence upon
arrogating to his own country the sole right of intervention.
Consequently his actions thus far might appear, not as a liberalizing factor, but as the studied tactics of a scheming imperialist.

Here, however, Ito was confronted with a condition, not a
theory.   No leader of note in Japan thought more conscientiously than he, in a large way, of the ultimate right of the Koreans to govern themselves. When conditions again made possible the advent of an era of serious reconstruction in Korea, he
would offer her people every assistance in instituting a healthy
regime on the Western basis which would eventually enable
them to become truly self-sufficient and thus to fashion their
own destiny.   But the immediate task at hand involved something far more grave. The situation had long since developed
—despite the pious platitudes of Russian officials—into an
emergency replete with perils, wherein the paramount necessity
of the moment was not one of deciding questions of self-determination, however legitimate, in Korea, but of preventing an
impending clash of arms.   The necessity, in short, of holding
in abeyance all questions of a theoretical character until some
future date in order effectively to undertake the more vital, the
more pressing mission of saving the people of Russia and of
Japan from the horrors of an unnecessary war.

Ito's proposals constituted the irreducible basis for a compromise, both to stop the mad tide of Russian aggrandizement
on the one hand, and to prevent, on the other, the demand for
a forcible show-down, which was the proud challenge of Japan's

military leaders. And to him the only possibility of a compromise lay in recognizing some legitimate activity of Russia in Manchuria, particularly in the management of railway enterprises, in somewhat the same manner that he had insisted on a recognition of Japan's paramount protective interest in Korea. This might appear like political bargaining, with all its sinister commercialisms, at the expense of China and Korea for the sole selfish benefit of Russia and Japan. It would not in reality, however, be exploitation in that sense, for the mutual recognitions as he conceived them would apply merely to legitimate interests already acquired or inherent in those spheres, these to be unequivocally defined through subsequent negotiations with the governments of Peking and of Seoul. Any other compromise would have been futile in the face of the onrushing forces which were now plunging recklessly, blindly, to a head-on collision in the Far East.

Consequently Ito's attempted negotiations were, inevitably, the only possible peaceful solution, the only possible liberalizing factor in that mad stampede of aggression and of rivalry. The merit of his proposals lay precisely in the fact that within their mutually restricted sense they were acceptable neither to the Tsarist regime nor to the leaders of his own country.

The alternative was war—and come it did!

CHAPTER XIV
MAN OF PEACE

I

Two months after the public announcement of the Anglo-Japanese alliance Russia agreed to withdraw her army of occupation from Manchuria within a year and a half. This would be accomplished from three designated zones, each such zone to be evacuated in consecutive order within a six-month period. At the time it was believed in certain quarters that this change of front on Russia's part was motivated by circumspective scruples—a rare phenomenon indeed for Russia—originating from the singular effects of the alliance; that it presaged a general halt on the predatory movements of Russia in Manchuria. By no means, however, was she influenced by any such susceptibilities in which prudence plays the principal rôle. Nor was she, at any moment of the crisis leading up to the final crash, concerned with matters of conscience. She was merely playing her game in the most cunning fashion appropriate to the occasion.

The first zone, which comprised that region lying between the Liao and the Great Wall, was to all intents and purposes evacuated without revealing any breach of her agreement with China. Actually, however, the troops were simply transferred to her naval base at Port Arthur, also to the next zone. This was not evacuation in the proper sense but expediency characterized by treachery and deceit. In the second period, she massed her troops on the Korean frontier. Here she paused in her movements to demand further concessions from China as additional compensation. If China complied, Russia would have regained complete control of Manchuria, together with the adjoining territory beyond the Great Wall. But China refused. Thereupon Russia regarded the evacuation convention as a mere scrap of paper—a gesture the like of which had tarnished many a brilliant page in history but did not become a popular symbol of international rape until the summer of 1914.

In Korea the private timber concessions along the Yalu had meanwhile been acquired by the Russian Government. This was now exploited to its fullest possibilities. An additional concession of a similar nature along the Manchurian banks was secured. A railway from the Yalu to the Korean capital was contemplated. So also was the leasing of Yongampo as a naval base. Russian troops in disguise prepared to occupy the Yalu region.

On June 23, 1903, at an extraordinary council convened in the Emperor's presence to formulate a decision regarding Japan's course of action in her relations with Russia respecting Korea and Manchuria, Ito again chose to disagree with the principles laid down by the government. The government was represented by Premier Katsura and his Ministers of Foreign Affairs, of the Navy, and of the Army, all of whom were united in advocating forceful negotiations with Russia—negotiations which would take the form of a firm and positive attitude calculated to place Japan's cards on the table and to compel Russia to come to a final show-down. Ito, alone among the five Elder Statesmen in attendance to oppose this plan, still adhered tenaciously to his original doctrine in which peace with Russia through reasonable concessions constituted the dominant motive. True, in 1894 he had approved of the war with China for causes substantially similar to the present activities of Tsarist Russia, but with this significant difference: China in 1894 had repeatedly resorted to *armed exploitation* and *armed resistance* to Japan's peaceful overtures on spurious assumptions of suzerainty over Korea. The quarrel with Russia, where it concerned Korea, the only region where Japan in Ito's opinion could claim legitimate rights of self-defense, had not, on the other hand, developed to such proportions wherein a *peaceful gesture* for an understanding and a compromise should be regarded as hopeless. But outvoted in the council, his pleas were of no avail.

His actions thus far meanwhile led the warlike Premier to assume that in his joint capacity as Elder Statesman and President of the Seiyukai Party, Ito commanded too much power for an assailant of the policies of his government; that he was in consequence an obstacle, rather than an aid, to the successful operation of his, Katsura's, programme. For this reason Katsura demanded that he divest himself, "for the good of the State," of one of his mantles of power.

The status of an Elder Statesman, Ito replied, was without substance or constituted authority. It was merely a recognition of one's past services upon which the Emperor ultimately relied in formulating decisions on questions of national import. Obviously one could not resign from such an anomalous state. Katsura was fully aware of this, of the utter unreasonableness of suggesting it as one of the two alternatives. It was simply a ruse with which to compel Ito into quitting his influential post at the head of the Seiyukai Party. Ito immediately saw through this sinister insinuation. He was, however, conscious of no convincing reason why he should renounce his leadership of the party, particularly as he had organized it solely with the object of diverting the masses from participating in promiscuous politics, and not for purposes of personal aggrandizement. Katsura next threatened to resign himself. This was merely another trick of his for putting over his scheme. For he knew full well that the popularity of his administration gained through the successful conclusion of the Anglo-Japanese alliance was still unassailable, and that his wishes would consequently be assiduously catered to.

True to his plans, Yamagata and Matsukata, two Elder Statesmen representing the military and the bureaucratic cliques now solidly at odds with Ito, of whom the former was the power behind the Katsura Ministry, here besought the Emperor to intercede. Through an arrangement manipulated by these veterans with astonishing cleverness, the fulfilment of the Premier's desire was greatly facilitated. Under this arrangement Ito was requested, through the medium of an Imperial rescript, to return to his former official habitat among the bureaucrats as President of the Privy Council, thus compelling him indirectly to surrender all party affiliations—a most effective way of muzzling the man of peace who would otherwise have blocked the programme of the government through the Diet. He had been virtually plotted against by those desiring a war with Russia, and he knew it. He could have easily refused the proffered post and told the plotters to let well enough alone. But in the end he yielded, for the mandate of his opponents had likewise become the mandate of the Emperor.

2

The Katsura Government now cleared its decks for action and began those "firm and positive" negotiations with Russia. It strove desperately to contend for the integrity not only of Korea but of Manchuria also, because it felt that this was the only way in which it could insure Japan's security. Russia, on the other hand, endeavored to tell Japan, somewhat scornfully, to mind her own business. Though manifestly guilty of aggression in Manchuria, she had not, so far, committed a single act in Korea which did not find a parallel in the activities of the Japanese in the same region. But aggression was evidently only one of several aspects in the Russian advance to which the Katsura Government particularly objected. It was not so much what Russia had done in Korea and Manchuria as, judging from her course of action, what she was obviously bent upon doing and what she might do after she had secured supreme military, political, and economic control of these two strategic regions, which made its leaders so determinedly anxious to call a halt upon her movements. Considering the particular brand of Russian imperialism so brazenly demonstrated in the Three-Power intervention of 1895, in her refusal to evacuate Manchuria, and in her economic penetration of Korea, what she might do then was not at all difficult for them to surmise. They shuddered to think of what might befall Japan when the last great barrier on the Asiatic mainland had been surmounted by hordes of Russian military despoilers and an unobstructed path leading to her very shores had been made accessible to these invaders. Korea and Manchuria were, moreover, fast becoming vital factors in the development of Japan's economic life. Forced by physical limitations to become, like Great Britain, a nation of manufacturers, she was now dependent upon these two neighboring regions, not only as her principal source of raw materials, but also as her chief foreign market for the disposition of her finished products. The time for

Japan to act, Premier Katsura and his supporters felt, was now. Russia was advancing swiftly in her conquering march to the south. Work on the Trans-Siberian Railway to perfect her troop movements from the far corners of her prodigious empire was being pushed forward with all possible haste; was nearing completion. Only that portion partially encircling Lake Baikal remained unfinished. A delay in the negotiations would prove fatal. Japan proposed the establishment of a neutral zone between Manchuria and Korea—her last peaceful gesture. Russia deliberately stalled. While Baron Rosen relayed the Japanese notes from Tokyo to Admiral Alexeieff, the newly appointed Viceroy of the Far East with headquarters at Port Arthur, who in turn kept up a long drawn out telegraphic tête-à-tête with the Tsar, who next confounded the issue with the political intrigues of central Europe in which he had become, through the Kaiser's cabalistic artifices, inextricably enmeshed —while all these bureaucratic indulgences were being freely practiced by the Russians with apparently no intention of satisfying the pressing demands from Tokyo for a summary decision, Japan prepared to mobilize her forces. On February 4, 1904, at another of those grave councils specially convened in the Emperor's presence, the Katsura Government decided, with the approval of the majority of the Elder Statesmen, to sever diplomatic relations with Russia. War between the two countries became a stark reality.

On March 7 Ito was summoned before the Throne to be invested with the office of "Consolation Envoy" to Korea. His mission, as propounded in an Imperial rescript, was to proceed at once to Seoul and there convey to the King of Korea the assurances of the Japanese Emperor for a continuance of Japan's good will and protection.

This was in line with the protocol concluded by Minister Hayashi on February 24, which established a modified protectorate over Korea—the first of a series of agreements entered into during the course of the war and after, between an exacting Japan and a docile Korea. Japan, having engaged in one costly affray and being now involved in another and still more stupendous war to prevent the domination in Korea of a hostile neighboring Power which would imperil her own interests, was persuaded that the whole sordid affair had gone far enough; that positive action to end the nuisance had at last become necessary. Korea had thus become a pawn in an immense rivalry for power in the Far East, in which the egregious imperialism of the West as typified by Russia was pitted against a paternal type of aggrandizement conceived in self-defense, which Japan undertook to exemplify. In the final analysis, Korea's own inherent weakness and perennial misgovernment constituted the pivotal cause, for they encouraged the movement by serving to whet the appetite of the one while prompting the other to interpose strong defensive measures. There was no other choice, as Japan's leaders chose to view it, but to decide whether a decent respect for the rights of the Koreans and for the dictates of international rectitude should compel her to continue to restrict her policies on the dubious basis of intervention and thereby tolerate the existence of a perpetual menace to her peace and security, or whether she should, for her own guarantees of safety, take such steps as were deemed imperative in bringing Korea more effectually under her control.

Hence the mission upon which Ito was dispatched by the Emperor was designed as much to receive, as to give, those solemn protestations of cooperation between Japan and Korea which had become so necessary in the prosecution of this war with Russia.

Leaving Tokyo on the 13th, Ito boarded the converted cruiser, "Hongkong Maru," at Kobe, arriving at Chemulpo on the 17th, after cruising past the Tsushima Strait, now rendered perilous by the presence of Russian warships. At Chemulpo he was met by a special representative of the Korean Court, who escorted him with all due formality to Seoul. The next day he secured the audience of the King and performed the "consolatory" functions appertaining to his visit. This was followed by a graphic description of the affairs of the outer world, for the benefit of the King whose knowledge on the subject with particular reference to the fate of his own unfortunate realm was far from adequate. At the end of ten days, his mission accomplished, Ito entrained for Chemulpo and took his departure on the "Hongkong Maru," which awaited him there, for Japan.

Throughout this visit Ito was actuated solely by the pressing needs of the moment. His influence, as a man of peace, was temporarily eclipsed by other powerful leaders who had succeeded—and no one could truthfully say that their policy was wholly wrong when viewed in the light of the Russian penetration—in making a sacrosanct issue out of the war. Much as he disapproved of their colossal programme, he had reconciled himself to it out of a patriotic desire for harmony, and it was his intention to make the best of a bad situation.

Despite the stark inevitability associated with the birth of the Protectorate, which presaged other drastic eventualities, Ito made no effort to prepare for the absorption of Korea. For his policy had always been, and would continue throughout his life, to aid and to protect Korea, not to rob her. If he had found it necessary at times to resort to desperate measures wherein her independent action was temporarily suspended, it had been to save her from the rashness and imbecility of her own leaders. Whether the Koreans appreciated his services and his particular line of action is, of course, another matter. But if the Emperor had agreed to capitalize his abilities and his enormous reputation chiefly to interpose a moderating influence which would counterbalance in some measure the suspicion and ill-will of the Koreans against Japan, then he did so with notable success. No open resistance of any consequence interrupted Japan's activities during the course of her war with Russia.

3

As the war progressed the Russians were driven out of Korea. The area of hostilities was thereafter confined to Manchuria, where the Grand Army of Russia prepared to defend its occupied strongholds. With the possibilities of internal disturbance in Korea thus appreciably minimized, Japan felt that the time for those administrative reforms stipulated in the protocol of February 24 was quite opportune. Again the Emperor made a wise choice in designating Ito for the supervision of this important work.

On July 9, 1904, Ito set out for Shimonoseki, where Minister Hayashi repaired from Seoul to meet him, and to whom he gave the necessary instructions for signing a new agreement. These instructions required that Korean affairs be directed under Japanese guidance until such time as she had achieved the capacity to stand on her own feet. The first of the reforms was thus effected on August 22, by virtue of which Korea accepted the appointment of Mr. Megata, a Japanese educated at Harvard University, and Mr. Stevens, an American, as financial and diplomatic advisers respectively. It was Ito's wish that Korea should have the most enlightened and disinterested leadership; and considering the policy to which Japan was now committed and the sacrifices involved, no better plan could have been devised.

BOOK IV

THE REDEEMER

CHAPTER XV
WHITHER KOREA?

I

In August, 1905, Japan and Russia—the former victorious but ruinously impoverished and the latter confronted with defeat and a rising proletarian revolution—terminated the war through Roosevelt's intercession and signed the Portsmouth Treaty, which conceded, among other things, Japan's paramount political, military and economic interests in Korea.

This provision was tantamount to a recognition of the right, on the part of Japan, to exercise an exclusive control—a free hand—over Korean affairs. It gave her practically the same privileges which Great Britain, in April, 1904, had secured over the Egyptian domain; which France, under the same instrument, had proclaimed over Morocco; and which the United States had established over Cuba when her rough riders ran rough-shod over the Spanish rulers in this misgoverned island. In a way, considering Russia's reckless policy of economic and military penetration, it was inevitable. In a way, too, it was justified by past events, by the hopeless incompetence of the Seoul Court, by the utter inability of the Korean Government to provide those safeguards which Japan regarded as vital to her problems of national defense.

This was precisely what Ito had hoped to achieve by friendly negotiations, but which, with the Katsura Government preferring to obtain by force, had cost Japan millions of yen and hundreds of thousands of lives. Now, at all events, the realities of the situation, which held a deep significance for the future, must be squarely met. Thus the question which came preeminently to the fore, creating a rift in the policies of the nation, was: how far should Japan go in exercising this control over Korea? Would she, in view of the events which precipitated it and of the sacrifices it entailed, be justified in rendering this control permanent and irrevocable by a gradual process of absorption? Or should she confine her activities, as Ito insisted, to purely redemptive measures and relinquish her hold when the Koreans had attained their requisite national strength?

The Katsura Government was determined, as a matter of course, upon a policy calculated to forestall any effort by others that might provoke a repetition of the causes which brought on the late war. If anything, it was to tighten the hold on Korea. Not, however, for purposes of economic gain, as the facile critics of Japan are asserting with astonishing verisimilitude a quarter century later, but principally for creating a logical outpost of defense against the two Powers whom she had driven out of Korea. "Had Japan been at liberty to annex the peninsula," wrote Lord Curzon, from personal observations made in 1896, "and to treat it with her own instruments and' in her own way, she might in time have evolved a new order out of the existing chaos. But this she has been prevented from doing by her own pledges and by the fear of others. She has cut the single cable by which the crazy little ship rode precariously at anchor in the Far Eastern roadstead; and she has left it to drift, without helmsman and without rudder, upon the stormy waters." But that "fear of others" no longer constituted a towering obstacle. What is more, the Tokyo Government proposed not merely to supply the "helmsman" and the "rudder," but to soothe the "stormy waters" as well. Precedents were not lacking, for seven years before the United States had acquired the Philippines and annexed Hawaii for reasons just as significant and in which native aspirations had necessarily been ignored.

Public opinion in Japan supported this policy, though it was not yet clear as to what precisely would be its ultimate expression in terms of action. The question at issue, as the mass saw it, no longer concerned the fate of Korea alone. The war to drive the Russians out of this ill-administered land had drained so heavily the vital energies of Japan that no future measure would be tolerable which did not consider the joint interests of the two countries as indissoluble.

But such a policy would have all the earmarks of "manifest destiny." In spite of the many provocative circumstances which had made intervention necessary, the desire of twenty million

Koreans to determine their own destiny was an inalienable right which Japan must ultimately reckon with. Ito bore this fact consistently in mind. Hence it was clear to him that whatever policy his government was bent upon pursuing must be firm but tempered always with humanity and with due respect for the aspirations of the benighted whenever their capacity for self-determination convincingly evinced itself. The line of demarcation which prescribed the limits of intervention demanded by the exigencies of the times, beyond which loomed the ugly spectre of imperialism, was so vague and yet so fraught with the possibilities of international misunderstanding that the utmost discretion must be used in exercising legitimate rights. In his desperate long-range duel with his colleagues over the Russo-Japanese understanding he had fought hard and lost. In his long and abiding commitments regarding Korea, now faced with possible subversion, he was determined not to repeat his defeat.

Thus with the scheme of his colleagues held effectually in check, the Korean experiment went on cautiously apace. For three years Ito dominated the scene. Firm in his resistance to acts of imperialism proceeding from men at the helm of the Tokyo Government, but equally firm in his insistence upon reforms which would lift Korea from the mire of corruption and ignorance, he instituted a healthy regime which was the only possible compromise between perpetual impotence and eventual absorption. Severely misunderstood by his associates, distrusted by his opponents, and hated by the very ones whom he took under his wings and to whom he elected to bring salvation, he carried on the world's most thankless task, earning for himself nothing but malignant opprobriums which were as inevitable as they were unmerited. After the lapse of three years, the Koreans, ignorant of their destiny, realized when it was too late —when Ito was no longer of this earth—that the only alternative to his regime was an eternity of sorrow and humiliation.

2

The first definitive gesture over which Ito and the existing government at Tokyo found a common basis of agreement took

shape in November, 1905.   On the 9th he set out for Seoul
and there, after a series of stubborn sessions with the King and
his Ministers, he negotiated a convention which brought
Korea's foreign affairs directly under the control of Japan.   The
protocols signed in February and August of the previous year
had been aimed chiefly at the strengthening of Korea's internal
administration.   The present treaty was designed particularly
to obviate that constant threat which lurked in the palace at
Seoul, the scene of many a sanguinary revolution, where the
King, surrounded by eunuchs, yang-bans, conspirators, and
foreign exploiters, wallowed in intrigues in defiance of all legitimate powers reserved for Korea's Foreign Office.   Here
the King, through the use of a private cipher, had been in
secret communication with the various Korean Ministers stationed at the foreign capitals.   Through them he had managed
to carry on a systematic campaign of misrepresentations and
distortions of the truth, thus to subvert the ties which were
now regarded by Japan as a *fait accompli.*

The King knew full well that this would deprive him for-
sooth of his immemorial privileges to which he owed his politically gluttonous state.   When Ito outlined the substance of the
new treaty, placing Korea under the rule of a Japanese Resident-General, he consented only on condition that he be permitted to continue maintaining Korean legations abroad.   This,
he explained with his customary shrewdness, was merely to
retain an outward semblance of control for no other purpose
than to preserve his dignity as king.   With such naïveté—
with such transparent pretexts for keeping intact the outward
form—he sought to secure longevity for the channels of intrigue
between himself and his foreign co-plotters as a means of nulli-
fying, underhandedly, the substance of what he would be required, publicly, to accept.   Ito replied that inasmuch as both
the form and the substance of control were, in diplomatic practice, productive of a similar effect, he could not accept any
compromise along that line.   He then intimated that it would
be useless, perhaps inadvisable in the extreme, for the King to
bargain for loopholes as he could not now recede a single step
from the decision he had arrived at with his government.   A

refusal on the part of the King to accept the present convention in toto might, he suggested, precipitate measures involving harsher extremities—extremities the fatal effects of which he, Ito, would be powerless to ward off for Korea.

The King next attempted to complicate matters by declaring his intention of submitting the treaty to his "people at large" for their consideration. For a ruler who had withheld even the rudiments of a parliamentary medium of expression from his people, this sudden reference to the popular will would have been ridiculous had it not been for the quality of deception which it unmistakably betrayed. Either it presaged a desperate move calculated to arouse public indignation, or else it was a ruse for stalling off Ito until the King had received the awaited assurances from Mr. Hulbert, an American associated with Korean propaganda work, whom he had dispatched to Washington earlier in the month to seek the President's intervention with a view to dissolving the Japanese protectorate. Ito reminded the King, in all sincerity, that such a procedure was likely to provoke incalculable harm, for which none but he, the King himself, would be held accountable. The success, he showed, of introducing needed reforms, or of concluding arrangements embracing similarly radical steps in a relatively backward State, depended upon the absence of popular excitement and the disclosure of sound leadership which could function intelligently in the briefest possible time.

The King, finding no other convenient recourse readily accessible, finally yielded. The convention was then referred to his Ministers, who, however, abided by Premier Han's move for its rejection. Ito pressed for a reconsideration on the strength of the King's prior approval. Meanwhile the King suggested an amendment entitling Korea, after she had achieved "national strength," to resume her autonomous functions. This was precisely what Ito himself had intended doing and was cheerfully incorporated. Late that evening the convention, as amended, was signed.

There was no question about the agreement having been secured under duress. Most treaties of this character and under these circumstances are, for that matter, secured under

one form of duress or another, and every first-rate Power has
a closet full of rattling skeletons.

No individual or nation, say the liberals, possesses the right
to impose one's will upon another. Hence if the Koreans
were determined to be enamored of corruption and misgovernment in their national life, it was not for an outsider to say
whether or not they should commit self-extermination through
self-determination. Say the conservatives: though liberty is
an inalienable right of every individual and nation, it nevertheless ceases to be so the moment it is abused to the extent
that it imperils the liberty of others. It then becomes a nuisance. It must then concede to those whose liberty has been
jeopardized the right to provide adequate safeguards against
its further abuse. Here Ito, situated as he was between the
proverbial devil and the deep blue sea, felt impelled, in view
of the stark realities looming in the post-war horizon, to make
the needful concession to the conservatives' stand. Otherwise
he would have met with incorrigible resistance in interposing
his redemptive policy. Every consideration within reason
must be given the fact that Japan had fought two costly wars
within ten years on Korea's account, and it would be a grave
mistake to expect the government at Tokyo to be satisfied
with anything less than an absolute certainty that such wars
would not be necessary in the future. There was no other
choice. And it was infinitely more desirable than outright
annexation. As long as the Emperor could be persuaded to
sanction the most effective yet the most reasonable efforts short
of a sentimental disregard of the existing evils under a civil,
as opposed to a militaristic, regime, Ito believed that the end,
which was Korean salvation, must justify whatever means that
seemed to offer the greatest assurances of success. The conditions imposed by the convention, moreover, were to remain in
force only during the interim in which Korea, with Japan's assistance, would endeavor to attain " national strength."

Though his admiration for the King, for reasons widely
known, was anything but profound, Ito's sympathy for the
Korean people was genuine indeed. All doubts on this point
should have been dispelled when, on December 21, 1905, he

accepted from his Emperor, at the advanced age of sixty-four, the first resident-generalship of Korea. Thus would he undertake to fulfill the responsibilities pledged in the agreement secured by himself.

There could have been no more salutary turning-point in the history of the Hermit Kingdom. For whatever Ito had achieved for his own country, he was now determined to accomplish for Korea. Not even his most rabid dissenters could have found justification for heaping castigations upon a mission so generously conceived. It was not to exploit the resources of a weaker nation temporarily bereft of independent action, nor to assume the vicious rôle of an overweening tyrant bent upon oppression and robbery, but to teach the people of Korea, out of the profound treasure-house of his accumulated knowledge and experience the modern arts of national self-development, self-government, and self-defense. Any other purpose would have been revolting to his moral sensibilities as a friend of humanity and his responsibilities as a patriot.

But the very ones whom he essayed to teach turned against him. To them he was at best an insufferable usurper. They greeted him with a smiling, deceptive hostility. Anything, even the basest example of misgovernment, as long as it had been perpetrated under native leadership, would have been preferrable to a regime that had been foisted upon them by a foreign Power, however enlightened or benevolent its purpose and effect. The more readily was their spirit of resistance aroused when it was remembered with consternation that Ito had been the very one, alone among Japan's Elder Statesmen, who had striven so meticulously in the past for their independence, yet had himself wrested it away from them as a hostage for reforms which were repugnant to their centuries-old habits and tastes.

Nor did they seem even remotely conscious of the fact that the most obnoxious impediment to their free and tranquil development lay imbedded in the core of their own body politic. Their political life was almost hopelessly decadent. The privileged mortals who constituted their ruling class plied their trade amid circumstances of degradation and ignominy. Much as they chose to disregard these evils, it was more than crystal clear that for them to profit under such conditions from the measures of rehabilitation deemed necessary for their national betterment was an utter impossibility.

Added to this intrinsic handicap, which rendered the execution of Ito's uplift work supremely difficult, were the innumerable evils created by the rabble of adventurers from Japan who had migrated over to Korea to engage in selfish pursuits following the termination of the war with Russia; the obstructionist movement carried on with an astonishingly destructive malignity by hypercritical foreign missionaries; and the poisonous propaganda engineered by the British editor of the Korean Daily News and the American publicist and educator who ended by becoming the King's personal agent.

3

Surrounded thus by hostile groups on every hand, and with his own government regarding with extreme dubiousness the nature of the Herculean mission which he was about to undertake, Ito initiated a new era for Korea with progress on the Western basis as the ultimate objective. Beginning with physical improvements, believed to be the most immediately conducive to the people's happiness, he engaged an able staff of scientists and engineers to assist him in his work. The building of roads, of bridges, of railways, of schools, of hospitals, of sanitary facilities, was soon under way. Then followed the reclamation of uncultivated lands, of marshes, of dry beaches; the rehabilitation of forests; the regulation and improvement of mines; the founding of experiment stations; the improvement of agricultural yields through the distribution of rice seeds from Japan and of barley and wheat from America and Europe; and the inauguration of experimental work on new products, notably cotton and tobacco.

Turning his attention to the system of public justice, Ito found it wallowing in incredible corruption. There was no such thing as a Korean national code under which an impartial meting out of justice could be carried out. The people, instead of seeking to remedy this state of affairs, presumably because of its proven futility or because of sheer indolence, had become accustomed to the comparatively simpler process of bribery and extortion. All this, under Ito's administration, was destined to change. A number of competent jurists were assembled at Seoul "to devise a written code under which the ancient customs and common laws of Korea, as representing its best efforts to enact and establish justice," could be "made available for future use."

Ito's first gesture in the interest of political reformation was the "purification" of the Seoul Court. The King's palace, despite whatever traditions of culture and reverence it had inspired, had become a strange rendezvous of rogues and promiscuous politicians. A center of intrigue and corruption, with the King himself constituting the most skillful protagonist, it had enticed into its folds a motley group of adventurers, conspirators, fortune tellers, knaves, thieves. All these people of doubtful origin and sinister intentions combined to render the Court a most villainous assemblage wherein it was a sheer impossibility to hope for virtue, order, and discipline. The process of "purification" relieved the palace of all those people, women as well as men, who could give no legitimate reasons for their presence. For every undesirable thus weeded out, Ito added one more member to the long list of enemies, active and potential, who threatened to subvert his work. And there was none more thoroughly frustrated in the continuance of his multitudinous designs and none more profoundly alienated, despite outward appearances, than the King himself!

Finally, in the course of about a year's intensive work, came, inevitably, the Ministry's reorganization. The existing government under Acting Premier Pak, though it represented a few docile converts to modern theories and practices, functioned none the less under a system as archaic as it was destructive of human liberty. Lacking proper concentration or division of power or responsibility, it constituted a dangerously haphazard affair, susceptible to all the evils of slavish antiquity. The King was still the privileged autocrat, with powers unlimited to do as he pleased with the lives and property of his subjects. Not only must the many powers hitherto exercised by him be transferred to a proper administrative body, but a change in

the personnel of the ruling classes must be made to enable
them to adhere with greater consistency and with increased
efficiency to the requirements of a changing Korea.

Under the reorganized scheme the Ministers would assume
the management of all important affairs of state, including the
appointment and dismissal of officials, the promulgation of all
laws and edicts, the fixing of the national budget, and the
granting of amnesty and pardon.   All the Ministers were required to act in unison and in pursuance of a common policy.
They were now enabled to act independently of the King's
manifold whims.   But they must at all times formulate their
programme of action in consonance with the Resident-General's
view.   Ito, in providing for this last arrangement, denied any
intention of usurping the position formerly held by the King.
For his powers were merely *advisory* and his purpose to give
constructive guidance to the Ministers; whereas the King,
who was wholly incompetent and selfish, had possessed the
power to *enforce* his wishes.

Determined to avoid friction and confusion and perturbation
as much as possible, Ito brought about the dissolution of the
old Ministry in a quiet audience with the King lasting five
hours.   There was no opportunity for intrigue, nor for the
mischievous clamor of the opposition press, of the designing
politicians, of the discontented mob.   Within two hours following this audience, Yi Wan-yong, Ito's choice for Premier,
created a new Cabinet.   The ex-Ministers were then appointed
to the Privy Council and provided with sufficient dignity and
remuneration to preclude the possibilities of their attempting
any destructive movements against the new regime.

"Korea's urgent need today," declared Ito, addressing the
newly-formed Cabinet, "is improvement in its administrative
functions.   It must, on the one hand, foster education so as to
enable its people to absorb the benefits of civilization.   On
the other hand, it must develop its national strength by formulating means of rising from its present state of impotence.
This will be of direct benefit to Korea.   It will, at the same
time, indirectly promote Japan's interests.   Further, it will
affect the whole of the Far East—in fact, the whole world.   I

trust, gentlemen, that in achieving these ends you will perform your duties faithfully. As for myself, I am constantly striving to do my utmost for Korea, with the conditions, not only of the Far East, but of the world itself as a background. Thus, under no circumstances do I place Korea alone in the path of my perspective."

Firm in his hostility to petty intrigues, he counselled loyalty to the new dispensation. "Koreans everywhere," he said, "seem to be clamoring for independence with increasing force. A nation cannot, however, exist without effort. Nor can other Powers enable it to stand on its own feet. A nation desiring the realities of independence must devise the proper means of achieving them. I fear that if Koreans continue as at present to have recourse to heedless, ill-advised attempts, they will surely bring about national suicide. I have not forgotten for a moment the grave responsibility of promoting the joint interests of Korea and Japan, and it is my belief that the very existence of Korea will depend upon her cordial relationship with Japan, upon her determination to rise or fall together with Japan. If anyone disagrees with me in this respect, I should wish to be fully informed. If you are willing to agree, do your utmost for Korea by discarding your selfish motives and by cooperating for the common good."

His first "advice" respecting the immediate tasks at hand was two-fold: "What I particularly wish to call your attention to at this time are, first, to encourage the opening up of Korea's rich natural resources by releasing the flow of capital and combating the bogey of pessimism; and, secondly, to disregard the prejudice in your own hearts and induct into the service impartially such leaders as will be of genuine benefit to society."

CHAPTER XVI
A DYNAST FALLS

I

Every indication pointed now to the inception of a truly beneficent era. Neither treachery nor corruption within the Ministry, nor yet the customary intrigues from without,seemed likely under the new arrangement to hamper the orderly functions of the government. Better still, the new Ministers were men possessed of a relatively higher capacity than those who had been obliged to retire, in administering the affairs of the state on a modern basis. Cooperation with Ito, under whose guidance the numerous redemptive projects were being rapidly executed, became an assured fact. The belief among them seemed to prevail that the type of government which Ito had introduced, embracing as it did not merely the political regeneration of the nation but its economic salvation as well, was after all productive of real benefits to all concerned. Not a few of them had a particularly poignant dislike for the pitiless fashion in which the King had been wont to weave his webs of intrigue. Compared with this wretched misrule, Ito's regime was infinitely more desirable, though it was admittedly humiliating in the sense that it was a foreign imposition.

Had the nation as a whole been reconciled to this manner of thinking and all pending problems met on the basis of this understanding, Ito most certainly would have had recourse, from time to time, to such measures as would have lessened, not increased, the control of Japan. He would indeed have labored sedulously in a progression of emancipating acts for the complete restoration of Korean autonomy. But the realization of his sincerity, of his concern for the well-being of the Koreans, and of the fact that inasmuch as he was endeavoring practically single-handed to save them from a worse fate, there could be no further compromise, was shared, unfortunately, by only a diminutive group of intelligent officials and their supporters. Those who were most vitally affected—the mass—were hopelessly prejudiced. The King, though he was still smilingly acquiescent, developed a growing suspicion. With each enlargement of the power of the Korean Government, and hence with each lessening of his own powers, his resentment increased. Meanwhile his baffled mind groped with desperate subtlety for some positive means of relief......

Ito seemed to be unaware of this. "Since assuming my present post," he said, "I have, without faltering, concentrated my attention upon a single objective: the fulfilment of the responsibilities which Japan must bear toward Korea. These responsibilities are indicated in the treaties between the two countries, the most important of which is to preserve the integrity of Korea. The second is to render constructive advice respecting administrative reforms. The third is to guarantee the safety of the Korean Imperial House."

But his difficulties multiplied. The drawbacks inherent in an arrangement wherein he could merely "render constructive advice" to a recalcitrant people, and was denied the power to enforce it, were obvious. "Though I am fully exerting myself in encouraging the present Ministers to accelerate the necessary reforms, the situation is precisely the reverse of an independent government formulating its own policies and executing them on its own initiative. Thus it is impossible for me to accomplish anything without first convincing them respecting the desirability of each phase of the reforms and obtaining their approval. There is no other recourse. The Ministers seem to be aware of this, but the local officials do not at all understand what is involved. Hence it is extremely difficult to avoid the dilatory evils from which the Administration inevitably suffers."

Nevertheless, it must always be remembered, he said in extenuation, that Korea was a country of twenty million people whose origin went back to an antiquity as remote as that of Japan, whose people had always been Koreans, and who had survived as a compact nation through the ages to the present era. It was thus only natural that they should possess a strong nationalistic feeling, a racially cohesive spirit which refused to adopt the counsels of foreigners, however well-meant and sincere.   Japan's responsibilities must consequently be borne with a firmness matched with infinite tact and patience.

No substantial improvements, he said, could be made without capital; and since it was difficult for Japan to advance state loans, it had been his policy to encourage Korea in the accomplishment of her aims through an intensive development of her own resources.   These, however, were by no means sufficient to attain anywhere near the requisite national strength.   He therefore recommended private investments from Japan.   But here he advised extreme caution.   " The Koreans," he said, "are a particularly mistrustful people.   Many of them harbor the suspicion that Japan, as likely as not, will annex Korea.   This, however, is a most natural state of affairs.   No one ever hopes that his country will be absorbed by another. I have especially been careful on this point, shedding light on misunderstandings, and explaining that Japan's only desire is to assist and to enlighten Korea, and that the two countries must prosper together."

He was especially mindful of the power of the press, for evil no less than for good.   A single destructive word in the daily paper possessed more power to mould the ingenuous thoughts of the Koreans than a thousand constructive words uttered by himself.   "There are," he said, "certain foreign newspapers which are in the habit of stirring up the Koreans and heaping abuse upon Japan.   Whether their intentions are to profit from this, or simply to hearten the Koreans, the fact remains that they *are* indulging in these things, and their voices have been echoed throughout the world."

Suddenly, like a clap of thunder, came the report from The Hague that a Korean delegation had appeared at the peace conference, at the behest of the King, to make an appeal before the delegates of all the Powers for release from Japanese control.

This was in obvious contravention of the existing treaties between Korea and Japan.   What was more, it amounted to a direct slap at Ito's patient efforts in the interest of Korean redemption.   Yet it was the only feasible remedy to which the King could have turned for the solution of his great and irksome dilemma, short of rapine and murder and open resistance.

The Tokyo Government, faced as it was with the necessity of preserving its prestige, could hardly be expected to ignore so significant a gesture. The one ray of hope which might possibly avert a tragedy for Korea was seen in the fact that the Korean Government had been entirely unaware, and consequently innocent, of the whole unsavory proceedings. At The Hague it was readily apparent that owing to the extraordinary relations existing between Korea and Japan, secured through treaties on which the King's sanction had been given, the Powers could not properly intervene.

When this fact became known to the King, he at once dispatched the Minister of the Imperial Household to Ito to deny complicity in the work of the delegation. Further, he suggested a fitting punishment for its members, whom he characterized as unauthorized offenders!

Ito was in great perplexity. The weight of evidence was far too patently incriminating to admit of any plausibility for the defense of the erring King. Nor was the King entitled to much sympathy since he could not even remain true to those whom he had employed to execute his bidding. The situation was not only delicate; it was embarrassing in the extreme—embarrassing to all concerned. Something must be done, but what? What could Japan do to such an ingenuous, defenseless ruler, and for something he had done out of the most natural and the most human of desires—the desire to throw off the yoke of constraint? Yet, would not this appear in Tokyo as the outcome of that over-generous policy to which its leaders, advocates of a sterner policy, had reluctantly, and purely out of respect for Ito's humanitarian counsels, submitted? Would it not, in their minds, attest the foolishness and the futility of prolonging the life of a nation that they had condemned to become eventually a part of Japan's scheme of empire? And would not this spell defeat and collapse of his, Ito's, cherished plans for Korea's redemption?

Seoul meanwhile became literally agog with genuine perturbation. The smiling King, no longer confident of the efficacy of his subtle tactics, became increasingly apprehensive of his security. Even his own henchmen and those other conspirators who, through some ingenious social contrivances, had managed to remain unmolested within the palace precincts, there to continue plying their infamous trades, became alarmed. But here, with a serious crisis at hand, the Korean Ministers, acting with commendable zeal, proved adequate to the occasion. They utilized every means within their power to prevent, through pacific and conciliatory measures, the uncertain fate into which the King had plunged the nation.

2

On July 16, 1907, the Tokyo Government decided to take definitive action in Korea. Viscount Hayashi, the negotiator of the Anglo-Japanese alliance and now Minister of Foreign Affairs, left for Seoul with the object of executing certain mandates the precise nature of which was withheld from public knowledge pending a consultation with Ito. When announcement of his departure from Japan was made, the Korean Ministers endeavored to obtain from Ito, who was assumed to have been previously informed, the probable nature of the plans of the Tokyo Government and to seek his counsel respecting the most desirable course to pursue.

Ito declined to make any premature declaration. Nor did he render the advice sought. He believed, and rightly, that whatever individual action he might choose to take during this critical period must necessarily be remedial and as such would later be construed as involving a punitive intent—as seizing a convenient pretext for yielding to the harsher policy of his colleagues.

Thus the Ministers, compelled to act on their own initiative without guidance or restraint from the Resident-General, now faced the realization that one of two possible courses must be adopted. They must either submit with penitent meekness to whatever measures the Tokyo Government might decide to take, or else—proceeding on the assumption that such measures were likely to prove extremely humiliating—they must strive to prevent their adoption through some voluntary act of restitution. And the only form of restitution commensurate with the seriousness of the offense appeared to them to be the King's abdication. The King had repeatedly shown his ineptitude as a ruler, and he had repeatedly disregarded the welfare of his subjects. Hence the worldly ignominy which he must bear in renouncing his throne would not be nearly so disastrous to Korea as the loss to which the people must otherwise submit under the tightening reins of Japanese rule. The Ministers urged the King to retire in favor of the Crown Prince.

But the King would not hear of it. To yield would have been to admit his criminality. When the Ministers insisted, he waxed wrathful and contumacious. On July 18 he requested a meeting with Ito, at which he reiterated his innocence and demanded whether the Resident-General had brought pressure to bear upon the Ministers to force his abdication. Ito assured him that, not being a subject of Korea, he did not presume to dictate in any manner whatever over a question which, like that of the King's abdication, concerned the ruler and his people only. The Ministers, as far as he knew, were acting, he said, on their own responsibility and volition. He demanded, in turn, what preparations the King had made in the nature of positive remedial measures. The King admitted that he had no suggestions to offer, save to repeat the face-saving charge that the members of the delegation alone were guilty.

That evening Viscount Hayashi was expected to arrive at Seoul. His arrival would presage a number of portentous events. It would undoubtedly mark the beginning of a most humiliating era for the people of Korea. The days of hectic speculations became hours of weighty suspense. The series of crises that had developed since the first of July neared their inevitable climax.

At about five o'clock in the afternoon, barely three hours before the Viscount's arrival, the Ministers assembled for the last time before the King to explain with an array of invincible facts that nothing short of abdication could now save Korea. The King still refused to budge. The Ministers then resorted to a boldness and an audacity which under circumstances less pressing would have been the height of indelicacy and perhaps of treason itself......

The train bearing Hayashi steamed impressively into the South Gate Station. Suddenly the King showed signs of relenting. He summoned the Elder Statesmen and sought their opinion. These men, all former reactionaries, were likewise agreed that for him there was no other alternative. He had come, it was evident, to the end of his tether. Baffled, defeated, miserably alone, he is said to have contemplated the utter darkness of the moonless night. Then, with an enigmatic look on his mask-like face, he capitulated.

3

"In abdicating my throne,"* his announcement of this fact to Ito and, incidentally, to the world at large, read, "I acted in obedience to the dictates of my conviction; my action was not the result of any outside advice or pressure. During the past ten years I have had an intention to cause the Crown Prince to conduct the affairs of state, but, no opportunity presenting itself, my intention has to this day remained unrealized. Believing, however, that such opportunity has now arrived, I have abdicated in favor of the Crown Prince. In taking this step I have followed a natural order of things, and its consummation is a matter of congratulation for the sake of my dynasty and country."

But though his attempt at face-saving was transparently futile, there was consistency at least in his general attitude. Earlier in the day, when the fact of his abdication was published in the official gazette, one thousand loyal Koreans had gathered in the vicinity of the Kwang-song Gate to make public demonstrations of their protest. Infuriated over the action of the Ministers and sullenly resentful of the Resident-General, who was suspected of having precipitated their decision, these rioters proceeded on a mission of murder, destruction, and vindictive incendiarism. The ex-King, touching upon this phase of the problem, wrote: "I am grieved to have to observe that some of my ignorant subjects, laboring under a mistaken conception of my motives and an access of wanton indignation, may be betrayed into acts of violence. In reliance, therefore,

*From "In Korea With Marquis Ito," by G.T. Ladd, LL.D.

upon the Resident-General, I entrust him with the power of preventing or suppressing such acts of violence."*

With the restoration of public order Ito disclosed for the first time his plans for the future control of Korean affairs. These were formulated following a series of conferences with Viscount Hayashi and only after the most careful consideration had been given the circumstances attending the recent revolutionary events, together with their probable effects upon the future cooperative possibilities between the Resident-General and the Korean Ministry. Thus they represented something close to a compromise between his habitually moderate views and the strong aggressive policy favored by the Tokyo Government. No punitive measures were involved. Nor was there even the semblance of annexation, such as the Korean Ministers and even the outer world had regarded as imminent, hinted at. True, Ito's faith in the sincerity of the nation he was sacrificing much to uplift had been severely shaken; but even if voluntary restitution as conceived in the King's abdication had not been made, his plans would not have been rendered any less conducive to Korea's ultimate redemption. Nor would he have given his assent to any harsher suggestions from his own government. As long as he remained at the helm, Korea was assured of a genuine friend, though a firm and forthright reformer, regardless of how refractory she proved to be on occasions.

His plans consisted merely in bringing Korea's internal administration, in addition to her diplomatic affairs, under the rigid control of the Resident-General. They provided (1) that the Korean Government should follow the direction of the Resident-General respecting administrative reforms; (2) that the Korean Government should first obtain the approval of the Resident-General when enacting any law or adopting any important administrative measure; (3) that Korea's judicial affairs should be differentiated from the regular administrative affairs; (4) that all official appointements should be made subject to the approval of the Resident-General.

The significant point was that these provisions were de-

*From "In Korea With Marquis Ito" by G.T. Ladd, LL.D.

signed specifically for "the early attainment of the prosperity and strength of Korea" and "the speedy promotion of the welfare of the Korean people." The principle conveyed by the stipulation made in the convention of November, 1905, namely, that Korea's right to direct her own affairs would be restored to her on the day she showed her fitness again to exercise the powers temporarily intrusted to the Resident-General, was still tacitly acknowledged. These provisions were made the subject of a new convention which, having after a number of conferences received the approval of the youthful King, Yi, and his Ministers, was signed on July 24, 1907.

This placed Korea under the full protectorate of Japan. Japan, for her part, was now required to offer full military as well as diplomatic and administrative assistance. There being no further need for Korea's standing army, it was formally disbanded by a decree endorsed by the young successor to the throne; and the money which would otherwise have been spent for its maintenance was diverted to channels of industrial activity.

In assuming these additional responsibilities Japan did not, however, wrote Ito, "violate" Korea's independence. She merely *suspended* it. And in justifying this act he pointed out that it was he himself, to be specific, who first proposed to recognize her independence and Japan herself who, adopting his suggestion, secured it for her by releasing her from Chinese suzerainty. This gave Japan the right, during a period of emergency which threatened her own security, to hold it in trust, and to restore it to her when those conditions which created the emergency improved. "It is said that Japan has done this from questionable motives," he declared, "but the truth is that she did so because it became inevitable from the standpoint of her national safety." Consider, he said, the "gigantic forces" of the world. No matter how powerful a country might be, it could not, through its own efforts alone, safeguard the peace of the whole world. It could only preserve the peace of particular regions. This was precisely why alliances between nations were deemed a universal necessity, and why Japan could not positively permit Korea to be on terms of hostility with her. "By no means, however, will she resort to uncivilized or inhuman measures which can only mean the prostration of Korea. On the contrary, she earnestly hopes that Korea may prosper and progress. And in order that she may expand and grow, Japan will approve of any conceivable methods she may choose to adopt, with but one proviso, namely, that Korea must always make common cause with Japan." Touching on the expressed fear of the Koreans that Japan's principal motive was imperialism, he said: "*There is no necessity for Japan to annex Korea. Korea by all means should have self-government.* But without Japan's guidance and supervision she cannot adequately achieve self-government. That is why the present treaty has been concluded."

It must be remembered that Ito, in 1907, was confronted with serious realities, not with the working out of theories. Japan had fought two defensive wars for Korea's protection, and each time she had been cheated out of her legitimate claims. What was more, the conditions which had brought on those wars had not improved, nor did they seem ever likely to improve under the status quo; and the only permanent safeguard her leaders could conceive, which would justify the enormous sacrifices already made, was the outright absorption of Korea. Ito's specific problem was to ward off this stroke of imperialism, however justified. He had succeeded in compelling his colleagues in Tokyo to meet him half way, and it was now the duty of the Koreans, if they had any appreciation of the imminence of their doom, to meet *him* half way. This was the alternative.

CHAPTER XVII
THE ACID TEST

I

On August 11, 1907, Ito left Seoul for a visit to Japan, there to confer with his government. His object, notwithstanding the suspicion of the Koreans, was simply a matter of fulfiling certain routine tasks of importance. For the full protectorate made possible for the first time a free development of Korea's internal administration under the guidance of the Resident-General, and this necessitated the securing of assistance from Japan in the form of loans and experts in all the technical aspects of government which went under the name of public welfare and of public improvements. His mission, moreover, was one which required not only a genius for organization, but a marked aptitude as well for developing the latent capacities of the Koreans themselves—for establishing harmony and cooperation within practicable limits, no less than for furnishing progressive leadership. "Korea's needs today," he said, "are money and leadership. She has, however, no capitalist of note. There are many men of noble lineage but practically all of them are in penurious circumstances. The average Korean's ambition is to become a government official, for officialdom begets wealth and advantages, whereas to be out of it breeds grievances and discontent. The conditions here are such that to create a new administration will require men conscious of their responsibilities and possessed of a great determination. But if Japanese are appointed to the service, it will mean widespread hardship, for it will deprive the Korean officials of their only means of existence. Here lies my difficulty."

Arriving at the Japanese capital on the 20th, he received a tremendous ovation in which the officials and the populace combined to extend the nation's welcome to its returning hero in a most spontaneous and unrestrained manner. It was the courage and the unselfish devotion with which he had fared

forth, at his advanced age, upon the dangerous mission of up-
lifting a hostile, benighted race, no less than the high quality
of his work, which won for him the unstinted applause of his
people. The Emperor, whose appreciation was equally as
ardent, elevated him to the Princedom, the highest Imperial
reward within reach of a Japanese subject. Thereafter it was
"Prince Ito," the idol of Japan, the greatest of her public servants.

But much of that optimism which was once so characteristic
of his hopes for Korea was now gone. The treachery of the
ex-King and the continued resistance interposed by the palace
politicians and the local officials, despite his liberal and humanitarian programme, had exacted their inexorable tolls. At
a reception tendered him by the city of Tokyo on September
14 he said: "Though the situation in Korea, as well as her
future, embraces some measure of hope, I regret that in view
of the perturbation which still exists as a result of the intrigues
and popular agitations of past years, it is impossible for me to
make any predictions at the present time. One thing, however, must be said. It seems to me extremely doubtful whether
a complete orientation of her present state of affairs can be
effected and a national policy formulated."

Elaborating the basic causes which made progress supremely
difficult, he continued: "In my attempts to rehabilitate the
country by bringing her administrative and diplomatic functions under the guidance of Japan, by rescuing her from an
affliction of several centuries' duration, and by directing her to
the ranks of civilized nations, I do not infer that her people
are decadent, or that they do not grasp the genuineness of our
sincerity. Nevertheless they are incapable of accomplishing
any reforms on their own initiative. Further, they do not
take kindly to any act of guidance on the part of others. Hence
there is no assurance that they will not, in the future, rise in
opposition to our regime. Should such an eventuality come
to pass, it would not be a case of destruction from without but
of extinction from within. I fear that such a time might come.
Certainly this is not in accord with the wishes of our ruler,
nor of our people, toward the Koreans. Even so, in my excess

of solicitude I fear that events might assume an aspect contrary
to expectations.   Thus it is my desire to strive to the fullest
limits of my power to induce them to rectify the error of their
ways, to foster them, to teach them, to let them bask in the
benevolent rays of our ruler's good will.   If, through some
desperate action on their part, our scheme should meet with
failure, the consequences may be unavoidable but at any rate
contrary, from the outset, to our wishes.   I shall continue, in
all sincerity, with the same principles by which I have been
guided to this day, thus to fulfill the full measure of our responsibilities.   I feel apprehensively of the future, but in any
case the difficulties are almost insurmountable, and I shall look
for support and cooperation from the government and the people of Japan."

His contemplated improvement projects for Korea were without exception given unanimous approval at a joint meeting of
the Cabinet and the Privy Council.   Among these was a provision for the appointment of an Assistant Resident-General to
aid him in the performance of his enlarged duties.   Viscount
Soné, the man who held the portfolio of Justice in his third
Cabinet, was selected for this post.   With the preliminaries
thus accomplished, Ito returned to Seoul with the new ap-
pointee early in October to inaugurate a yet more extensive
programme of reconstruction.

His attention was meanwhile directed to another channel,
for two weeks later Crown Prince Yoshihito of Japan paid a
good-will visit to Korea.   Ito at once exploited this opportunity to its fullest extent to strengthen the special ties which
now linked the two royal Houses.   Partly as a result of this
friendly mission, but more especially in consequence of the
great influence exerted by Ito through his wisdom, his humanity, and his cheerful labors, the young King of Korea decided to
give Prince Ri, his son and heir, the advantages of a modern
education befitting the future ruler of Korea, such as the
schools of Japan afforded.   This singular apprenticeship was
to be served under Ito's personal supervision.   The responsibility of training the young heir for the arduous rôle of ruling
a benighted race, upon whose ultimate strength or weakness

depended the peace of the Far East, was thus placed in Ito's hands. Satisfied that this decision was for the best interests of Korea, he took his princely protégé to Tokyo and placed him in the Peers' School.

Returning again to Seoul, he plunged at once into the voluminous work for which he had so laboriously planned. Within a year, with the aid of a corps of experts, he revolutionized the Korean judicial system. The medieval monstrosity reeking with bribery and corruption was displaced by a modern institution based upon Japan's judicial organization. This consisted of an imposing array of houses of justice, including 113 subdistrict courts in as many towns and cities, 8 district courts in such regions as were deemed eminently representative, 3 appeal courts in three of the largest cities, and 1 court of cassation (supreme court) in Seoul. Until the Koreans could produce men of qualified abilities to preside over these courts, and until such time as their impecunious government could afford to meet the financial burdens which they imposed, Japan, through her Resident-General, undertook to provide for their administrative personnel and for their maintenance. Aside from such laws and ordinances as were specially prescribed in existing agreements, the people of Korea were given the benefit of the newly-codified laws of their own land.

2

Despite these many blessings the Koreans, with the exception of the newly-enthroned King and his Ministers, persisted in opposing, in obstructing, in resisting Ito's administration. To them all such efforts at modernization were both repugnant and intolerable. Repugnant because they represented the innovations of a foreign intruder; intolerable because they led inevitably to the abolishment of those ancient practices under which they had so long enjoyed a peculiarly satisfying freedom —a freedom suggestive of utter decadence but suited most admirably to their national temperament. As the improvements progressed and the opportunities for indulging in their corrupt pastimes became correspondingly less, their smouldering resentment turned to burning hostility. With the completion of each unit, this hostility was galvanized into action. It culminated in a series of spasmodic riots, revealing only too clearly the hopeless irreconcilability between the aims of Ito, however humanitarian in concept, and the desires of the Koreans. It was the same old tragedy, repeatedly experienced, in all places, in all ages: the tragedy of the strong forcing the weak to accept his philosophy of government, of defense, of well-being. The strong lacked patience and the weak intelligence.

Nevertheless Ito believed that if the proper contact with the people were established, they might still be persuaded, through sheer enlightenment, to believe in the desirability of his reforms. He decided to create this contact by organizing a personal tour of the King throughout the realm. Such a tour was without precedent in Korea's history. It would constitute an indubitable manifestation of the King's love and solicitude for his subjects. He would himself accompany the King. *He would thus demonstrate the spirit of cooperation existing between himself and the King.* Together they would attempt, each in the manner most suited to his particular position, to win the good will of the people.

The King, when the proposition was presented to him for his consideration, gave his immediate assent. Unlike his royal father, he had been an early convert to Ito's doctrine of modernity. Though he was not particularly gifted with a strong will and intelligence, he was nevertheless possessed of sufficient knowledge of his country's affairs to understand the fundamental weaknesses inherent in her national life; and he was more than willing to rely upon Ito's indefatigable efforts at redemption.

Accordingly, on January 4, 1909, the King, accompanied by Ito and a magnificent entourage, departed from Seoul on this extraordinary tour. Throughout the southern provinces they were given a most enthusiastic reception. Ito, in his numerous speeches delivered at the principal cities, denied the widespread imputation that Japan's policy in Korea was one of hypocrisy and dissimulation. Her constant aim, he pointed out, was not, as it had been so often maliciously presumed, to destroy Korea's political entity through sinister efforts concealed in gestures of pretended altruism, but to promote the genuine prosperity and happiness of her people. The ancients, he said, solved their problems of aggrandizement through conquest and confiscation and regarded their exploits in the light of splendid heroism. The tendency in the modern age was its very antithesis. Only through cooperation, through joint action beween nations in which the stronger lent its support to the weak and the weak benefited by this assistance, could peace in their respective spheres be effectually maintained. Were Japan bent upon conquest, she would not, he explained, undertake to *strengthen* Korea through the introduction of enlightened institutions and modern industrial methods. Nor would she take particular pains in securing the *good will* of the Koreans or in assisting their ruler to guide them to the path of virtue.

Between the King of Korea and the Emperor of Japan there was not, he said, the slightest cause of suspicion. Their friendship was, in fact, bound by an understanding so close and serene that not even the ordinary ties of brotherhood could surpass it. This cordiality, moreover, was being particularly strengthened in the course of the tour by a constant interchange of telegraphic messages of sympathy and assurance. Such a relationship, it was obvious, could hardly exist were it not for the fact that there was perfect confidence between them. These, he said, ought to be self-evident proofs of sincerity.

"Today Japan's only request of Korea," he said, "is that she discard her ancient practices, encourage her people to aspire for knowledge and industry, bestow upon them the same blessings of civilization which the people of Japan enjoy, and make common cause with Japan. It stands to reason that were she to ally herself with Japan, their combined strength would conduce so much more to the protection of the Far East. This constitutes Japan's sincere aspiration in Korea."

No untoward incident occurred to mar this visit. Whatever animosity the people harbored against the protectorate, and against Ito's regime in particular, was discreetly suppressed, presumably in deference to their King.

The tour was completed in nine days. It was considered a

splendid success, and the gratifying results which it accomplished encouraged both Ito and the King to repeat their exploits throughout the northern provinces without delay.

But here they were doomed to a crushing disappointment. The northerners, due apparently to their relatively isolated status and consequently their ignorance of the material benefits accruing daily under Ito's redemptive measures, differed radically from their southern brethren. They greeted Ito's speeches with demonstrations of vengeful discourtesy. Everywhere, save among the more responsible groups, he was made to feel the deep resentment of the natives against himself, against Japan, against what they conceived to be an unwarranted intrusion upon their national affairs.

Meanwhile In Sun-jun, the Home Minister, and a member of the King's entourage, strenuously objected to the tour. He had become an insistent advocate of annexation, not because he recognized its desirability, but because in his opinion Korea had already surrendered to Japan every vestige of sovereignty, which rendered it futile to pretend any further that she was in reality anything but a dependency. All this show of kingly solicitude, all this blare of benevolence, seemed to him merely a gigantic farce. He showered Ito with exhortations. He created a dangerous dissension among those most closely associated with the work of national uplift at a moment when the lowest ebb had been reached. Rather than continue with this "farce," he resigned from the Ministry en route, took his departure from Korean soil, and proceeded to Japan, where he undertook to make himself heard.

The tour of the north thus ended in a dismal failure. Ito returned to Seoul an extremely disappointed man, a man smitten to the very depths of his soul by the pangs of Korean ingratitude. Within a week, after placing in Viscount Sone's hands the complete management of the residency-general, he left Seoul for Japan, never again to return in the capacity in which he had served Korea for three laborious years.

This decision was pregnant with dramatic significance. It meant that the man who had stood persistently for the integrity of Korea had at last lost faith in the sincerity of the Korean people. It marked the turning point in Korea's dark history of intrigues and resistance to progress. It afforded the Katsura regime the long-awaited opportunity to prepare the way for annexation.

In a way Ito quit entirely too soon. Three years of redemptive work, no matter how intensive, could not have possibly elicited from the Koreans that response and that cooperation which alone would have ultimately precluded the necessity of annexation. But it seems reasonable to suppose that he would have resigned from the resident-generalship before long in any event, despite the ingratitude of the Koreans. To a man of his distinguished status in the political life of Japan, three years was much too long a period to devote to the dubious work of tutoring a benighted race, especially in a spot so far removed from the beaten tracks of civilization. Others must carry on where he had left off. For at the hub of the Japanese universe there were innumerable other problems affecting more vitally the foreign affairs of his country which required his close personal scrutiny.

CHAPTER XVIII
THE HARBIN TRAGEDY

I

Though he had ceased his uplift work for Korea, Ito remained the same well-wisher of the Koreans. He revisited Seoul for a brief unofficial sojourn to bid farewell to King Yi and his Ministers. In his subsequent speeches delivered on a lecture tour of his own country he continued to stress the fact that harmony between the two countries was an indispensable factor in the preservation of peace in the Far East. Wherever he went on this mission of enlightenment and peace, he took with him the twelve-year old Crown Prince of Korea, whose education had been placed in his hands, both for the purpose of giving him the benefit of an early contact with the Japanese and of offering the latter the opportunity to develop a friendly regard for the welfare of the Korean royalty.

His declining days were the busiest of his extraordinarily busy life. Though weighted with sixty-nine years of incessant labor, his body was still blessed with the vigor of his prime. His mind was alert; it had never ceased to function with that singular precision and that indomitable sobriety which were his greatest attributes. Everywhere he turned, he observed the bustling evidences of modernity. Within fifty years Japan had emerged from the somnolent depths of medieval obscurity and achieved a measure of success in matters political, military and industrial, which was little short of miraculous, and which enabled her, after two defensive wars, to take her place among the preeminent Powers of the earth.

He reviewed the part he had played in this memorable drama. The modesty characteristic of men of his race would not permit him to assume any credit, however deserving, for individual feats. Nevertheless he was satisfied that he had not been remiss in his manifest duties to his Emperor and country. His life throughout his career had been in constant peril of assassination, for his foes, like his admirers, were legion.

He had not satisfied everyone with his moderate tactics, with his perennial advocacy of peaceful measures. Certainly the radicals and the militarists, the two extremist groups, could observe nothing but opprobrium in his conduct during the period of his greatest influence. Had it not been, however, for his particular qualities of leadership, Japan would have lost her equilibrium in the inordinate zest for hastening the attainment of political liberty and international prestige. The result would have been disastrous. Perhaps, at a later date, when she had become measurably secure in her new position as a world Power, she might move forward with a greater acceleration of speed. But after forty-two years of public service, he was still firm in the belief that the most desirable policy was one dedicated to righteousness, to rational progress, to peace.

His private life had been almost always overshadowed by the spectre of weighty responsiblities of state looming ponderously over his realm of consciousness. So much so, that with the exception of a few months in the year spent irregularly in his seaside villa at Oiso, there was precious little opportunity for relaxation or for those affectionate indulgences in domestic affairs which constitute the quintessence of a blissful life. Like all privileged men of his race, he had made the rounds of the various inns where wine, women and the noisy twang of the *shamisen* served to conjure up that delectable freedom of oblivion for one brief night. But those houses of dissipation, evil as they undoubtedly were, had served in many instances as the only safe retreat for the deliberation of important affairs of state. Most of the significant decisions respecting the early developments of the reconstruction period had been reached over the wine cups in those sumptuous quarters, securely sheltered by the camouflage they afforded from the attacks of murderous critics. The life of a political leader during those formative years was thus a precarious gamble, existing from day to day without any semblance of assurances for the future. Such men were optimists of the first water, not so much by temperament as by force of circumstances, who ate, drank, and served the state with cheerful selflessness, for there was no telling what the morrow might bring. And perhaps the greatest of these opti-

mistic sinners who sinned through love of country as well as
ephemeral pleasures of the flesh was Ito himself.

A furious smoker, an inveterate drinker, and an inordinate
lover of beautiful women, his had been the gay, cheerful life
whenever he had found the time for Bacchanalian pursuits.
His reputation as the Japanese equivalent of the gay Lothario
was only surpassed by his fame as a carver of governments.
Nevertheless—and this is significant—he is once reported to
have said that the only notable difference between himself and
his reputedly virtuous colleagues was that, whereas his friends
went about their business in a quiet, unobtrusive way, seducing
maid-servants and other men's wives, he, on the other hand,
enjoyed his fun in the bright public spotlight, showering his
affections on none but professional *geisha* girls.

He was often seen, this illustrious leader who had ripened
into a great and lovable commoner, dressed in a simple *kimono*
and swopping yarns with the humble fisherfolk of Oiso.   A
great talker, with a ribald sense of humor, and a keen relish
for the reminiscences of the past, he recounted the many
tight fixes in which he, as a rebel and adventurer, had often
found himself in his youth.   He spoke of them with the cheerful gusto of a born story teller, living over his many embarrass-
ments and enjoying it hugely.

2

No sooner had he returned from his lecture tour than he
busied himself with preparations for embarking upon yet another mission.   It was to be decidedly the most significant one
of his varied career.   Furthermore, it was designed to be the
first of a *series* of missions embracing a vital international import to be undertaken for his country.   How urgent this sudden
burst of increased activity on his part was may be realized
when it is stated that Japan's post-war conduct in Manchuria
had precipitated fresh disagreements which threatened to involve her in serious difficulties, not only with a reawakened
China, but with two great nations who alone among the Western Powers had supported her throughout her conflict with
Russia—the United States and Great Britain.

His first declarations of policy regarding Manchuria were enunciated in a measure he submitted to a joint meeting of the Elder Statesmen and the Cabinet Ministers under Premier Saionji called, at his request, on May 22, 1906.*

The defense of Korea, in his opinion, constituted a problem of life or death to Japan, but the only conceivable interest she could entertain in Manchuria was one of creating a military and commercial hegemony, with Port Arthur and the South Manchurian Railway as the respective bases of operation. Nor would the Western Powers having some commercial stakes in this region look favorably upon any move which tended, through military intervention, to nullify the policy of the open door and the principle of equal opportunity.

Within six months following the consummation of the Portsmouth and Peking treaties, the Japanese, he pointed out in a speech delivered before the assembled leaders, had received, both privately and officially, severe notes of protest, notably from the United States. In Great Britain the question had even assumed Parliamentary importance. "At the time," he said, "I felt considerable anxiety over this state of affairs, for it constituted not merely a diplomatic problem for Japan alone, but possessed grave possibilities as well for creating, indirectly, an unfortunate effect upon Korea. Should Japan, through her activities in Manchuria, invite criticisms from the various Powers and denunciatory attacks from the foreign press, the Koreans, who have by no means become completely reconciled with our government and who are in fact in that condition of mind which will eagerly seek to disrupt Japan's political policy, are more than likely to enter into intrigues with Russia and devise various measures of a highly illusory character."

Typical of the protests from the Western Powers was a letter from Ambassador Macdonald, who represented the British Government in Tokyo. This letter, which was presumably of an unofficial nature but confessedly intended for Ito's personal perusal, stated (1) that Japan, through her military activities in Manchuria, had closed this region to foreign trade even

*The details of this debate which follow are taken from "Ito Hirobumi Hiroku," pp. 392–404. See Bibliographical Note.

more thoroughly than did the Russians under the pre-war regime; (2) that the merchants of the United States and of Great Britain had been particularly discriminated against; (3) that for Japan thus to estrange the two countries which had assisted her morally and financially during her conflict with Russia was patently unwise; (4) that the principal reason why the two countries had supported her then was because she had championed the principle of the open door; (5) that while it might be a necessary policy for Japan to proceed with preparations in Manchuria in order to provide against a possible revival of Russian exploitation, at the same time she would be certain to lose the sympathy of the two Powers and perhaps suffer serious handicaps in her future wars should she herself persist in exploiting this region for her own exclusive benefit.

"Upon receiving this protest," Ito said, "my apprehension for the future of Japan increased. Meanwhile telegraphic reports emanating from Europe pointed out repeatedly that Japan was actually preparing for another war with Russia; that she regarded the Portsmouth treaty merely as a temporary armistice. This report was given credence in Peking, where the Russo-Chinese negotiations were purposely delayed, and Russia postponed the evacuation of her troops. Thus it became increasingly apparent that the situation in the Far East was developing into an extremely difficult impasse." It was subsequently revealed, he explained, that this "so-called revenge propaganda" had had its origin in Japan—that it had been manufactured by her military leaders to further their own ends—thus making the situation, as far as he could perceive, worse confounded.

General Yamagata meanwhile wrote to him, attributing the difficulties encountered with regard to Manchuria to a disagreement between the military officials and the Japanese Foreign Office and explaining Premier Saionji's contemplated tour of inspection of this troubled region. This explanation, however, instead of offering extenuating reasons for the activities of the military leaders, seemed to place the blame on the diplomatic division of the government, which was presumed to be ignorant of the actual conditions.

From China proper came further dispatches, Ito explained,

indicating that Yuan Shih Kai was considerably aroused by Japan's attitude; that he regarded her conduct in Manchuria as constituting a breach of the Peking treaty. "Were we," said Ito, "to pursue the present course Japan is bound to incur the enmity, not only of the people of North China, but of the whole twenty-one provinces. My opinion is that Japan's attitude toward China should always be that of a friend and adviser. China's present conditions reveal that her people are by no means blessed with peace and contentment. Many of them are advocating the recovery of their country's rights and prestige, and it would be a grave mistake to treat this movement with contempt. Westerners regard it lightly as an expression of anti-foreignism, but by whatever name one chooses to characterize it, the fact remains that the ultimate effects of such a movement will be the same. And from whatever premise one makes the observation, the only desirable situation in China so far as Japan is concerned is one which is free from agitations of any sort. Hence it follows that the most fitting policy for Japan to pursue is one which is least likely to arouse the hostility of the Chinese." Thus, when a man of the calibre of Yuan Shih Kai who, above all China's leading statesmen, professed the friendliest regard for Japan, voiced such a protest, the consequences were not likely, he said, to prove in any way palatable to Japan.

"At present," Ito continued, elaborating his measure, "we maintain a military government in Manchuria. By scrutinizing its provisions and regulations, one realizes at once that it is only natural the Chinese should feel resentful. No one would interpose objections if Japan were merely attempting to preserve that which Russia has assigned to her. But in reality she is proceeding beyond the limits of her rights. If our military authorities should fully carry out their contemplated schedule, the Chinese would be deprived of every opportunity for legitimate activity. Our authorities may have conscientiously considered their course of action from the outset, but nevertheless I strongly believe that our whole system of military government in Manchuria must be abolished at once. When this has been done, Manchuria must revert to the civil rule of the Chinese, for the responsibilities involved in the protection of the lives of the people of this region and the administration of their government are rightly China's." Should China prove incapable of functioning as the responsible government, Japan, he said, would perhaps be justified in rendering the necessary assistance.

"There is something about which I wish to speak very plainly," he cautioned, "in order that we may arrive at a clearer understanding of the situation. I give this warning because what I have to say may not be fully in accord with the views of our military colleagues; it may even ruffle their feelings in the matter. The members of our staff in Manchuria, judging from information which I have gathered from various sources whose authenticity I cannot doubt, seem to be laboring under the impression that inasmuch as the period of evacuation has been extended to eighteen months, it would be perfectly in order for them to take such measures until April of next year (1907) which are permissible under war-time conditions. Proceeding upon this basis, they are apparently engaged in various pursuits, such as the exploitation of industries and the imposition of duties. For them to take such action when, as a matter of fact, they should actually be evacuating now; when they should merely retain the railway guards; when the province of Antung should be opened to international trade on May 1; and when even Mukden should likewise be opened on June 1, is something which it is extremely difficult for me to understand. Not only do I believe that our military activities and the real situation existing in Manchuria are clearly incompatible, but according to the protests of foreign governments, all foreign goods destined for Dairen through the ports of Shanghai and Chefoo, are subject to duties imposed under the Chinese coastwise tariff, whereas Japanese goods are permitted to enter free of duty into Dairen, thus creating a discrimination in the treatment of their respective goods. Our Foreign Office, in replying to these protests, faces an embarrassing dilemma."

Thus was his measure, which suggested the immediate restoration of a normal peace-time regime in Manchuria at the close of the Russo-Japanese war, and the enforcement of the principle of the open door, presented to the veteran Tokyo council. Those supporting him in that memorable conference in 1906 were Count Inouye, Elder Statesman, and Foreign Minister Hayashi, who constituted, with Ito, the civilian leaders and hence the liberal voice of Japan. Opposed to him were the military group, to whom Japan's hegemony was the paramount consideration in the maintenance of Far Eastern peace. They included the great Yamagata; General Kodama, Chief of the General Staff; General Katsura, former Premier; Terauchi, Minister, of War; and Admiral Yamamoto, founder of the Japanese navy. Between these opposing groups stood Premier Saionji, Ito's successor as head of the Seiyukai party. (Field Marshal Oyama, Navy Minister Makoto Saito, Finance Minister Sakatani, and Matsukata, advisor to the Privy Council, refrained from active participation in the debate.)

But however great his offiicial solicitude for Korea, for China, for world opinion, which lent moral authority to his measure, Ito was not, at the time, an active member of the Ministry, then regarded as the only logical body to shape the policy of the nation; and this fact was at once seized upon by the military leaders as their basis of attack.

"What I first desire to know," began Admiral Yamamoto, "is what precisely is the opinion of the *Government* toward Manchuria. The Army and Navy merely carry out the will of the Government. Whether their regular peace-time conduct in any way differs from their mode of action in time of war need not be argued here. Suffice it to say that the necessary limits within which the Army and Navy should confine their activities must be fixed by the Government, which is the truly representative body of the nation."

General Katsura said: "Our military staff is facing some difficulty because of the *absence* of a definite Government policy. As soon as the Government decides upon a course of action for the Army, our men will assuredly strive to act within the limits of their authority. Let us not, therefore, discriminate between the military and the civil. Let us decide upon that policy."

Yamagata wound up the arguments of his colleagues: "I

agree with Admiral Yamamoto that the measure under consideration being Marquis Ito's, we cannot regard it as representing the sense of the Government. Let us first hear what the Government has to say."

"On general principles," Premier Saionji declared, "we are in agreement with the present measure."

"As a matter of argument," put in Elder Statesman Inouye, "it is clear that there is no apparent disagreement. As a matter of *fact*, however, the actions of our military are contrary to the will of the Government. Therein lies the source of our trouble."

Here Yamagata displayed the supremely realistic bent of the military-minded. "After all," he said, "the present measure does not constitute an important matter. If War Minister Terauchi and Chief of Staff Kodama should go over the matter carefully, I do not doubt that the matter can be settled easily."

The Premier, urged by Admiral Yamamoto to state his own views, said: "The Government must earnestly carry out the terms of the treaty with China. At the same time it is demanded that preparations be not overlooked for a possible return match with Russia. The spirit of our men in Manchuria cannot be ignored; in fact the Government adheres to the same spirit. Still, though Japan has not yet committed any breach of the agreement with China, if the Peking treaty cannot be enforced, the Government will find itself in a serious quandary. If because of this we should incur the criticism of the Powers, the situation would become really serious. I feel, therefore, that with the cooperation of the present political leaders of this country, we should, here and now, decide upon a fixed policy. ...... As to the present measure I have not yet given it a thorough study, my attention having been called to it for the first time last evening. The fact is, however, that our men at the front are exerting themselves with due diligence, though I feel that perhaps they are going a little beyond the limits of what the central (civil) authority has been considering."

This placed the burden of responsibility upon Chief of Staff Kodama, the man who was immediately responsible for the state of affairs in Manchuria. Confronted with the inescapable, Kodama denied vigorously that the situation was so serious as Ito had described it. With facile verisimilitude he described the peculiar difficulties with which he and his staff had been confronted. He strove to justify the course he had taken by "passing the buck" to the Tokyo Foreign Office which, because of its dilatory tactics, he said, should alone be held accountable for the long delay in lifting the war-time ban throughout the occupied areas. Particularly did he endeavor to show that the Foreign Office staff displayed little willingness to cooperate with his "administration" in the formulation of a *modus operandi* for the opening of Antung province. Wherever the military administrative offices possessed no jurisdiction, the Japanese consular agents should, he said, take the necessary action, but until the Foreign Office specified in unmistakable terms their respective spheres of activity, it was impossible to clarify matters.

Here Ito, in order to disprove the General's statement, quoted for his information from a published summary of military instructions regarding Manchuria, wherein the military offices were definitely instructed to undertake the civil administration of this region precisely as though it were a conquered territory.

The Chief of Staff declared that with the appointment of Japanese consular agents to assume the civil responsibilities, military intervention would become unnecessary.

"Our consular agents," Ito replied, "have no power over administrative affairs. They merely represent our commercial and industrial interests."

War Minister Terauchi came to the General's rescue: "It is not the purpose of this meeting to discuss such trivial details. Our difficulty lies merely in the fact that whereas the National Government is contending for the restoration of a peace-time regime, our Manchurian Administration is being conducted on a war-time basis. The Kwantung Government was created during the war, but if it is made to conform to a peace-time basis the problem will be solved. In other words, up to now it has been under the rule of the Army General Staff, and it merely remains for us to transfer its command to a representative of the National Government. Moreover, under General Kodama's administration the various steps to reduce it to a peace-time basis are being carried out, and it is only a question of time before a complete adjustment will have been made."

Ito next tried moral suasion. "Since," he said, "with the return of peace, the evacuation of our troops has been accomplished......our remaining task is simply to retain the Kwantung garrison and fifteen railway guards to each kilometer. The province of Antung should therefore revert to the civil rule of the Chinese. In reality, however, our military administrative offices are still functioning, so that many foreigners accuse Japan of harboring territorial ambitions, and the people of China are loudly denouncing our actions. Our authorities must consequently undertake appropriate steps to bring about harmony and mutual understanding with all concerned."

"Mutual understanding," Terauchi replied, "may be necessary at all times, but the usual procedures must be followed throughout."

The military leaders, speaking all at once, here agreed that the reduction of the Manchurian "administration" to a peace-time basis would solve the problem. "Wherever consular offices are established, the military sub-offices should be abolished," said Yamagata, "otherwise there will be unavoidable conflicts." He added: "Let the commander of the garrison take charge of the whole administration—that will be sufficient." The War Minister concluded: "It would be difficult to discuss each phase of Marquis Ito's measure at this gathering. On general principles, however, I approve of it."

"It won't do to say that you agree on general principles," Ito declared. "If an agreement is reached, appropriate steps must be taken to carry out the measure."

Count Inouye suggested: "How about referring it to the committee on Manchuria?"

"That won't do either." Ito preferred direct action. "That committee is not concerned with military affairs. Some other course must be followed. If appropriate steps are not taken our Foreign Office will never be able to take positive action." The alternative would not be pleasant: "We should particularly be cautious over the fact that in the United States public opinion is a powerful influence, and once it is aroused, no matter how friendly the Government may be toward Japan, it will be compelled to adopt such measures as the public may demand."

General Kodama was recalcitrant. "Those who bear no direct responsibilities can proceed as they will," he said, "but those who *do* shoulder such responsibilities cannot proceed in so careless a fashion. To name one instance, were we to return the administrative authority to the Chinese, these people would not be likely to give any consideration to the creation of sanitary facilities, and as a result epidemics would break out and our troops would suffer."

"No foreign Power," Foreign Minister Hayashi replied, "would interpose objections if Japan were endeavoring merely to provide sanitary facilities."

"The future of South Manchuria," General Kodama insisted, holding fast to his intentions, "is likely to be of varied interest to Japan...... Meanwhile in our administration of this region numerous problems are sure to arise, and once they spread into the interior we shall meet with prodigious difficulties in trying to settle them. Moreover, the open port of Manchuria (Dairen) which is operated under the rule of Japan differs plainly from such ports as Hankow or Shanghai. Therefore, instead of placing the power of sovereignty in the hands of one individual (Yamagata had suggested the Commander of the Kwantung Garrison), I should suggest the creation of an entirely new office where all the complex problems could be centralized and handled."

Ito's rejoinder was preeminently meet: "It seems to me General Kodama and others are laboring under a fundamental misconception regarding Japan's position in Manchuria. Her rights therein cover only that portion which was assigned to her by Russia under the terms of the peace treaty, namely, the lease of the Liaotung peninsula and the railway. Over other than these she possesses no authority whatever. The phrase 'the administration of Manchuria' has been in vogue among our people ever since the war, especially among our officials and even among our merchants and businessmen. Yet Manchuria is not a dependency of our country; it is obviously a part of Imperial China.   Under the circumstances there is no justification for our exercising the rights of sovereignty within that sphere."

Premier Saionji, summarizing the arguments, resorted to this compromise: "I conclude that on general principles there is no objection to the measure under consideration.   It is decided that the Kwantung Government as well as its sub-offices shall be reorganized so as to conform to a peace-time basis."

This, let it be repeated, was in 1906 when China was still under the old Manchu regime.   Between this date and September 18, 1931, when Manchuria was violently precipitated upon its course of political independence, many significant changes took place, necessitating a candid reappraisal of the whole Chinese situation.   China in 1906 was at least a nation with a common purpose and fulfiling her destiny as a united people, however inept, however corrupt, and however oppressive her rulers and viceroys.   China in 1931 had been through a disastrous revolution.   Furthermore, this upheaval had left in its wake only a simulacrum of cherished human liberties. It left a people torn with social and political chaos, a people ruled by the cruel hands of a succession of military brigands who, separately and by means foul or fair, sought individual power, profits and prestige.   Aided and abetted by Quixotic young intellectuals of the Western school, they threatened not merely to tear up treaties with friendly foreign States, but skilfully and without benefit of diplomacy to demolish their vested interests.   Admittedly China as a nation had many just grievances against the Powers which, indubitably, deserved an early and equitable adjustment.   But the methods pursued by its leaders plunged that country inevitably into the morass of national disintegration and of international confusion.

Ito did not live to see this spectre of a pitifully disintegrating China.   In 1906 he was principally concerned with helping Imperial China to achieve order, stability and political rehabilitation within her far-flung realm.   To that end he sought to guide the policies of his own government, to temper its hard and realistic post-war policies vis-à-vis Manchuria with justice and moderation.   His motives, both as a liberal and as a patriot, were not to assist China at the sacrifice of hard-earned privileges extracted from Russia in Manchuria so much as to co-operate and to seek the cooperation of China in building up an invincible cordon of neighboring Asiatic States with common interests. For the menace to the security of the Far East came, at the time, not from within the common periphery of its component States, but from without. Nevertheless, his method of promoting peace with all the restless factors on the outside was not to meet challenge with challenge, or to maintain an attitude of collective intransigence, but to secure the harmony and good will of all on the basis of mutual respect and understanding.

3

Since then Japanese interests became solidly intrenched in Manchuria. The evacuation protocol was fulfilled according to schedule, but the loss of the Russian indemnity furnished a powerful impetus for exploiting the South Manchurian Railway to its fullest possibilities as a means of liquidating the enormous war debts; and an era of feverish development characterized by activities eliciting all manner of foreign criticism set in. Japanese merchants flocked to the great cities and seaports. A magnificent merchant marine linking the Dairen terminal of the railway with the industrial centers of Japan was created within a miraculously short space of time. Commerce prospered. Japan's geographical proximity, coupled with purely commercial advantages accruing out of an unprecedented demand for Manchurian products, such as bean cake and bean oil, and the availability of a market eminently suited to Japan's particular articles of export drove the Western—especially American and British—competitors into a peculiarly unfavorable situation. It soon developed that the increasing volume of Japanese trade necessitated the exclusive use of their railway. "So Japan traded her textiles for beans and bean-cake and established a market by barter while the other fellows were ice-bound in Newchwang and couldn't move their goods except by cart. The Americans and British frothed at the mouth, sent deputations from Chambers of Commerce and parties of business men to investigate and report on conditions, flooding Washington and Downing Street with protests against Japan's unfair use of the railway."* Charges of violation of the principle of the open door, of unfair tactics, of unethical manipulations, were hurled at the Japanese with a bitterness seldom equalled in Western journalistic history. "Here was Japan with a hornet's nest of angry American piece-goods men buzzing around her, demanding the right of equal opportunity to get their goods into the Manchurian market; with Washington shaking its finger and reminding her of her obligations under the Hay Doctrine, and an equally persistent Ally (Great Britain) who had advanced the funds to rebuild the railway and confidently expected to book the orders for equipment, but could not guarantee delivery in time to appease the trade-hungry Americans."*

The Russians in the meantime renewed their erstwhile activities in the north, notably in those regions traversed by the Chinese Eastern Railway. But the significance of the Russian resurrection was almost totally eclipsed by the amazing feats of the Japanese. China, seemingly reanimated by a vigorous movement of social and political reform which followed close on the heels of the recent reverses, threatened to assert her rights. Unable, however, to rise to the occasion, she again resorted to her former tricks by enlisting the support of other countries, or their agents, in "checkmating" Japan in Manchuria. She first gave a concession to a British firm for the construction of a short railway between Hsinmintun and Fakumen. This was a breach of the supplementary agreement of the Peking protocol signed on December 22, 1905, which declared that "the Chinese Government engage, for the purpose of protecting the interest of the South Manchurian Railway, not to construct, prior to the recovery by them of the said railway, any main line in the neighborhood of and parallel to that railway, or any branch line which might be prejudicial to the interest of the above-mentioned railway." That this treaty was an arbitrary one, or that it was in violation of the principle of equal opportunity, could not properly be claimed by the British, for they themselves had obtained a similar advantage from the government of China in the so-called Shanghai-Nan-

*George Bronson Rea in The Far Eastern Review.

king Railway Loan Agreement concluded two years previously. The concession was ordered cancelled.

A group of American bankers working through the resourceful Willard Straight now sought a like concession for a proposed railway extending from Chinchow to Aigun, a distance of seven hundred miles, and running virtually parallel to the South Manchurian line. This was intended as a strategical move, a competitive project designed to force the Japanese railway out of existence, or to compel its sale to the Americans. But it was also a breach of the Peking protocol. Nor could the Americans, original guardians of the doctrine of equal opportunity, conscientiously dispute the point, for they also, through the American-China Development Company on July 13, 1900, had wrested a similar stripulation from the government of China in the agreement for the construction of the Canton-Hankow Railway reading: "It is further agreed that without the express consent in writing of the Director-General and the American Company, no other rival railway detrimental to the business of the same is to be permitted, and no parallel roads to the Canton-Hankow Line are to be allowed to the injury of the latter's interest within the area served by the Canton-Hankow main or branch lines."

At this point Mr. Philander C. Knox, the American Secretary of State under President Taft, contemplated putting an end to all these rivalries in Manchuria by securing a pledge from Great Britain, France, Germany, Russia and Japan to advance money to China for the purpose of enabling her to adopt one of two alternatives, namely, (1) to buy back the South Manchurian and the Chinese Eastern Railways, or, (2) to finance the Chinchow-Aigun line. These enterprises, however, were to be operated by an international board of management. Why, however, the railways of Manchuria alone were to be thus "internationalized" under American auspices, while those operated by other countries in other parts of China—the German railway in Shantung and those of the French in Yunnan and Kwangsi—were completely disregarded, was a question which could not be so easily answered. The only plausible reason offered was that it would effectually dispel all future possibilities of a renewed conflict between Russia and Japan. But the paramount motive was that it was intended, with all the pacific means at America's disposal, to restore equality of trade in Manchuria through concerted international *action*.

Such was the situation which confronted Japan when Ito decided to depart on his mission to the far corners of the earth. His plan, first of all, called for a conference with Russian officials; and the first of a series of meetings was scheduled to take place at Harbin. Arrangements for this initial meeting were completed by Shimpei Goto, Minister of Communications and former head of the South Manchurian Railway, whereby the Russian Finance Minister, Vladimir Kokovtsov, then regarded as the most influential leader of the Tsarist Government and under whose jurisdiction lay the supervision of Russia's interests in the Far East, was to proceed to the Manchurian metropolis and await Ito's arrival.

Korea meanwhile seethed with unrest. Ito's resignation from the resident-generalship had been construed as portending developments of the gravest import. He had never been genuinely popular with Korean officialdom, despite the many blessings he had introduced into the country. The mass, ignorant, unappreciative, resentful of his influence, hated him with a venom equal only to their colossal ingratitude. Now, on the eve of his unexplained mission to Harbin, their brooding suspicion turned to rank belief—belief that he was about to secure a Russian understanding for the annexation of Korea! And this when Ito had all his life worked consistently for their welfare and had been the greatest obstacle to the annexationists of Japan! Sinister movements, in which a nation doomed to an irreparable loss stood groping in a blind fury for that worldly justice which only the races that have had the sense to be far-seeing, alert, and powerful, have inherited from the ages, cast their gruesome shadows across the unhappy kingdom, across the beaten tracks of the Manchurian waste—across Harbin!

4

Blissfully unconscious of this inscrutable fate awaiting him in Harbin, Ito embarked upon his long journey on October 12,

1909. Proceeding first to Shimonoseki, he boarded the "Tetsu-rei Maru," which conveyed him to Dairen. A tremendous welcome was accorded him there by both officials and civilians alike.

Here, at what proved to be his last political speech, he gave the first public hint of the purpose of his mission. "My constant desire," he said, to begin with, "is to promote the peace of the Far East, for it has a direct and prodigious bearing on the destiny of the Japanese Empire. At the same time it must be remembered that Japan's share of the responsibilities in preserving this peace is obviously great. And Manchuria, because it is closely bound up with the fate of this sphere, holds the key to the situation."

Enunciating the course of action he had repeatedly taken to be the only sane and honorable one which his country, notwithstanding conflicting circumstances, must espouse, he opposed popular sentiment among the Japanese by stressing strict adherence to covenanted principles. "Japan's official policy," he said, "has always been to uphold the principles of the open door and of equal opportunity for the commerce and industry of all nations. The righteousness of these principles is eminently apparent, though it is an undeniable fact that Japan has been subjected to certain criticisms with regard to their execution. Nevertheless her true intentions are dedicated to a faithful carrying out of their purposes and effect. Those of you who are charged with official responsibilities in this region should consequently strive to devise means of enforcing adherence to these principles no matter what the circumstances. I should particularly advise Japanese nationals resident here to bear them constantly in mind and to respect them at all times. The fact that various enterprises are being constantly launched hereabouts is a matter for congratulation, but their development must at all times be consistent with these principles."

Finally, alluding to the future working out of an international policy in this storm center of the Far East, he declared: "Our neighboring countries have at last awakened to the need of a civilized regime. I sincerely trust that they will succeed in inaugurating their various reforms for if, unhappily, they should meet with failure, its effects upon the peace of the Far East would be incalculable. My conviction is that should Japan find it impossible to extend direct aid to China in helping her attain her objectives, she should at least endeavor to contribute indirectly to her success, the more so as her prior experience along this line would seem to render her duty-bound to lend a helping hand to a friendly neighbor. Thus the fate of Manchuria, as I perceive it, should rest on the fullest possible cooperation among the people of China, of Japan, and of Russia for the promotion of their common interests, for it is they who possess vital interests here."

In other words, he stood unalterably for peace and harmony in Manchuria, for he was not merely a realist and humanitarian with an international conscience, but a patriot as well who desired a safe margin of security for his country. But he was also convinced that the problems of the Far East, and of Manchuria in particular, concerned primarily the people whose interests, economically and strategically, were inextricably bound up with its singular resources; and for this reason they alone should unite to formulate a common basis of understanding. Commercially, he would insist on the principle of equal opportunity for all nations, and politically he would assist China in achieving the necessary reforms. Thus he hoped that China would develop a strong and unified government which would evince every capacity for fulfiling her responsibilities in Manchuria. Nevertheless, he believed that the people of the Far East—of China, Japan and Russia—should go about frankly to set their house in order without interference from other Powers.

In 1905, when the Russo-Japanese war which he opposed hung in the balance, he had sent Kentaro Kaneko on a friendly mission to the United States. Kaneko, in the course of a pleasant visit with President Roosevelt at Oyster Bay, had been advised by the latter to set up a so-called Japanese Monroe Doctrine of Asia. The President had also promised to support this policy, apparently believing it to be the only feasible solution for the salvation of the other independent Asiatic States. Apparently, also, he did not foresee that American business and political interests would in the future militate against such a scheme. Ito's policy, it would seem at first thought, possesses some points of similarity with Roosevelt's suggestion; and it is presumed he may have been encouraged in some measure by the President's forthright assurances in this respect. But his policy differed slightly from Roosevelt's recommendation. Whereas a Japanese Monroe Doctrine would suggest the foisting of Japanese hegemony upon Asia to which the other independent States must submit as a price of protection, Ito deprecated forceful dominance and advocated conciliation. Whereas Roosevelt's advice would incur the suspicion and enmity of the other Far Eastern States and lead them to believe that Japan was influenced by selfish motives, thus rendering the security of such a doctrine subject to the mere fact of her ability to hold them in subjection, Ito eschewed all suggestions of Japanese superiority and sought the cooperation of the countries of the Far East on a basis of mutual assistance. His policy, in brief, obviously amounts to applying the Golden Rule in the Far East for the purpose (1) of averting rivalry and enmity among the Far Eastern Powers themselves; (2) of obviating the temptation of the Western Powers to continue their exploitation of this sphere; and (3) of creating a common policy throughout the Far East so that the whole world might be free to trade here, unhampered by considerations of international greed and ill-will.

He had advocated the same sort of policy in 1901 when he went forth to meet the Tsar and his Foreign Minister in order to secure a Russo-Japanese understanding, as opposed to an Anglo-Japanese alliance. Once again he was on his way to achieve an understanding with official Russia. He did not foresee that, within a few years, a mighty debacle was to overtake both China and Russia, changing their political character and bringing forth new factors to be reckoned with on the old frontier. Nor, for that matter, did his opponents, the military leaders, who were about to seek a renewal of the Anglo-Japanese alliance on an entirely new basis, foresee that had they given him free rein from 1901 onwards, the tragedy of 1914, so far as Japan was concerned, bringing in its wake a host of connected blunders and insults from abroad, would have been averted.

Before entraining for Harbin Ito visited Port Arthur to inspect the site, marked by an imposing memorial, where thousands of stalwart Russians and Nipponese patriots had fallen in the war of 1904-5. Between Port Arthur and Harbin on the South Manchurian Railway lay the city of Mukden, equally reminiscent of martial splendor and the sanguinary exploits of heroes now resting silently in the cold grey bosom of the earth. Here Ito tarried yet awhile. Every day so spent in distractions prolonged his hour of destiny, which now, unknown to him, was hovering inexorably at his journey's end. On the 24th of October he visited the Fushun colliery. The following day he stepped aboard a special train which sped swiftly toward Harbin.

Arriving there at nine o'clock on the morning of the 26th, he was first greeted in his coach by Vladimir Kokovtsov, with whom he had come all the way from Tokyo to discuss the future of Manchuria. For about twenty minutes thereafter the two were deeply engrossed in conversation. What did the two discuss? What was the one solution which Ito believed would solve the Manchurian riddle? Some historians claim today, apparently on the strength of Kokovtsov's disclosures, that he sought a Russo-Japanese understanding on the sale of the South Manchurian and the Chinese Eastern Railways to China, a plan which Kokovtsov himself is reported as having favorably entertained. This is not substantiated by any of Ito's previous statements, nor directly hinted at in any of his writings or speeches. It is not unreasonable to surmise—it is in fact far more likely in view of the manifest drift of his last political speech delivered at Dairen—that he attempted to secure a Russo-Japanese rapprochement in order to present a solid phalanx of Far Eastern unanimity preparatory to seeking a desirable, a harmonious, an honorable adjustment of Manchurian problems with the various Western Powers. But the tragic incident which was about to occur, in a few minutes, shattered all possibilities of his revealing his secret plan to the world and to posterity.

Outside, at the station, a large and enthusiastic crowd of Russians and Japanese had assembled to extend a popular welcome. A company of crack Russian guards stood at attention on both sides of the platform. The Mayor of Harbin and a Japanese delegation headed by Consul General Kawakami then entered Ito's coach.

After a brief ceremonial greeting in which the city's official welcome was extended to him, Ito stepped off the train. He then, with Kokovtsov and the Mayor accompanying him, proceeded to review the Russian guards. Having completed the review on the right, he paused for a brief interval to receive the greetings of the consuls of the various nations who had in the meantime assembled near the platform. He was about to resume the review on the left when suddenly a mysterious intruder, attired in the customary clothes of a European, slunk past the Russian guards. The man's right hand closed tightly on a Browning revolver. In the tense formalities of the moment no one had perceived his presence soon enough to check his movements.

Springing noiselessly and with the faultless dexterity of an animated ghost, the intruder confronted Ito just as he started to walk briskly down the aisle, hat uplifted in salute, between his Russian hosts. The next instant a staccato chorus of flying bullets rent the air. With a cry of amazement and frustration, Ito staggered, reeled, and was about to fall when those nearest him supported his inert frame. Three of the six shots fired had entered his breast and abdomen. The assassin was immediately apprehended. He was a Korean.

It had all happened so unexpectedly and so swiftly and with such deadly precision that the whole thing seemed to those who witnessed the tragedy utterly incredible.

They carried Ito back into his coach. He was dying. He was dying, this apostle of Japanese liberalism, with his most important work left undone. He was dying in the midst of an important crisis which faced the country he had given his all to build up laboriously from an obscure State wallowing in medieval ignorance and turmoil to a great world Power. He was dying with a mind filled with apprehension for the nation he must leave behind him at the mercy of leaders who refused to heed the cry of moderation. He was dying—and no surgical feat could avert the end which was now coming.

He never lost consciousness. He asked for some brandy to allay the terrible thirst in his throat and the pain from his wounds which racked his body. When told of the identity of his assailaint, he said softly: "The fellow is a fool." Only a fool could have stooped so low as to seek the destruction of his benefactor.

Thirty minutes later Ito's heart, which had functioned steadily for sixty-nine years through every conceivable human crisis, ceased permanently to beat. With him died the guiding personification of modern, liberal Japan.

. . . .

The train bearing Ito's lifeless form slowly retraced its way toward Dairen, where the battleship "Iwate" had been dispatched from Saseho to convey it back to his native country. A nation of sixty million mourners contemplated this profound tragedy with sorrow and anger. Another—Korea—trembled in the imminent certainty of retribution. The whole world, moved momentarily by sympathy for the one and humanity for the other, turned toward the East with speculative expectancy.

THE END

BIBLIOGRAPHICAL NOTE

In preparing this book the author has relied chiefly on documentary revelations contained in the three definitive works in Japanese dealing with the different phases of Ito's life and career which have appeared since his death in 1909.

The first of these, the work of Mr. Hisatsuna Furuya, who was private secretary to Ito during the last ten years of the great statesman's life, entitled "To Ko Yoyei," was published by the Minyu Sha, Tokyo, on November 15, 1910. It deals with sidelights on Ito's personality and on the extraordinary incidents of his career. The only work of its kind in Japanese, it is devoted principally to reminiscences and was written at a moment when Ito's violent death was still fresh in the memory of the author. It is a strangely revealing account, but entirely uncritical.

The second work, in the order of publication, is "Ito Ko Zenshu," the complete works of Ito, in three large volumes. This monumental work was edited by Mr. Midori Komatsu and appeared under the imprint of the Showa Shuppan Sha of Tokyo, on August 30, 1928. It is a collection of his letters, his writings, his speeches, his poems, his calligraphic creations, his memoirs, and, in addition, sundry anecdotal contributions by his friends, admirers, and erstwhile political opponents. It also includes a brief biographical sketch by the editor.

The third in this series of definitive works, "Ito Hirobumi Hiroku," comes in two closely-printed volumes, published separately by the Shunshu Sha, Tokyo. The first volume appeared on March 15, 1929, and the second on November 15, 1930.

This is a complete collection of Ito's official papers photostatically reproduced in their original forms, with a running explanatory comment by the editor, Mr. Atsushi Hiratsuka. Its authenticity is vouched for by Ito's late heir, Prince Hirokuni Ito, who supervised its publication. It is an invaluable record inasmuch as it reveals, for the first time, important secrets in Ito's official life.

All quotations appearing in the present work, unless otherwise noted, have been translated from these sources into English
by the present author.   In doing so he has departed from the
usual practice by trying to follow the original Japanese text as
closely as possible in order to retain the precise meaning of
each phrase as it was expressed and understood from the Japanese angle.

Other works consulted are "Meiji Koshin Roku," by Mr.
Izumi Asahina, which devotes ninety-seven pages to Ito (pub-
lisher's name not given); "In Korea with Marquis Ito," by G.T.
Ladd, LL. D. (New York: Charles Scribner's Sons); "Makers
of Modern Japan," by J. Morris.

For verification of historical data I have used the works of
Dr. Payson J. Treat, Professor of History of Stanford University, on the Far East.

INDEX